IMAGES
of America

THE AVENUES

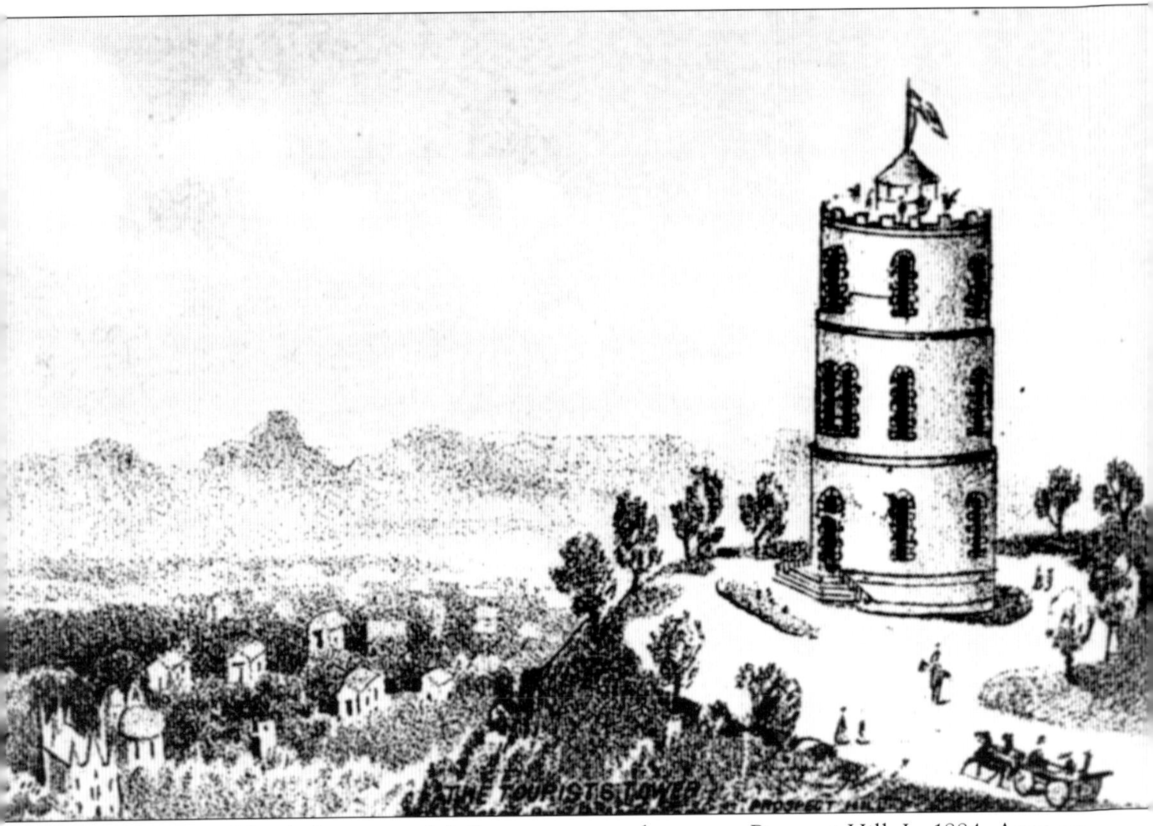

The corner of Sixth Avenue and A Street was once known as Prospect Hill. In 1884, Avenues resident Robert Anderson built this tourist tower to provide fee-paying visitors a panoramic view of Salt Lake City. The tower was known as Anderson's Tower or, derisively, Anderson's Folly. Tourists found that they could get just as good of a view of the city from the base of the tower as the top. The tower itself became a favorite subject of visiting photographers. Anderson, one of the first settlers on the north bench of the city, built a second home near the tower at 207 Fifth Avenue in 1913. He was manager of the Dinwoodey Furniture Company, private accountant for Brigham Young, and Utah's first bank examiner. Anderson's Tower stood until 1932. Today, the footprint of the structure is laid out in the small park commemorating the site. A photograph of the structure can be found on page 100. (Utah State Historical Society.)

On the Cover: A woman is bundled up in the back of car parked at 271 Fourth Avenue on a winter day in 1909. The home and vehicle belonged to William G. and Carrie L. Romney. Romney was a partner in the Romney and Ryan Printing Company. The enterprise owned the first linotype printing machine in Utah. Cars were a rare sight in the Avenues when this photograph was taken. Driving one of the neighborhood's first cars on unpaved, snow-covered Salt Lake City streets would definitely be a challenge. The Victorian home, built in 1891, still stands and is well preserved. Today, however, large brick apartment buildings flank the structure on each side. (Utah State Historical Society.)

IMAGES
of America

THE AVENUES

Cevan LeSieur

ARCADIA
PUBLISHING

ISBN 978-0-7385-8535-2

Published by Arcadia Publishing
Charleston, South Carolina

Printed in the United States of America

Library of Congress Control Number: 2011940760

For all general information, please contact Arcadia Publishing:
Telephone 843-853-2070
Fax 843-853-0044
E-mail sales@arcadiapublishing.com
For customer service and orders:
Toll-Free 1-888-313-2665

Visit us on the Internet at www.arcadiapublishing.com

To my wife, Heather, for her support and to all Avenues residents who have spent time, money, blood, and tears to restore our unique neighborhood.

Contents

ACKNOWLEDGMENTS

The Research Center at the Utah State Historical Society is a valuable resource for anyone interested in learning the history of their home, neighborhood, city, or state. The combination of their online resources, photograph collection, and publications are an asset to those interested in the history of Utah. Their photograph collections come from 14 different sources. The majority of the pictures used in this publication come from the Shipler Photograph Collection. All images that appear in this book are used by permission of the Utah State Historical Society, all rights reserved.

I wish to thank the Greater Avenues Community Council (GACC) for giving Arcadia Publishing my name. The GACC has been a great asset for Avenues residents concerned about preserving their community. Finally, I would like to thank my acquisitions editor at Arcadia Publishing, Stacia Bannerman, for her expert guidance.

INTRODUCTION

Salt Lake City was a rapidly growing western city when the first settlers built homes in what would eventually be known as the Avenues. In the early years, the area was plagued by a lack of water that restricted settlement up the hill. In 1876, 1884, and 1906, projects were undertaken to bring water to what was referred to by city residents as the "Dry Bench." City Creek Canyon, which borders the western edge of the neighborhood, provided the water, as well as future recreational opportunities to residents.

The Avenues is the only portion of Salt Lake City that does not follow the historical street pattern planned out by Latter-day Saints (LDS) Church president Brigham Young. The neighborhood's streets were laid out in a narrower grid pattern that created smaller blocks than those of Salt Lake City proper. Because of the smaller blocks, the first residents were businessmen and not farmers. The proximity of the neighborhood to the central business district and transportation hub made it a popular living location for citizens involved in many trades. The original streets were named mostly after trees, such as Pine, Spruce, and Fir. In 1885, the north–south streets became A through V Streets and the east–west streets became First through Fourth Avenue. Since the early 1900s, Salt Lake City residents have referred to the area as the Avenues. Brigham Young gave fellow Mormons the first land grants on the small blocks of what was then known as Platt D of Salt Lake City in 1857. Each block was broken up into four lots. Portions of Platt D came from Young's sprawling estate and included portions of the old city wall. Because of his involvement, nearly all of the area's first residents were members of the LDS Church. Population increase in the city was fueled by the growing local mining industry. The railroads also brought in new residents from other parts of the United States. Religious and ethnic diversity was a result of this growth. By 1910, only 45 percent of the district was populated by members of Utah's predominant religion. The Avenues neighborhood continues to have more religious diversity than the rest of the city and state today. After continued improvements in city services, including the increased availability of water, the neighborhood started to expand north up the hill and east towards Fort Douglas. By 1910, the highest street in the Avenues was 11th Avenue. Even though it is outside of the current historic district, 11th Avenue is the highest street where any older historic homes can be found. This expansion brought Salt Lake City Cemetery, a hospital, public and private elementary schools, new churches, neighborhood stores, a small amusement park, and homes that would be more permanent to the Avenues. The establishment and growth of what was originally known as Dr. Grove's Latter-day Saints Hospital would continue to influence the development and preservation of the neighborhood into the 1980s. Three different streetcar companies competed with each other by building lines on Avenues' streets. These trolley lines continued to spread through the area, bringing transportation options to the residents. The Avenues area was Salt Lake City's first streetcar suburb.

The majority of citizens in the neighborhood during the years 1860 to 1940 could be classified as middle class. However, because of the area's proximity to downtown and the mansions along South Temple Street, several of the city's leaders chose to build larger homes in the midst of the area. Among the more prominent Avenues residents were land developers, miners, medical pioneers, architects, and builders. They included Utah State Capitol architect Richard K.A. Kletting, early female physician Ellis R. Shipp, mining magnate Gill S. Peyton, LDS Church president and property developer Heber J. Grant, Utah governor William Spry, and pioneering photographer Charles R. Savage.

The first homes built in the neighborhood were small adobe structures. Over time, many of these original vernacular pioneer homes were replaced by new, larger Victorian houses and, later, Craftsman bungalows. Developers started building homes in the area around 1900. Because of the multiple landowners on each block, these builders were only able to construct homes on individual lots often separated by several streets. Each block face is very different because of the neighborhood's architectural diversity. This diversity makes the area unique compared to other residential historic districts in the United States, which often have a common home type or architectural style. While most of the area's home designs come from pattern books or stock plans, several of Utah's early architects designed houses in the neighborhood. These buildings stand out as fine local examples of Prairie style, Dutch Colonial, Craftsman, and Victorian architecture.

While neighborhoods near urban centers declined throughout the United States after World War II, the decline of the Avenues started even earlier. The onset of the Great Depression forced many owners of large homes to split their structures up into multiple apartments. Accelerating apartment construction also drove down the desirability of individual homes in the area. The continuing flight to new suburbs after the war eventually led to increased crime and urban blight. Salt Lake City political leaders reacted to the neighborhood's decline by changing zoning laws. They hoped to increase real estate values and stop the area's decline. Unfortunately, a series of ill-conceived decisions led to the demolition of numerous historic homes. Starting in the mid-1970s, a greater appreciation of historical architecture and the neighborhood's location near downtown Salt Lake City and the University of Utah led to widespread home restoration and preservation. Efforts of the neighborhood's citizens to preserve the area led to the creation of the Greater Avenues Community Council. The organization was instrumental in bringing the Avenues local, state, and national historic-district designations.

This book is the first publication to pool a large collection of historical photographs that reveal the Avenues neighborhood as it was during its first heyday.

One

Community Leaders

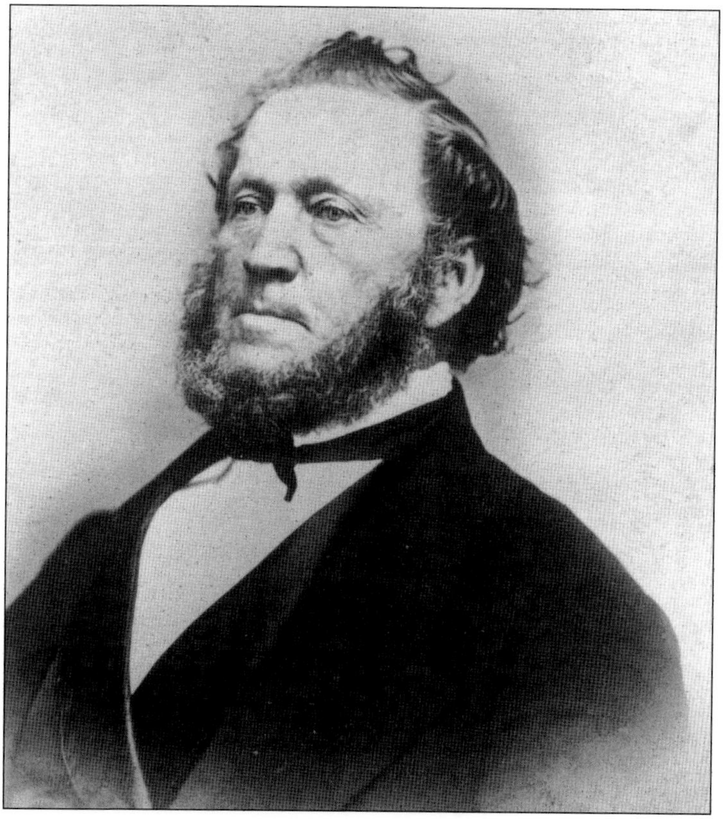

LDS Church president and territorial governor Brigham Young influenced development and settlement throughout Utah. His original estate made up much of the western portion of the Avenues. Most of the initial land deeds granted to the first settlers in the neighborhood were given by Young. By the 1880s, landownership split up rapidly. Leaders in politics, business, education, mining, and medicine moved to the neighborhood and called the Avenues home.

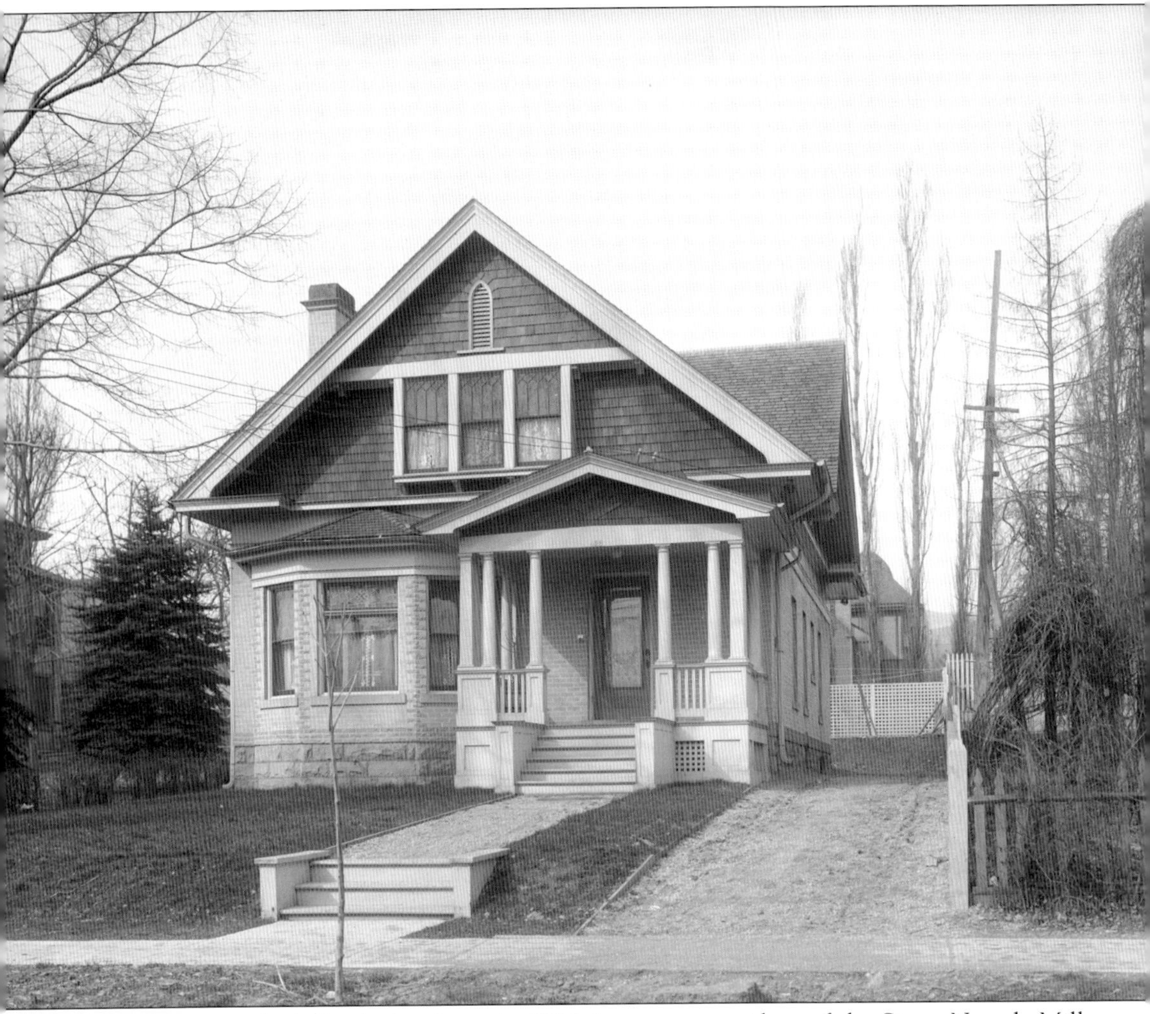

This home was built for Arthur Lynn in 1904. Lynn was president of the Sierra Nevada Mill Company. This was one of the first lumber companies established in Salt Lake City. A later resident, Hermann Harms, was proprietor of the nearby Brigham Street Pharmacy. Prominent Utah architects Alberto Treganza and Walter Ware designed the residence. Originally built as a one-and-a-half–story Victorian home, a Craftsman-style porch was added in 1920. In 1942, the home was converted into apartments.

Anthony W. Ivins served as LDS Church president Heber J. Grant's first counselor. Ivins was a resident of the Avenues during those years. Prior to his time on the church's first presidency, he helped establish the church in Mexico. He was also a member of Utah's Constitutional Convention in 1894. His home, which still stands, was at 299 Second Avenue.

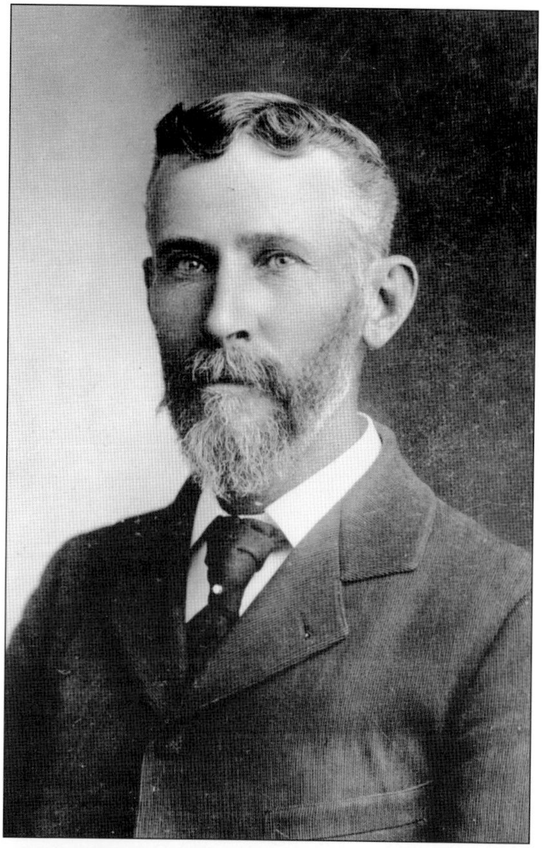

This stucco-covered bungalow's design was inspired by an English cottage. The home, located at 376 Second Avenue, was designed by Lewis Telle Cannon for his wife, Martha. Cannon's architecture firm designed several prominent buildings in Salt Lake City, including the Deseret Bank building on First South and Main Streets.

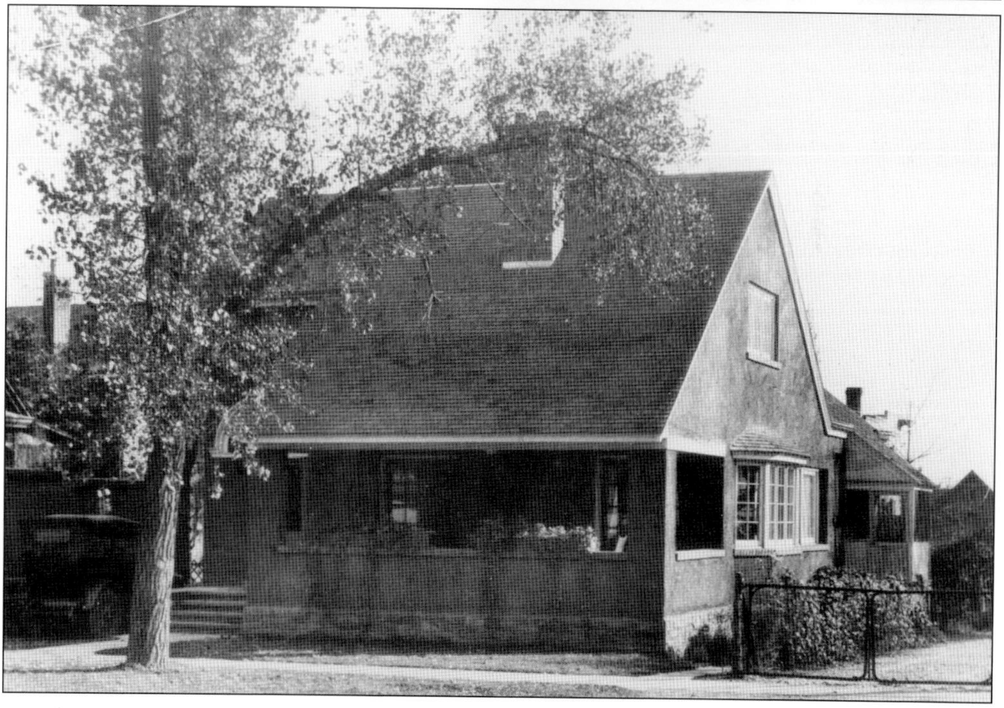

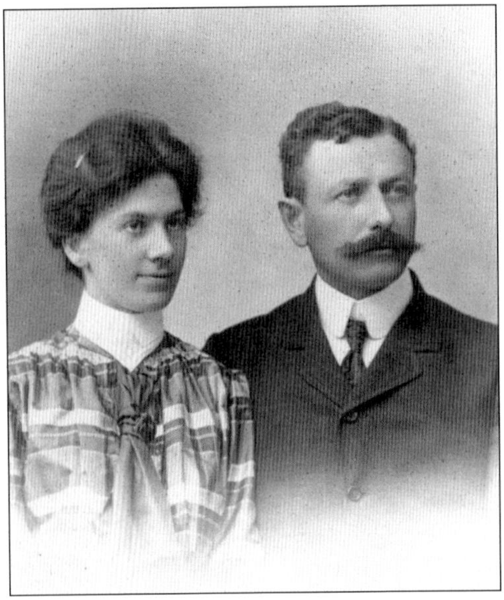

Prominent Utah architect Richard K.A. Kletting is pictured with his wife, Mary Elizabeth. Kletting, an Avenues resident, was the state's most influential late-19th century architect. In addition to several homes in the Avenues, he designed numerous important buildings in Salt Lake City, including the original Salt Palace, the Utah State Capitol, and the Saltair Pavilion.

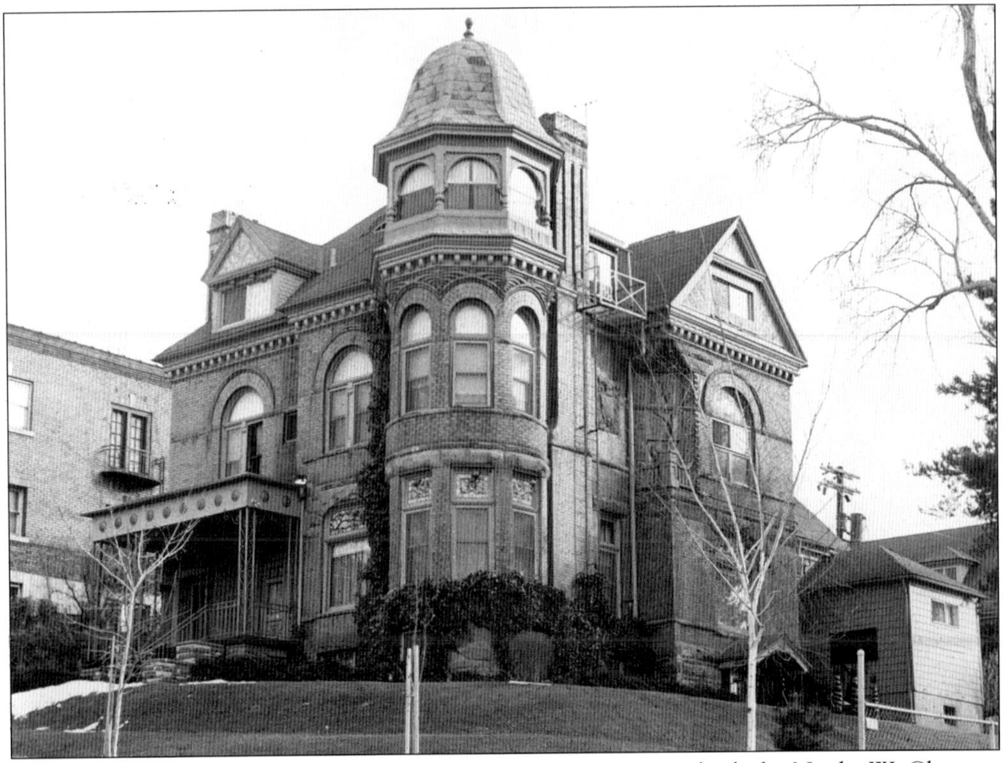

This prominent Victorian mansion at 140 Second Avenue was built for Nephi W. Clayton. Clayton was manager of the Inland Salt Company, a member of Salt Lake City's Alta Club, and developer of the original Saltair Pavilion at the Great Salt Lake. This photograph, taken in the late 1960s, shows the home after it was split into multiple apartments. This was a fate bestowed on many large Avenues homes. The original posts of the front porch have been replaced by iron posts. As the neighborhood declined, deferred maintenance led to the breakdown of original architectural elements, such as the posts.

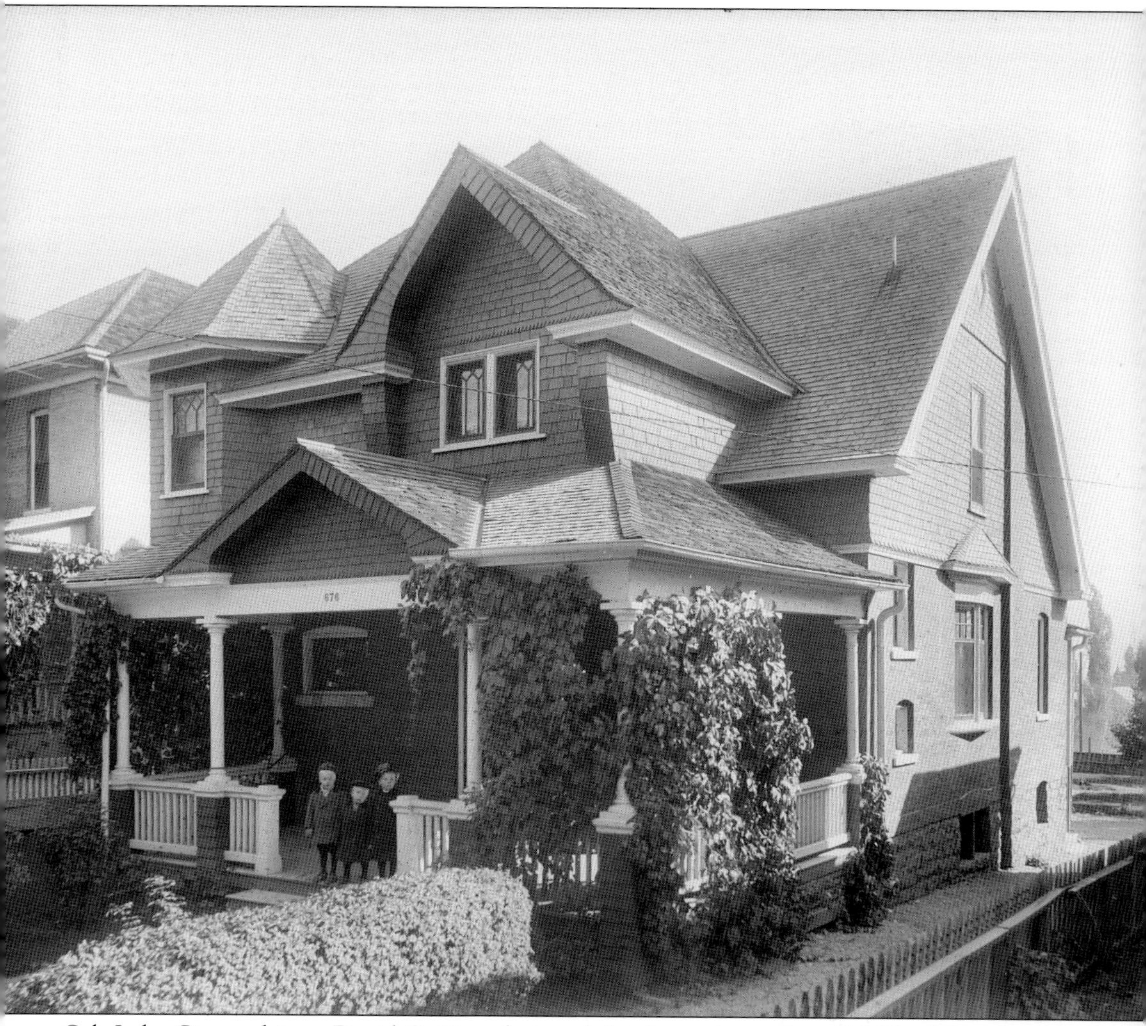

Salt Lake City architect David C. Dart designed this home located at 676 Third Avenue in 1899. Elements of both the Shingle style and Queen Anne style of architecture are found on the exterior of the residence. Brown shingles cover the upper walls, and an octagonal tower graces the northeast corner. Rachel McMasters built the home on speculation. McMasters was a draftsman for the Oregon Short Line Railroad. He apparently invested in real estate on the side. The home was split into apartments briefly before being restored into a single-family residence. Today, the home remains well preserved.

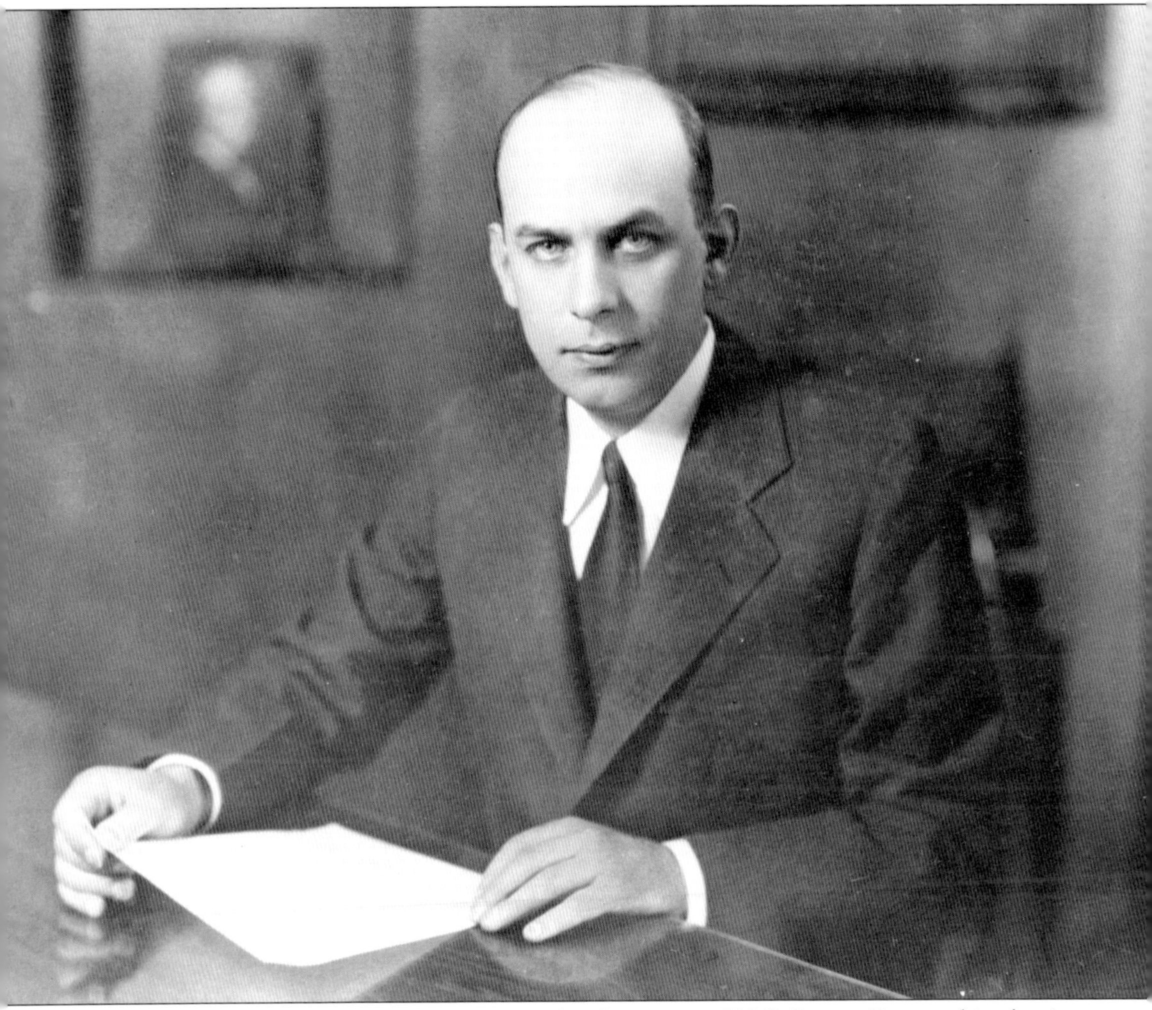
US senator Wallace F. Bennett grew up in the Avenues at 176 D Street. Prior to his election to the senate, he worked as a high school principal and as a paint manufacturer for his family's paint company. Bennett was also a hymn writer and composed "God of Power, God of Right" for the LDS hymnal. He was elected in 1950, defeating fellow Avenues resident Elbert D. Thomas. Bennett served until 1974, and his son Bob Bennett was elected to the same seat in 1992, serving until 2010.

John J. McClellan resided at 688 First Avenue, beginning in 1906. McClellan became organist for the Mormon Tabernacle Choir that same year. An influential musician in Utah during the first half of the 20th century, McClellan founded the Salt Lake Symphony Orchestra and the Salt Lake Opera Company.

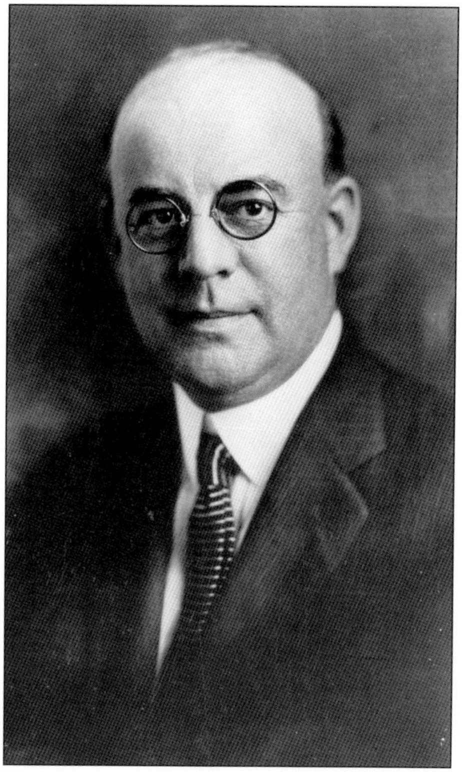

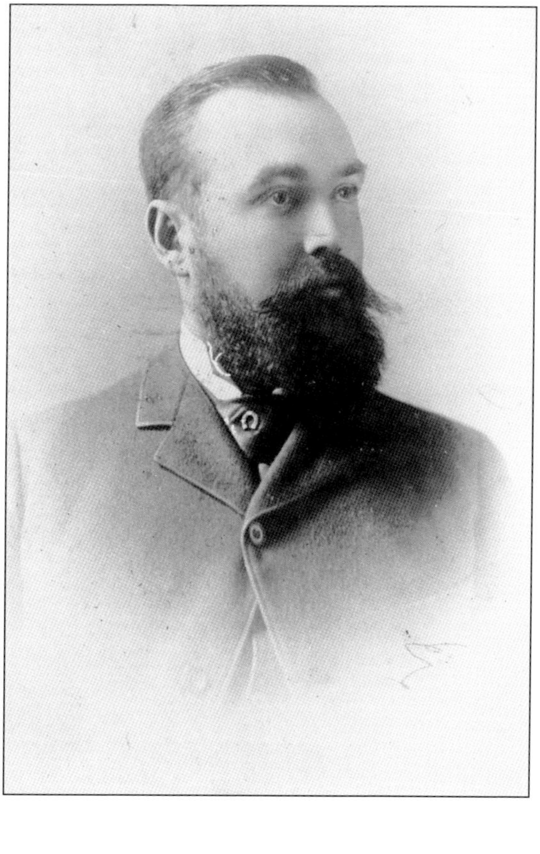

Noted Utah architect Carl M. Neuhausen was a resident in the Avenues when he helped with the completion of the Cathedral of the Madeleine. Among the other buildings designed by Neuhausen are the Kearns-St. Ann's Orphanage and the Thomas Kearns mansion and carriage house.

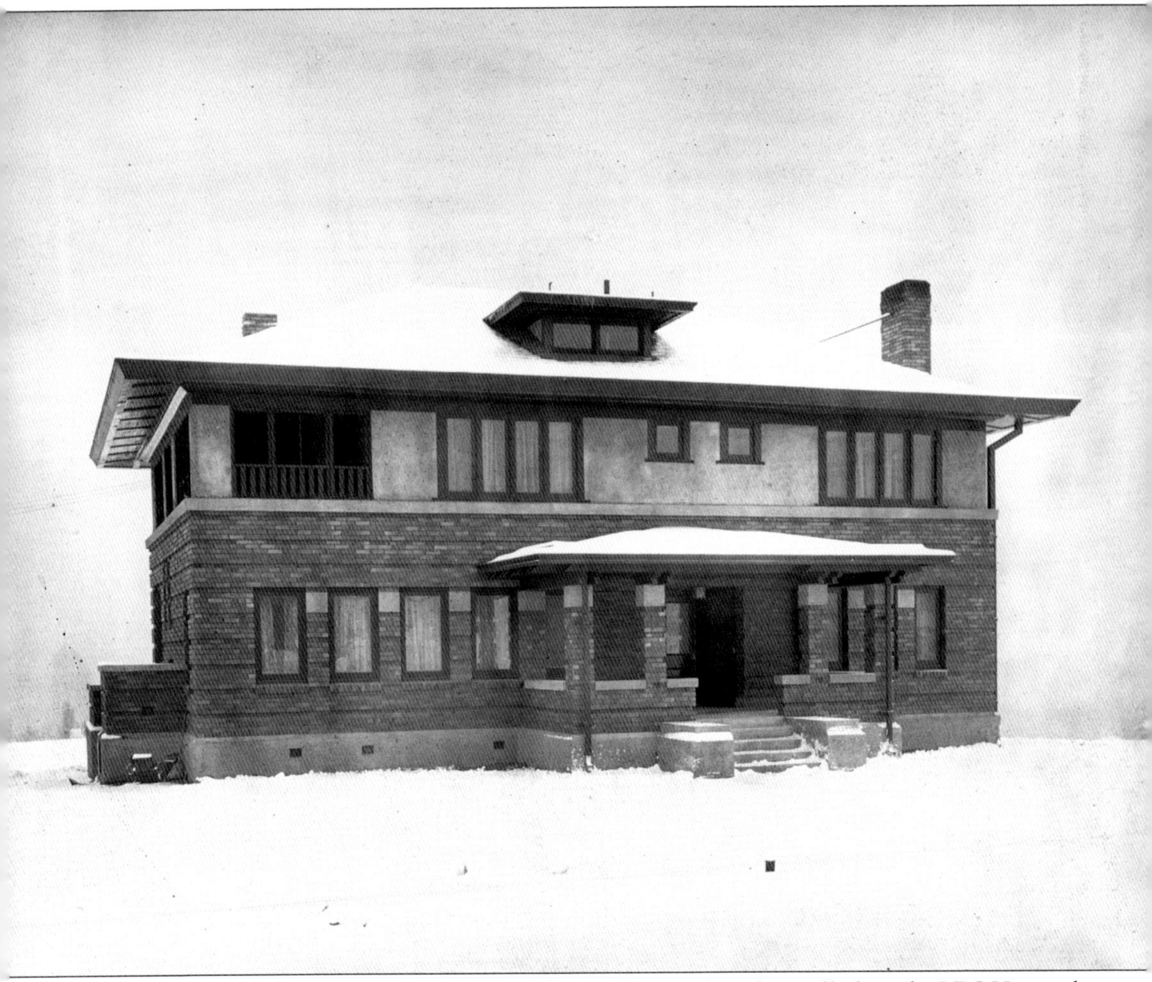

Dr. Samuel H. Allen formed the Salt Lake Clinic and served on the staff of nearby LDS Hospital. He had this Prairie-style home built in 1910 on the southeast corner of Eighth Avenue and A Street. Prominent Salt Lake City architects Walter Ware and Alberto Treganza designed the residence. The horizontal emphasis of the style can be found in the division between the stucco second story and brick first story. The broad eaves and heavy porch columns are also typical of the style. The home stands today but has been divided into a duplex.

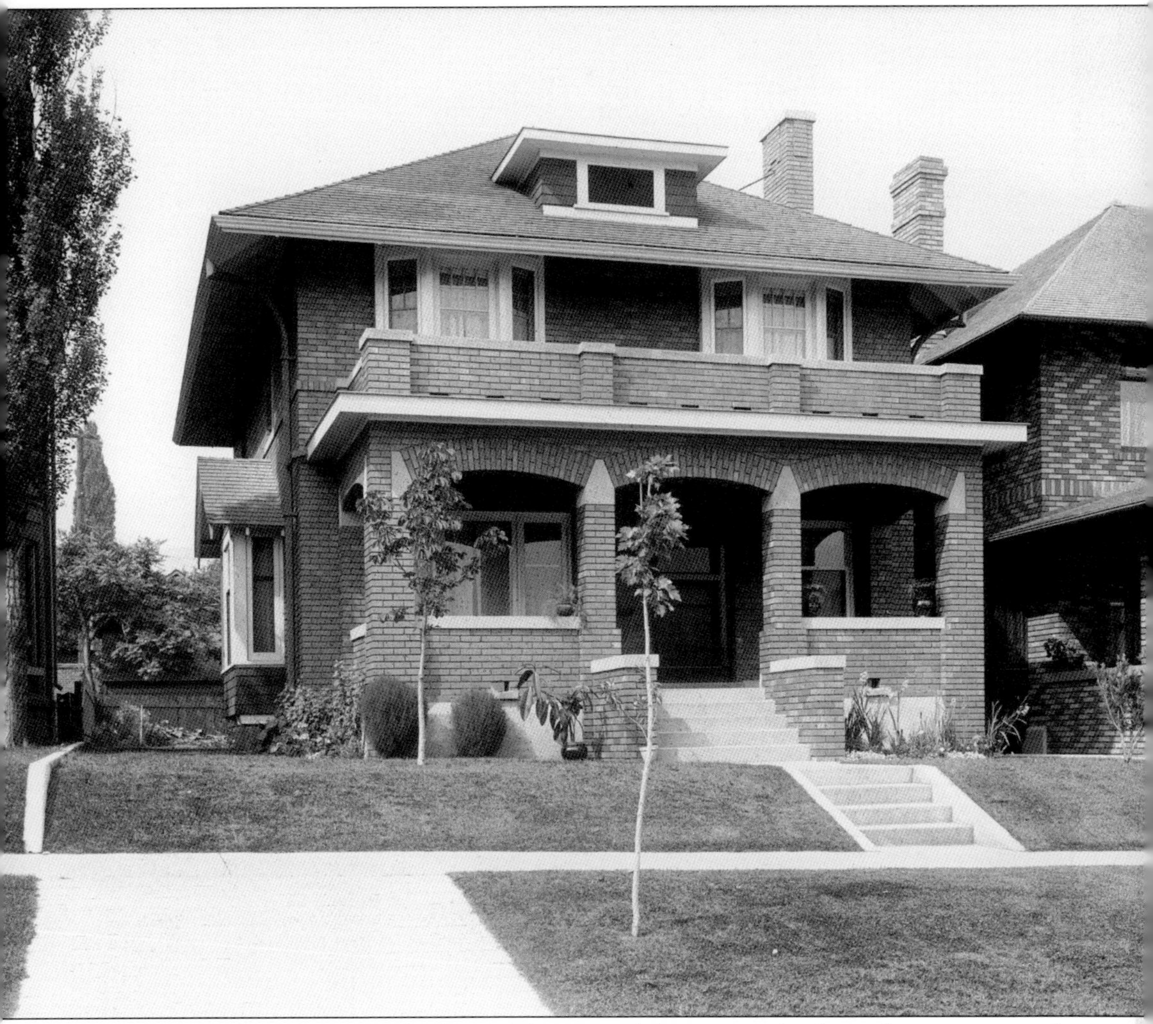

This two-story brick home at 271 Second Avenue exhibits exposed rafter tails consistent with Craftsman-style architecture. This is another residence designed by Alberto Treganza and Walter Ware. It was built in 1911 by the Schuyler Building Company for Henry Wallace. Wallace owned the Utah Cracker Company before selling it to the American Biscuit Company. His daughter Mary Ellen Wallace continued to live in the home until 1965. Today, the house looks nearly identical to the newly built structure in this photograph.

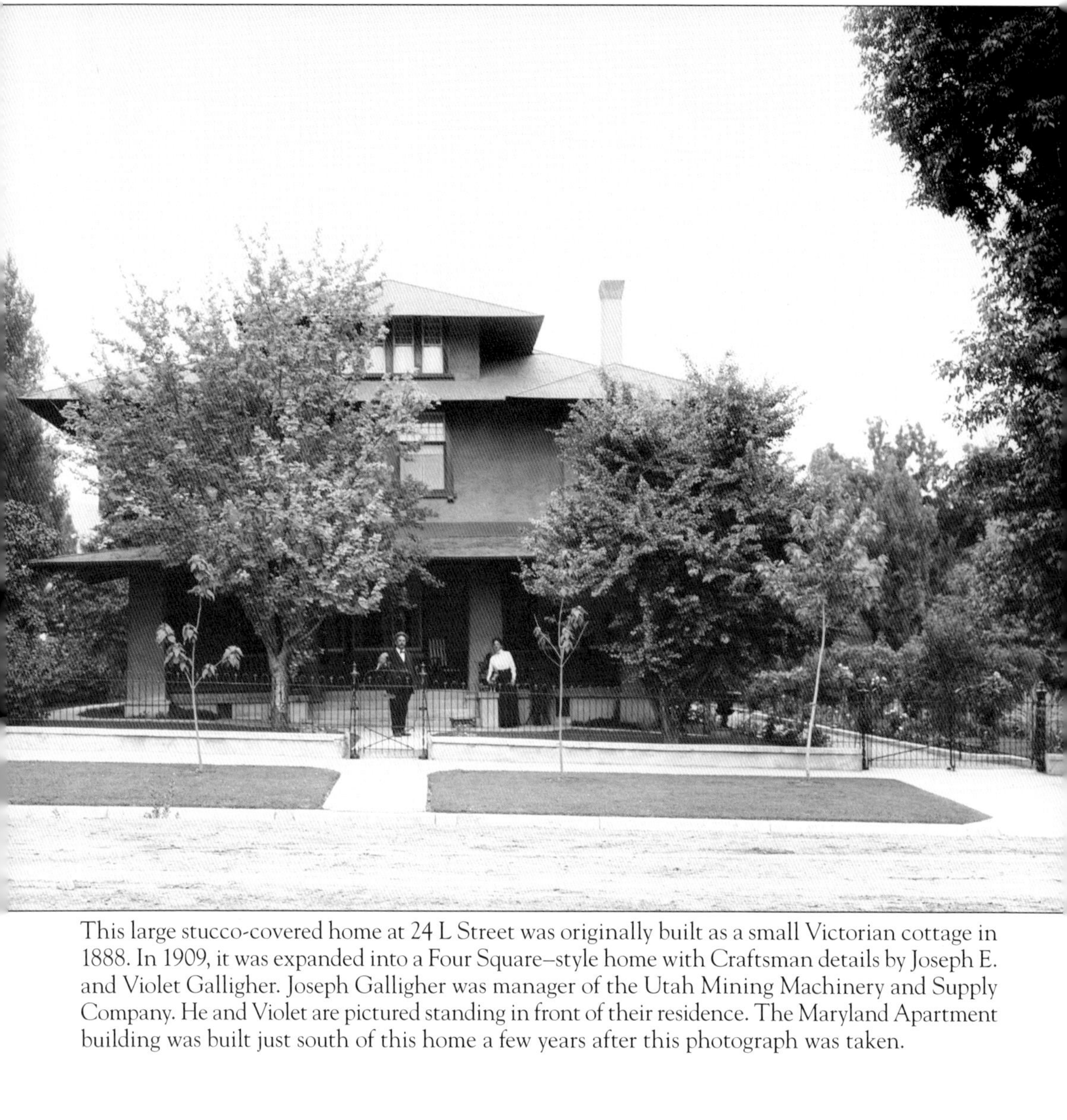

This large stucco-covered home at 24 L Street was originally built as a small Victorian cottage in 1888. In 1909, it was expanded into a Four Square–style home with Craftsman details by Joseph E. and Violet Galligher. Joseph Galligher was manager of the Utah Mining Machinery and Supply Company. He and Violet are pictured standing in front of their residence. The Maryland Apartment building was built just south of this home a few years after this photograph was taken.

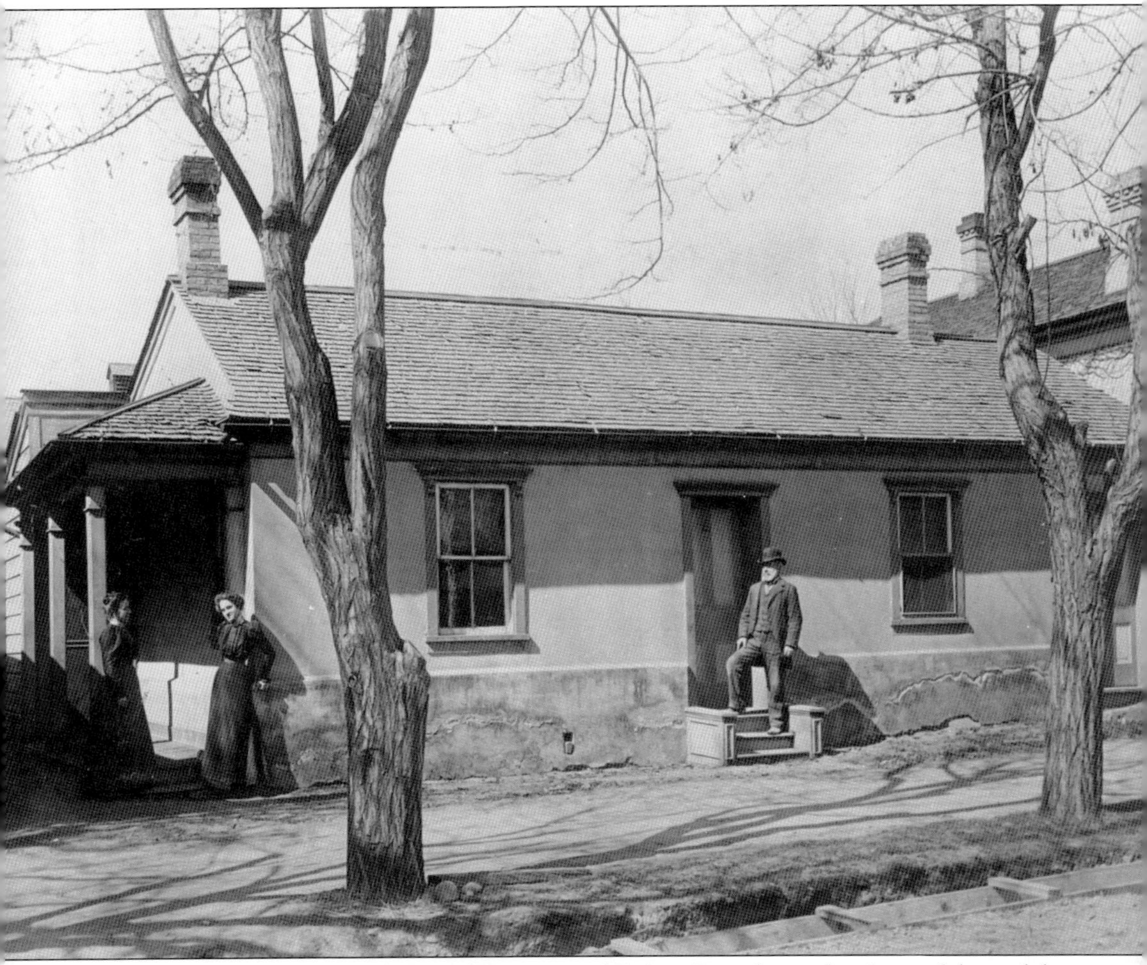

Rachel Patrick (far left), Maude Patrick Barnes, and Robert Patrick stand in front of their adobe home at 167 B Street. The Patricks were emigrants from Scotland. Robert Patrick was a city alderman and responsible for the early tree plantings and planning for the city's parks. This home was demolished in 1900 and replaced by a duplex. The Patrick family continued to live on one side of the duplex until 1923.

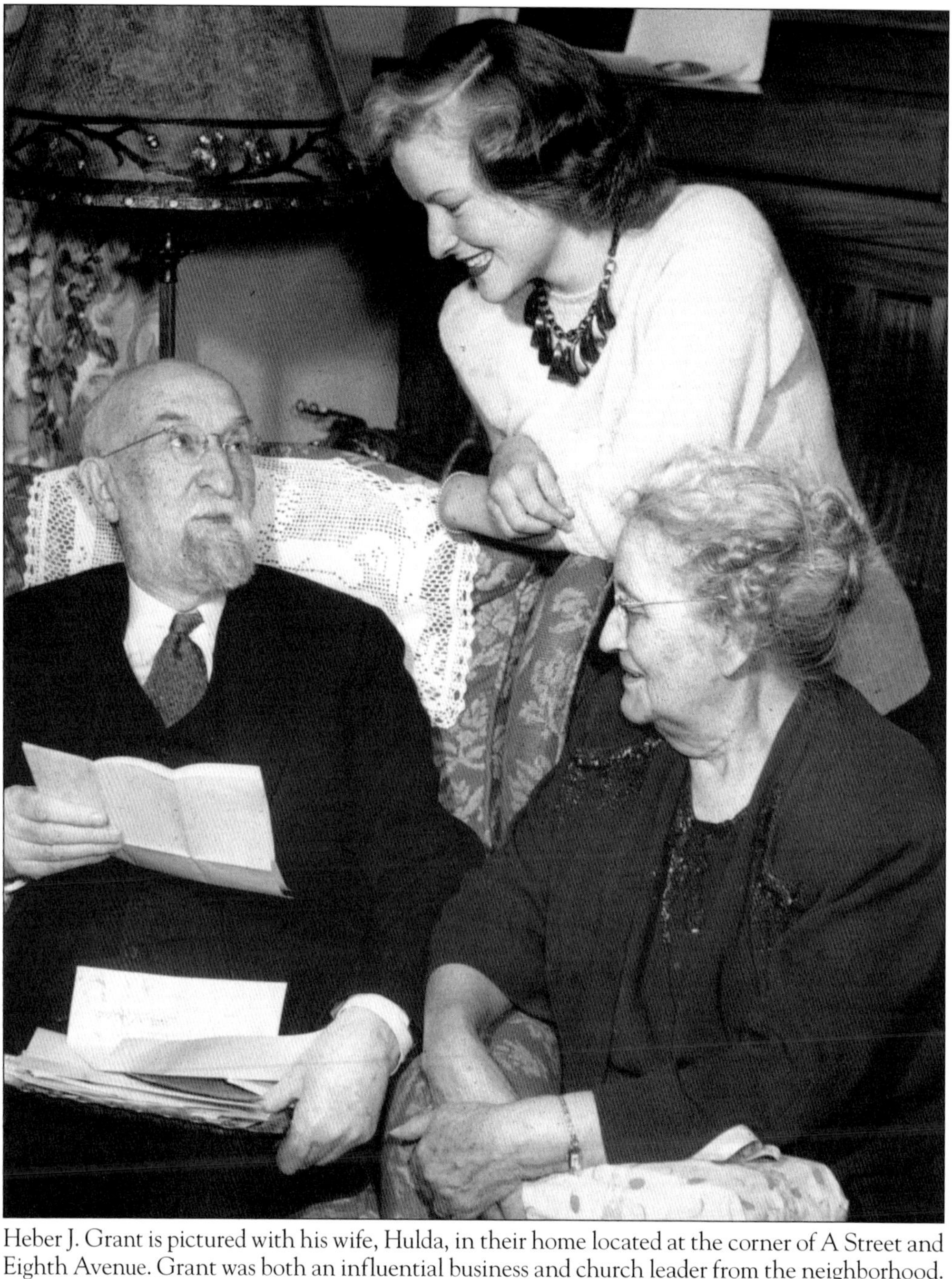

Heber J. Grant is pictured with his wife, Hulda, in their home located at the corner of A Street and Eighth Avenue. Grant was both an influential business and church leader from the neighborhood. His Heber J. Grant and Company developed homes in the area. Grant became the seventh president of the Church of Jesus Christ of Ladder-day Saints in 1918. He was one of the most important leaders of the church during the 20th century. During his time as president, he strongly enforced the 1890 church manifesto against plural marriage. He also authorized the implementation of the Good Neighbor policy to improve relations between the LDS Church and the US Government. His administration also emphasized practice of the LDS health code known as the Word of Wisdom.

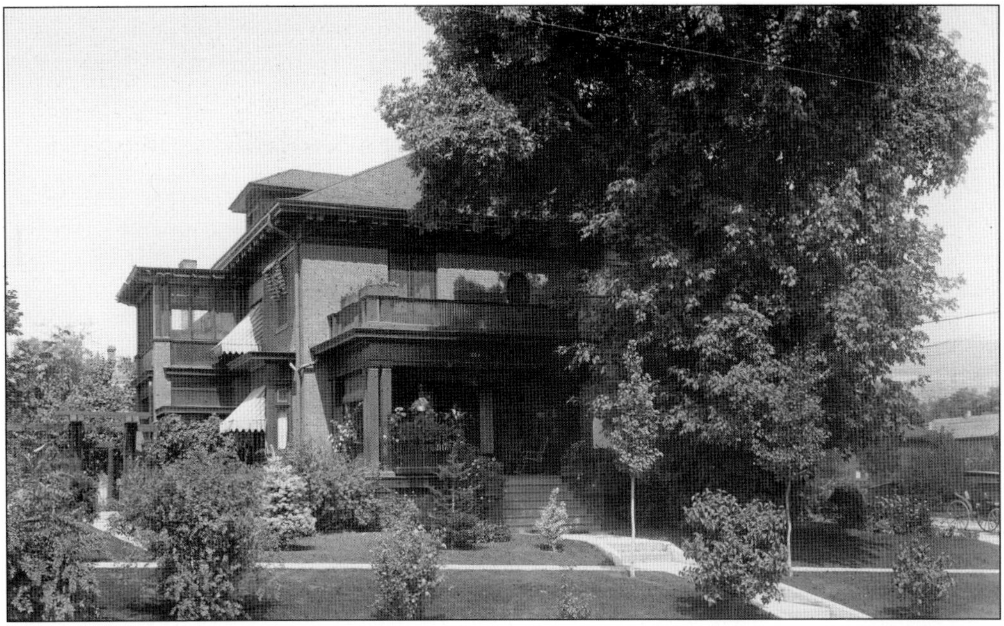

This home located at 299 Second Avenue was built for Willard Young, a son of Brigham Young. He was prominent in the LDS Church's education system and served as superintendent of the church's building activities in the 1910s. This house was later occupied by Anthony W. Ivins, a member of the Quorum of the Twelve Apostles for the LDS Church. From the Great Depression until the late 1990s, the building was split up into several apartments.

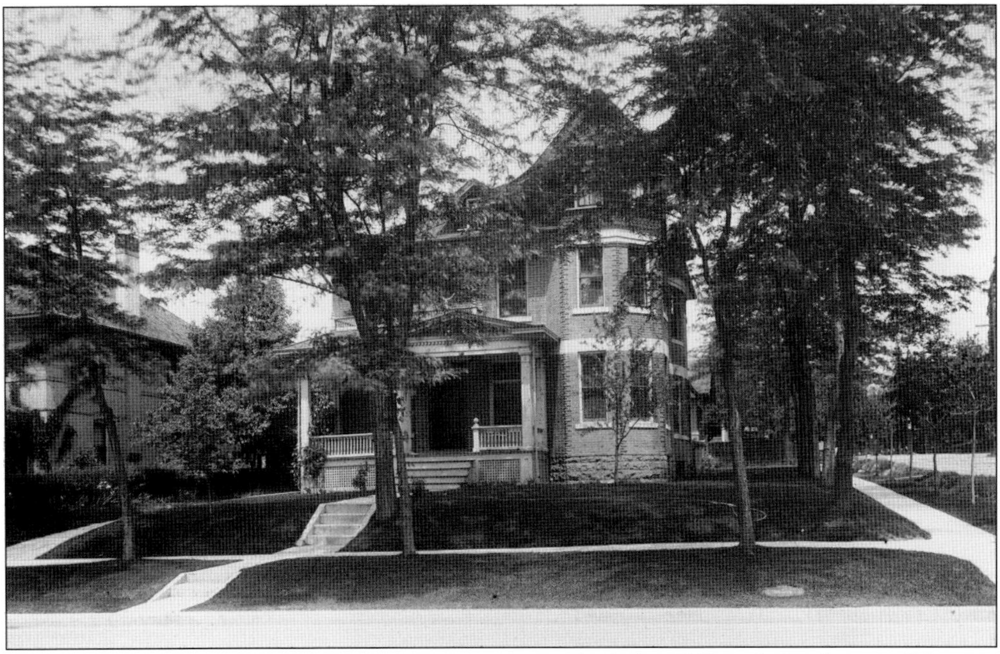

This Victorian home, located at 535 First Avenue, was built for William I. Snyder, a well-known Salt Lake City and Park City attorney. He was elected head of the Utah Bar Association in 1908. This well-preserved residence is still standing on the northwest corner of First Avenue and H Street.

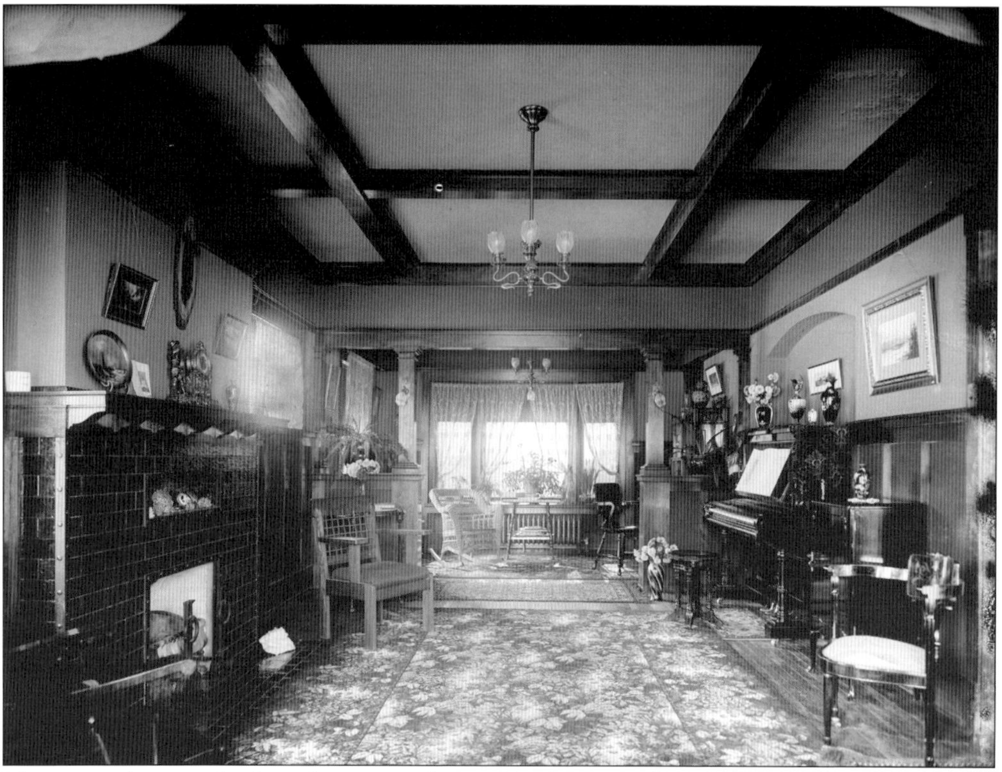

These two photographs show the interior details of architect Walter Ware's home on the southwest corner of First Avenue and U Street. The exterior of the home is a fine example of Dutch Colonial Revival architecture. Built in 1905, the interior details show a mixture of Craftsman and late Victorian styles. Walter E. Ware partnered with Alberto O. Treganza to form one of Utah's most important early architectural firms. The firm of Ware and Treganza designed several prominent commercial buildings in Utah and homes of varying architectural styles.

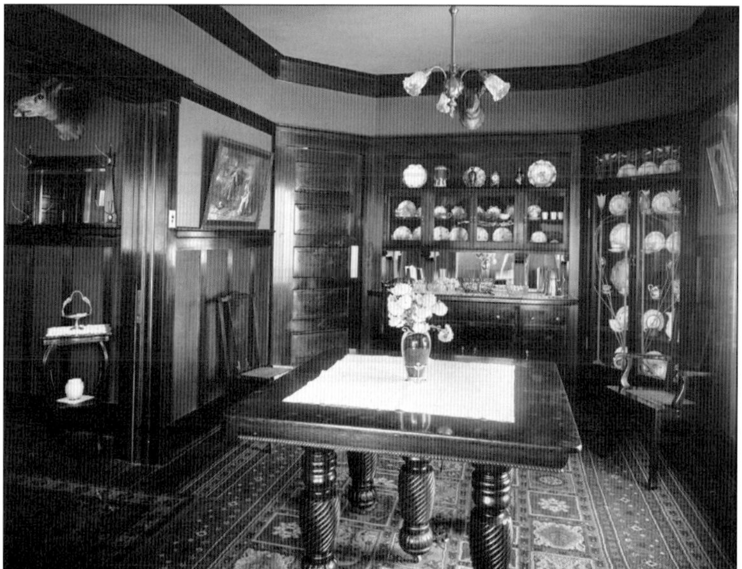

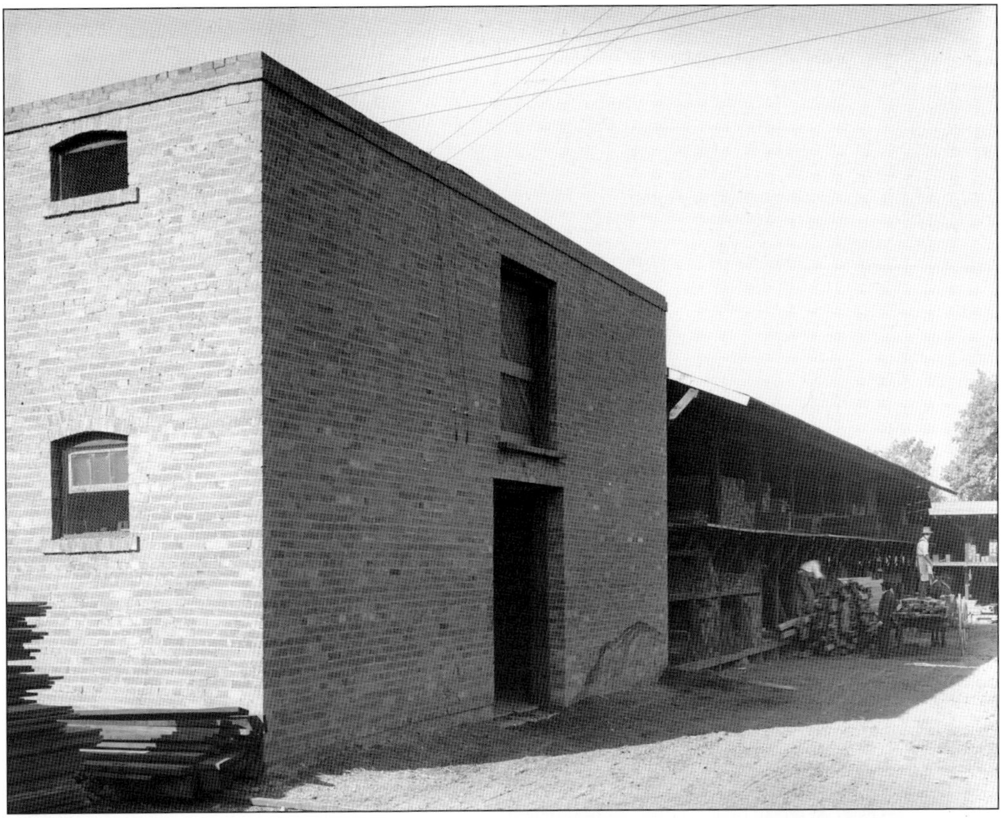

The George Romney Lumber Company was located at 65 North 100 West in Salt Lake City. Lumber used in the construction of numerous Avenues homes came from this yard. George Romney was one of the earliest developers in the neighborhood.

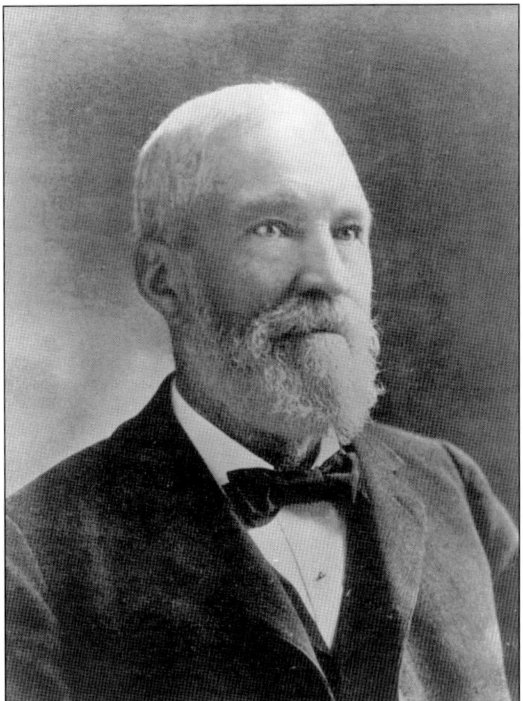

George Romney was a prominent business leader and developer of Avenues properties. He lived in the neighborhood at his C Street home until his death in 1920. Romney was president of George Romney and Sons Company and the George Romney Lumber Company.

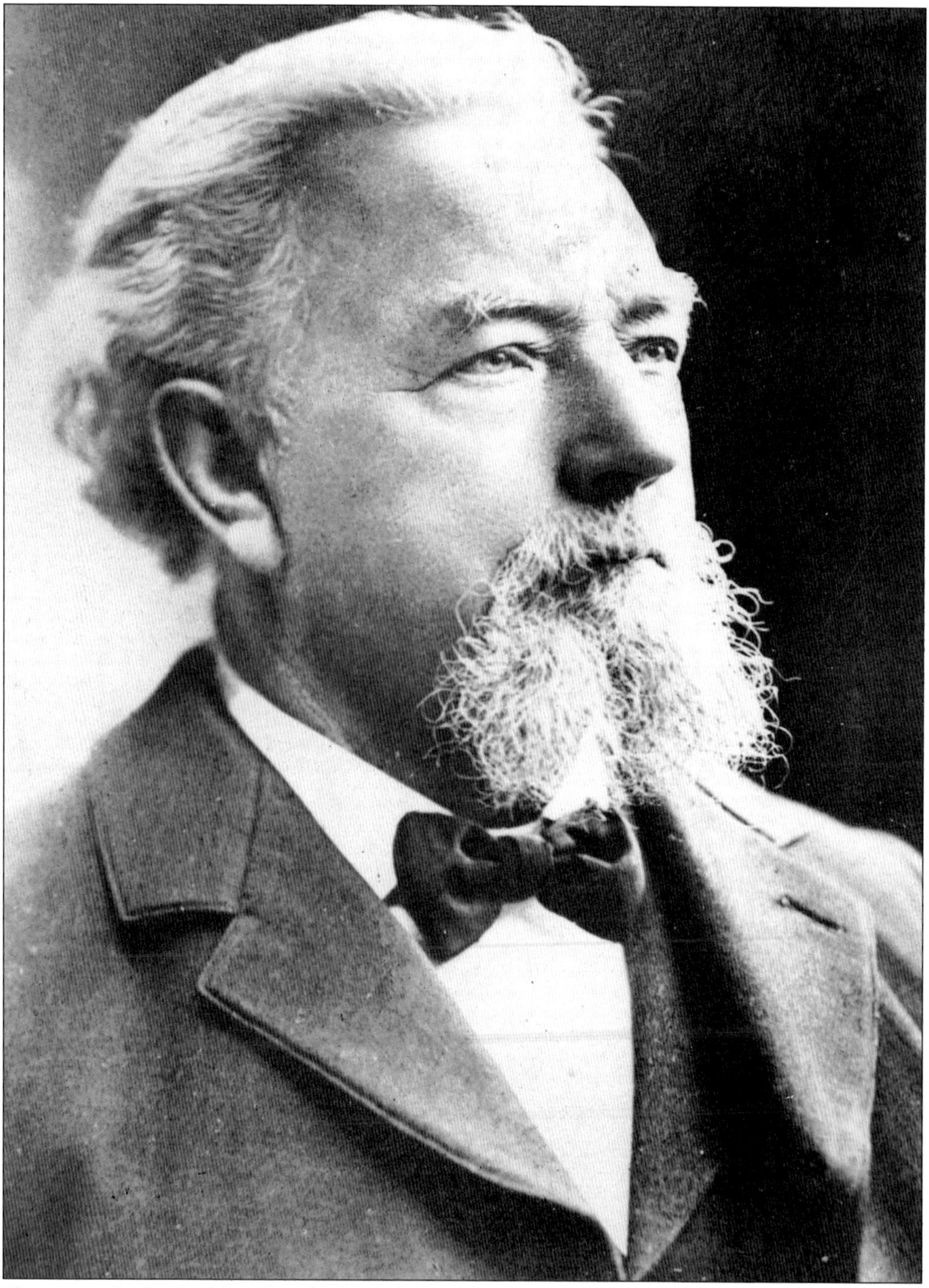

If a person finds an old studio photograph shot in Salt Lake City during the late 19th century, there is a good chance that it was taken in the studio of Charles R. Savage. Savage was Utah's best known early photographer. He was chosen to photograph the joining of the transcontinental railroad at Promontory, Utah.

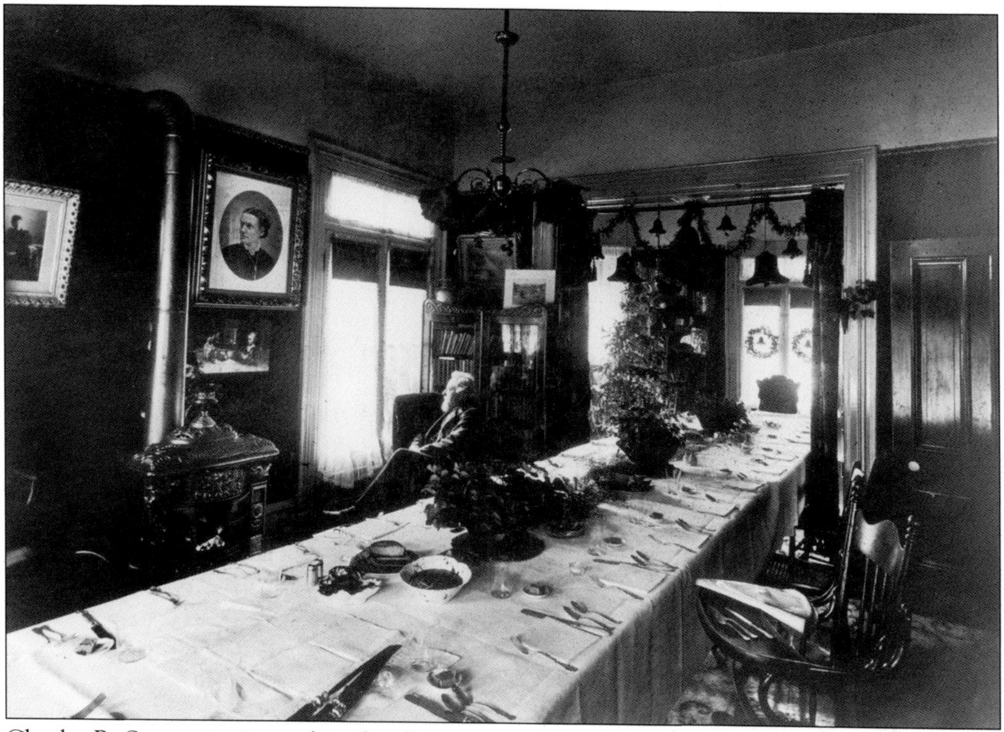

Charles R. Savage is pictured in the dining room of his home on Christmas Day in 1905. The oldest portion of his residence was built in 1871 and still stands at 81 D Street. Although Savage's studio was located on Main Street in downtown Salt Lake City, he also operated a print shop in the rear of his home. Below, employee Frank Pusey is shown outside the shop with some photographic plates.

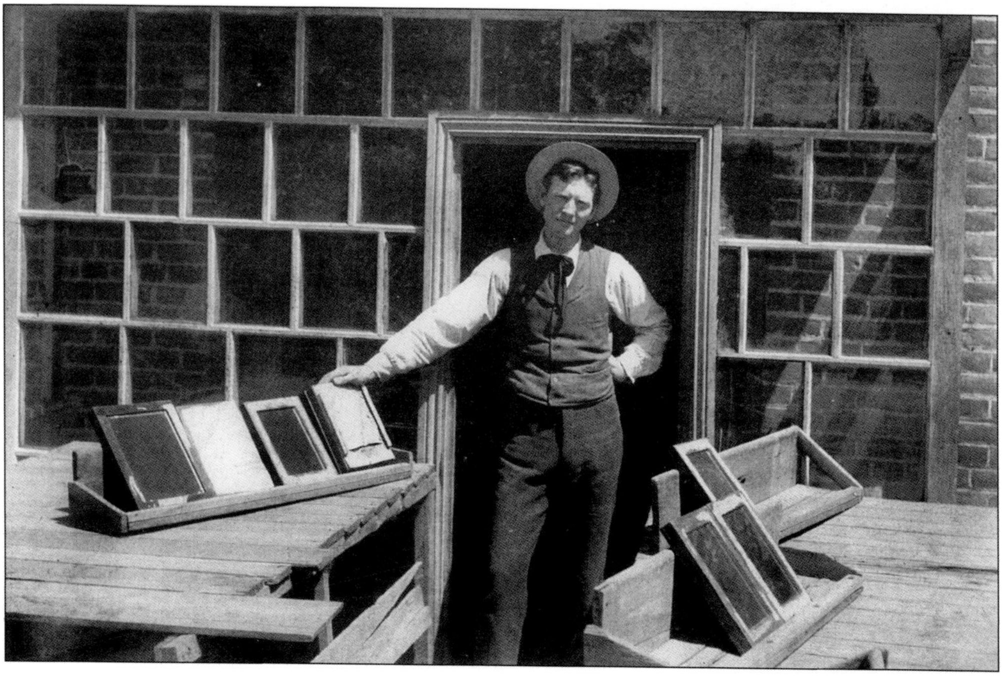

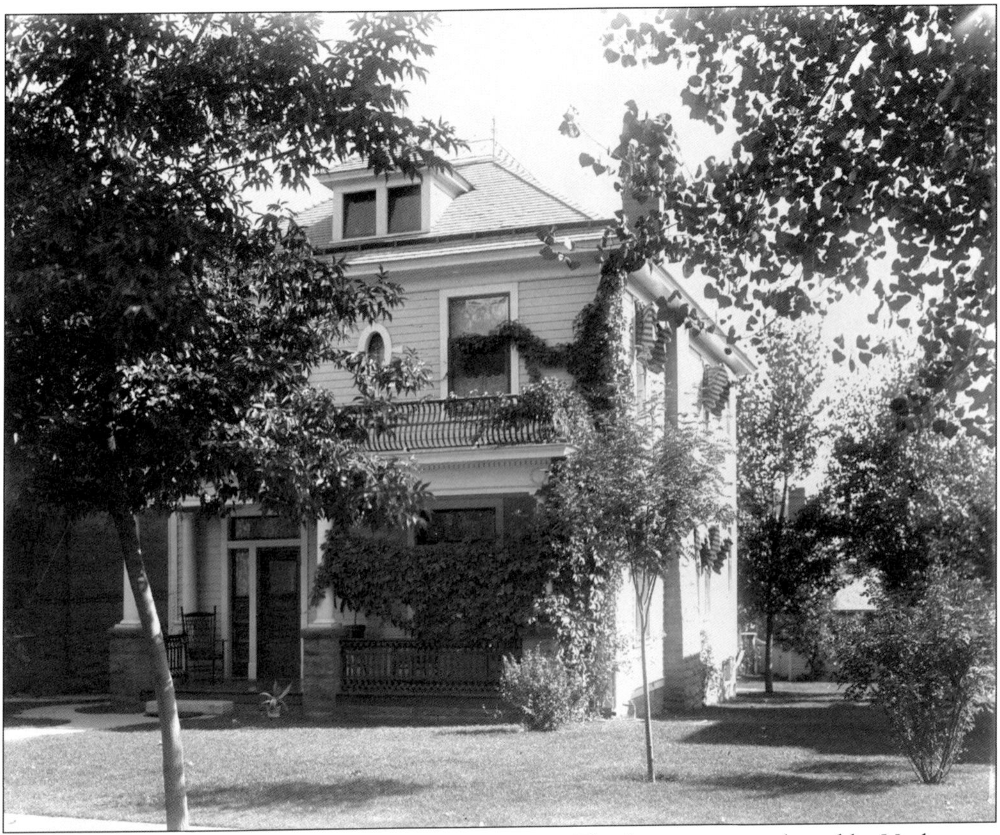

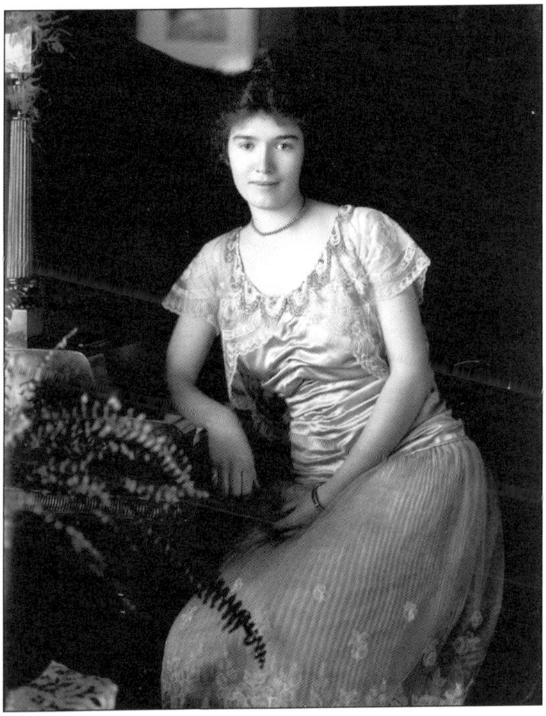

This home was purchased by Utah governor William Spry in 1911. The structure originally stood at 368 First Avenue. It was moved to this location in the mid-1970s when several homes were demolished along First Avenue to construct a parking garage for an office building on South Temple Street. During his time in office, Spry refused to overturn the death penalty of labor leader Joe Hill. Two failed attempts were made by Hill's supporters to blow up this house in 1915.

Lita Spry, pictured at the age of 22, was the daughter of Utah governor William Spry and a well-known figure in Salt Lake City's social circles.

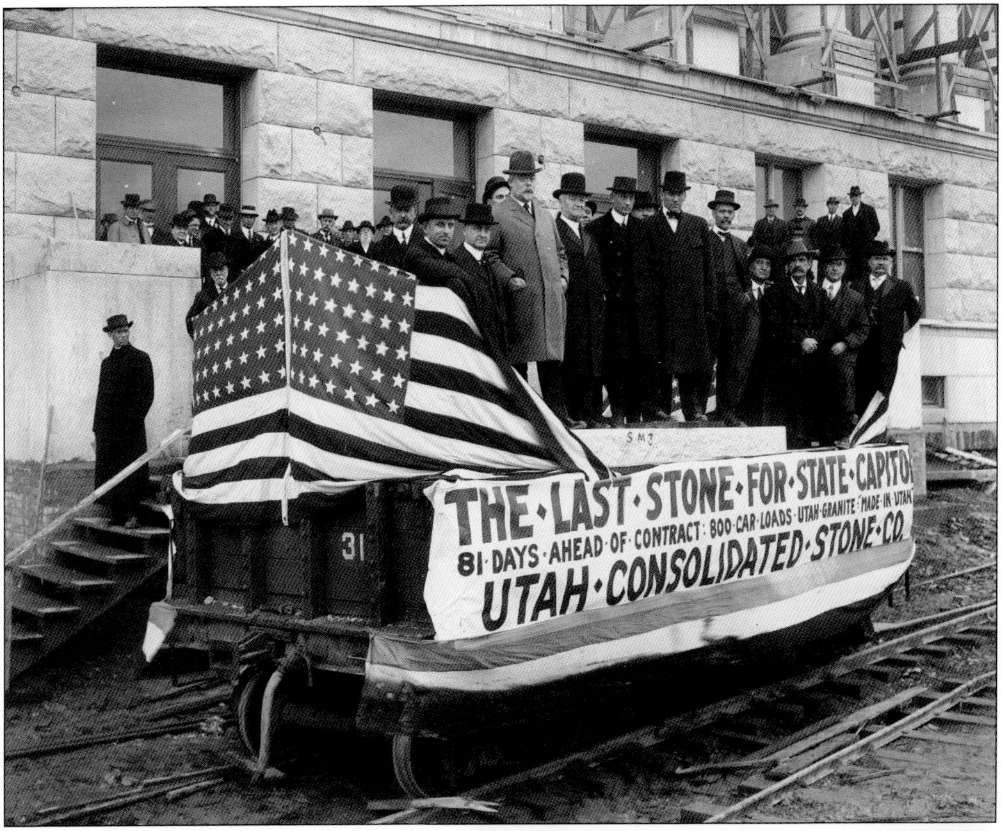

The Utah State Capitol was completed just across City Creek Canyon from the Avenues during the terms of Gov. William Spry. A group of dignitaries present a railcar that delivers the last piece of granite stone for the building. Spry is the tallest man in the grey coat.

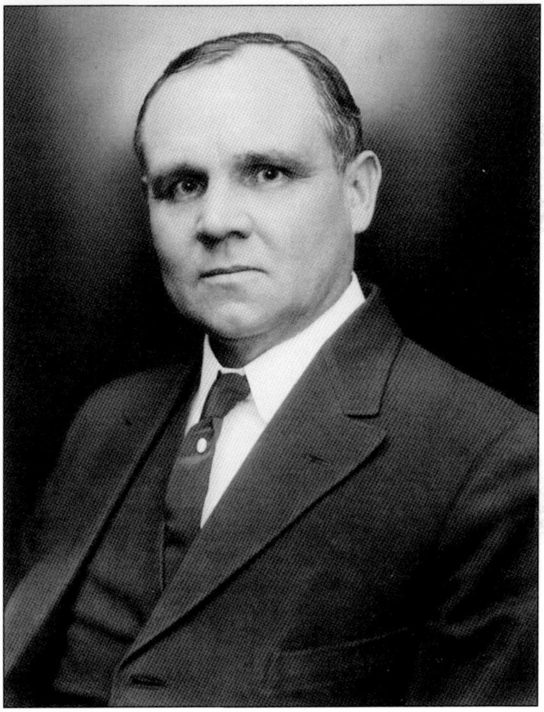

James E. Talmage was a member of the Twelve Apostles of the LDS Church. He was also a mining consultant and professor of geology. Talmage served terms as president of the Latter-day Saints College and the University of Utah. He wrote several books on LDS doctrine, including *The Articles of Faith* and *The House of the Lord*. From 1900 until 1912, Talmage resided at 970 First Avenue, and from 1912 until 1925, he lived at 304 First Avenue.

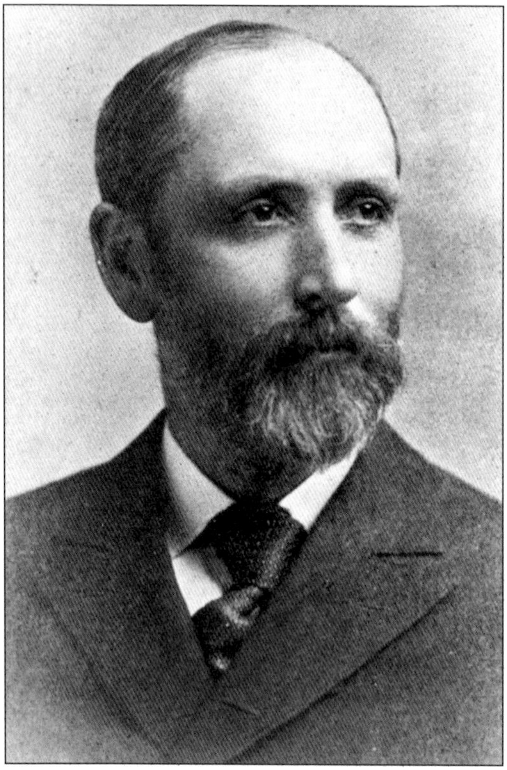

Clarence E. Allen was a member of the Utah Territorial Legislature beginning in 1888. After Utah became a state in 1896, he was elected to the US Congress. Allen was also a lawyer and manager of the Centennial Eureka Mining Company. He resided at 929 First Avenue.

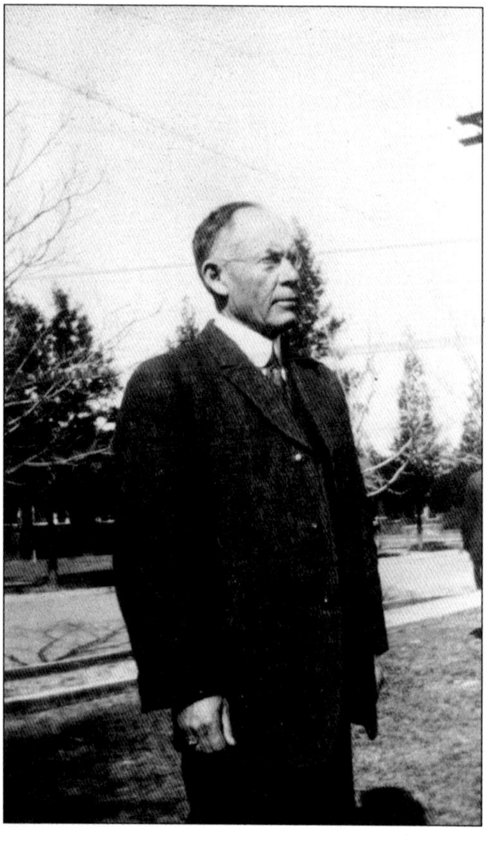

Attorney Joseph Rawlins resided in a Victorian home at 231 First Avenue. Rawlins was an apostate Mormon. He helped form the Utah Democratic Party in 1894 and served Utah as a US senator and congressman. Even though he was not a practicing member of the LDS Church, he supported legislation promoting the interests of the church. His home would become part of Rowland Hall school in 1922.

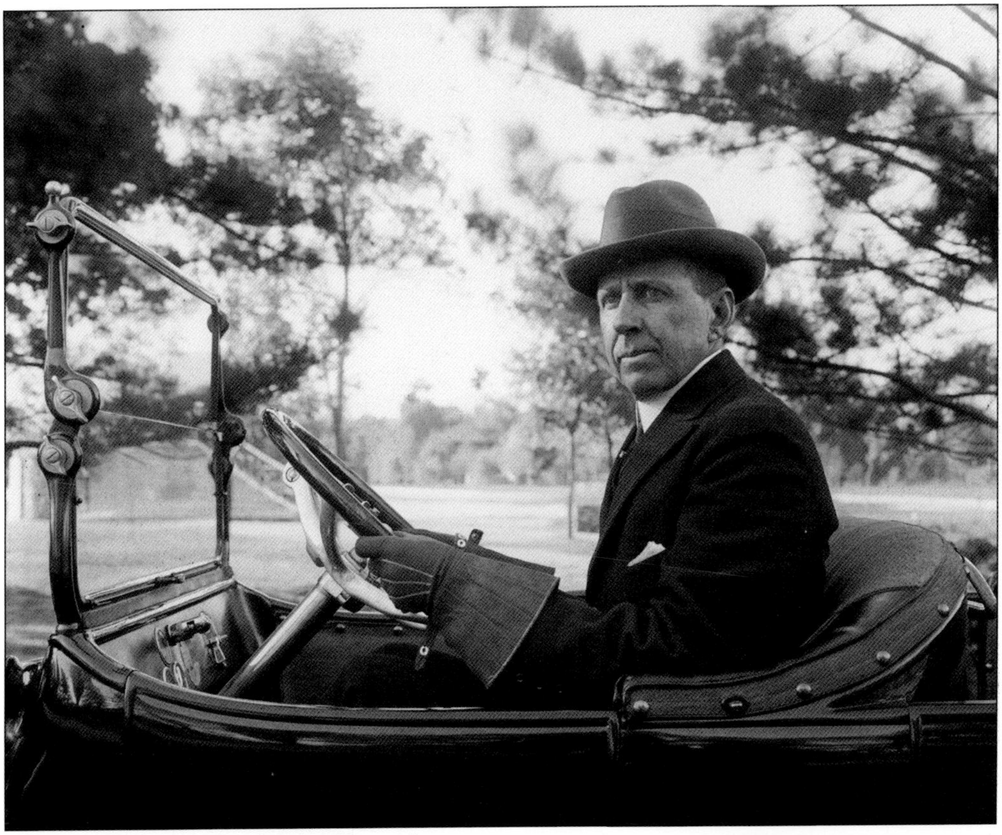

Russel L. Tracy was a noted banker and philanthropist in Salt Lake City. He founded Tracy Boy Scout Camp in Millcreek Canyon and the Tracy Aviary at Liberty Park. Tracy resided at 1024 First Avenue before building a Prairie-style mansion a few blocks away in Federal Heights.

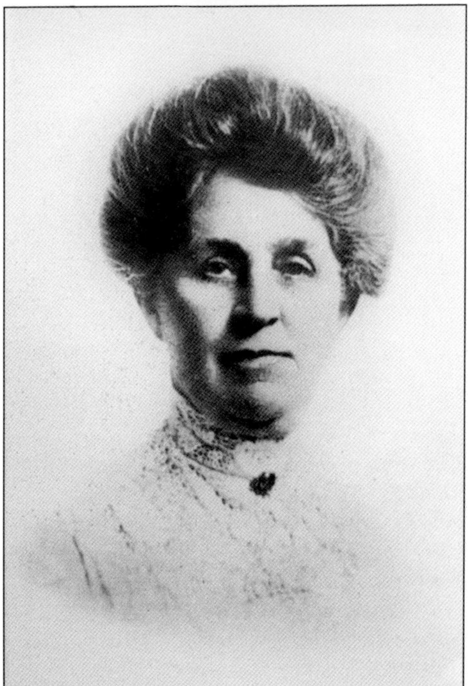

Mary Teasdel, the daughter of successful Salt Lake City businessman Samuel P. Teasdel, studied art in Paris for three years before establishing a successful art studio in her home on C Street.

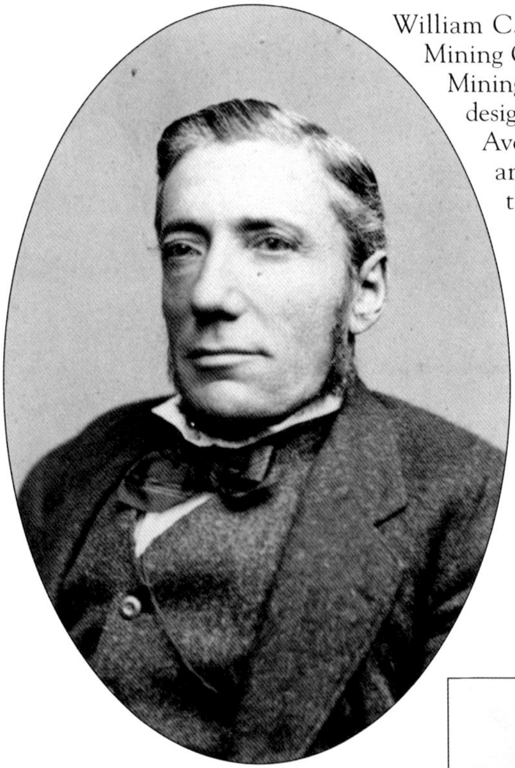

William C. Staines was president of the Cunnington Mining Company and the Cane Spring Consolidated Mining Company. He and his wife, Lillias, had a home designed by Walter E. Ware and built at 461 Second Avenue in 1892. Lillias Staines dealt in real estate and developed several empty lots throughout the neighborhood.

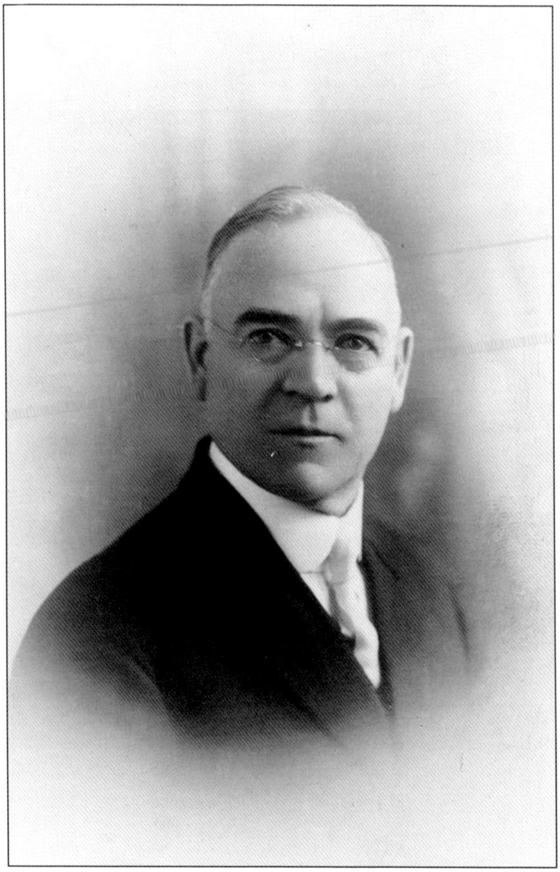

George F. Richards lived at 1010 Third Avenue from 1906 until his death in 1950. Richards was the son of LDS church historian Franklin D. Richards. At the time of his death, he was serving on the Council of the Twelve Apostles for the church.

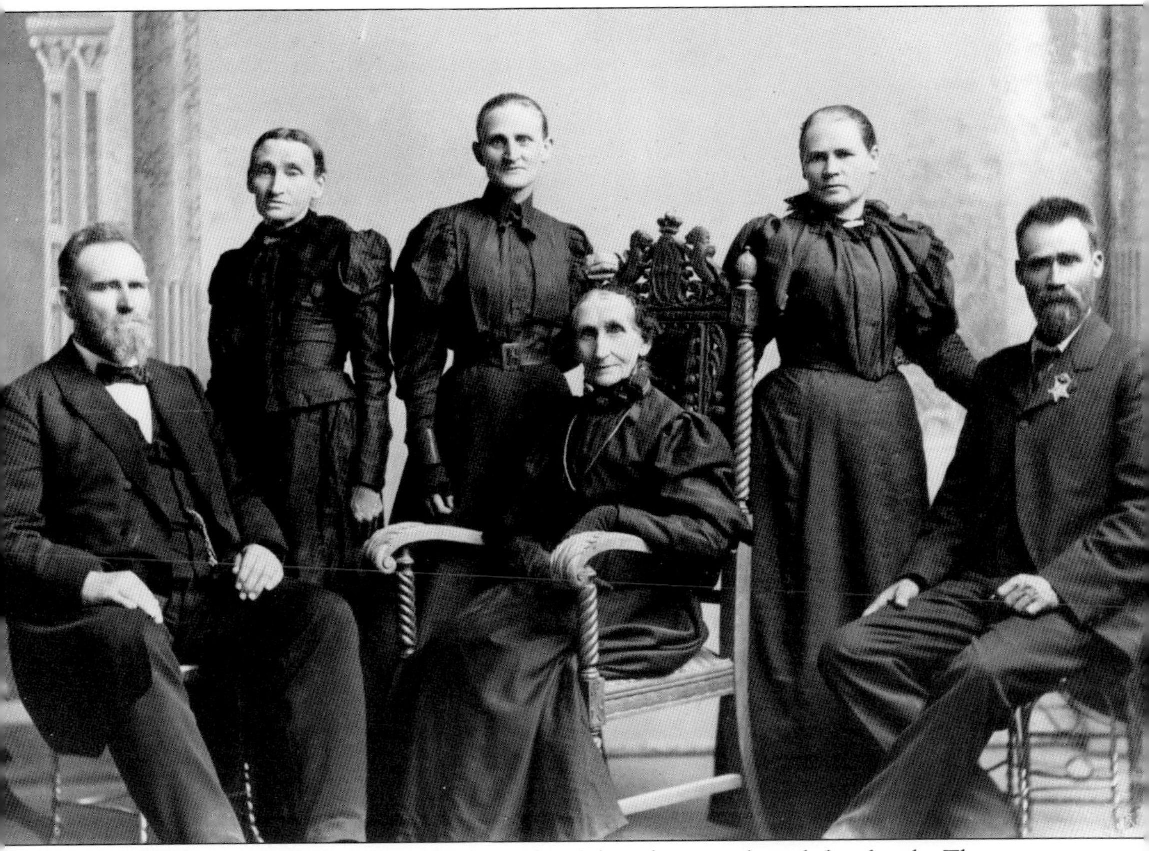

Francis M. Lyman is pictured on the left side of this photograph with his family. The image was captured at Charles R. Savage's studio in Salt Lake City. Lyman was also a member of the Council of the Twelve Apostles for the LDS Church. He lived next door to George F. Richards at 1014 Third Avenue.

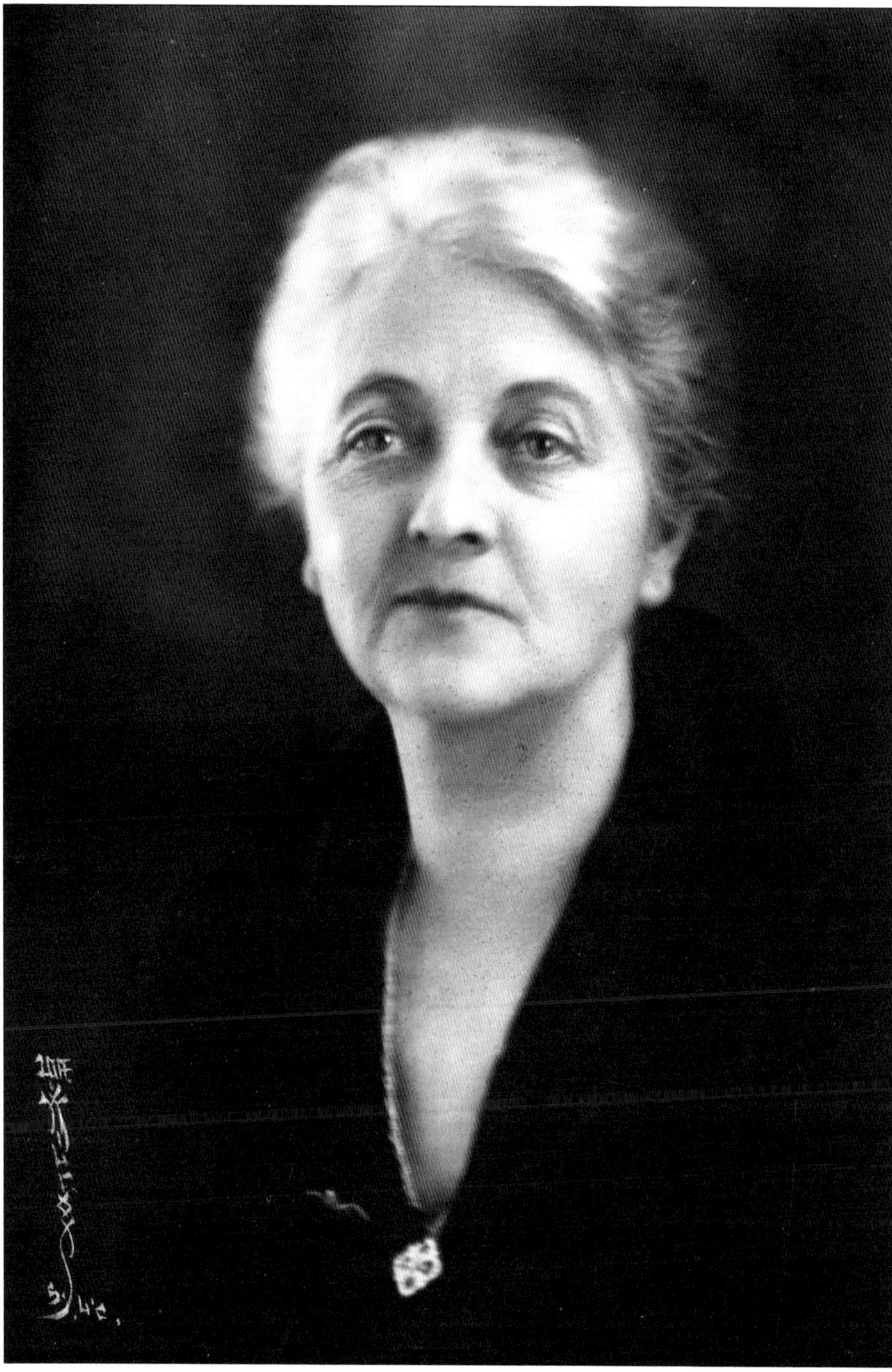

Alice C. Horne was educated at the University of Utah and promoted the arts in Utah during her life. She established the Utah Institute of Fine Arts and the annual state arts exhibit when she was a member of the Utah State Legislature in 1898. She was the author of *Devotees and Their Shrines: A Hand Book of Utah Art*. As an active member of the LDS Church, she helped establish their children's organization. She and her husband, George, purchased 868 Second Avenue in 1924. She operated an art gallery out of her home.

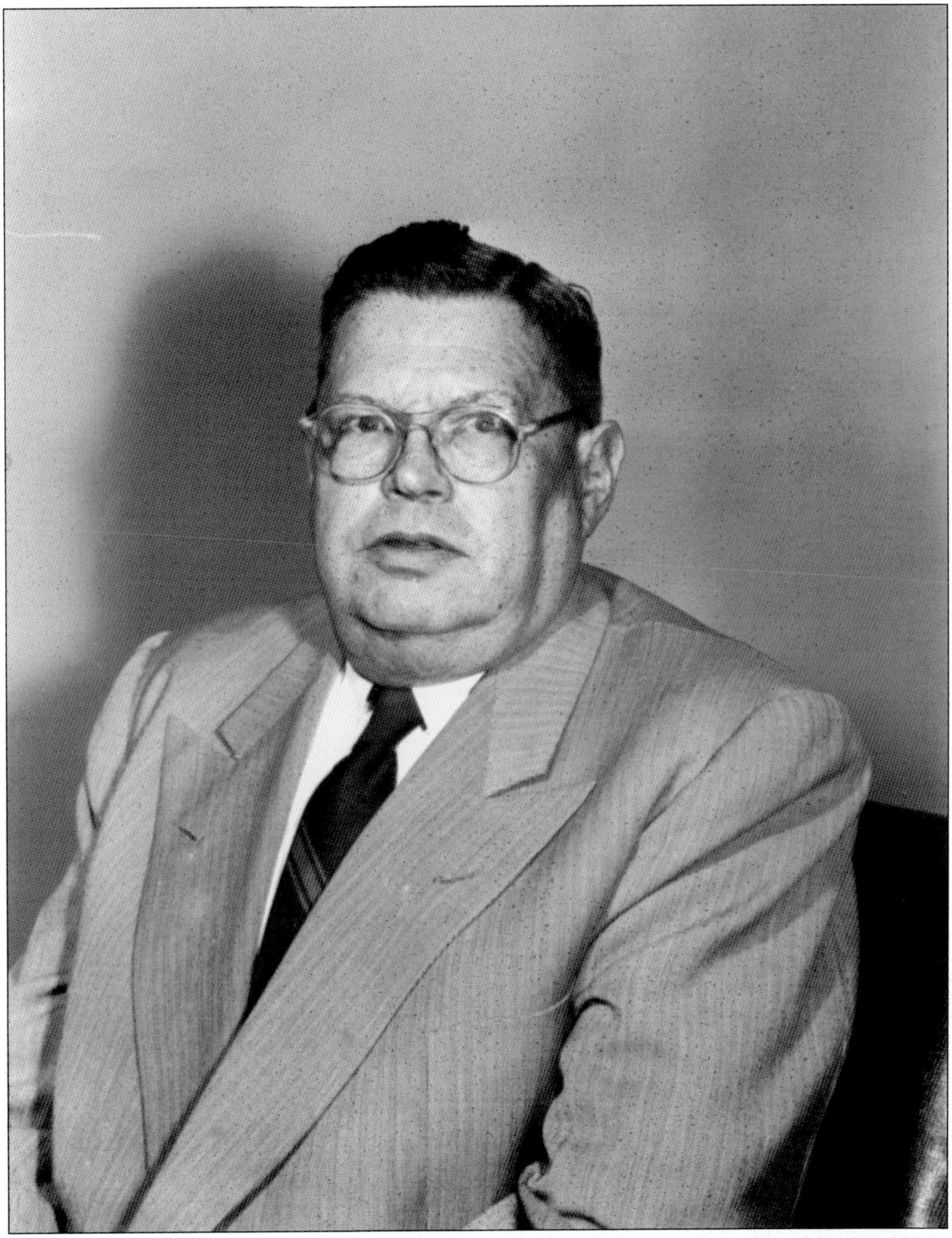

Carl W. Scott was a mining engineer before training as a draftsman for architect Richard K.A. Kletting. He established his own architecture firm in 1914, and his best-known works in Salt Lake City include the Masonic Temple, South High School, and the Shriner's Hospital for Crippled Children. He designed and built his own Period Revival–style home at 765 Eighth Avenue.

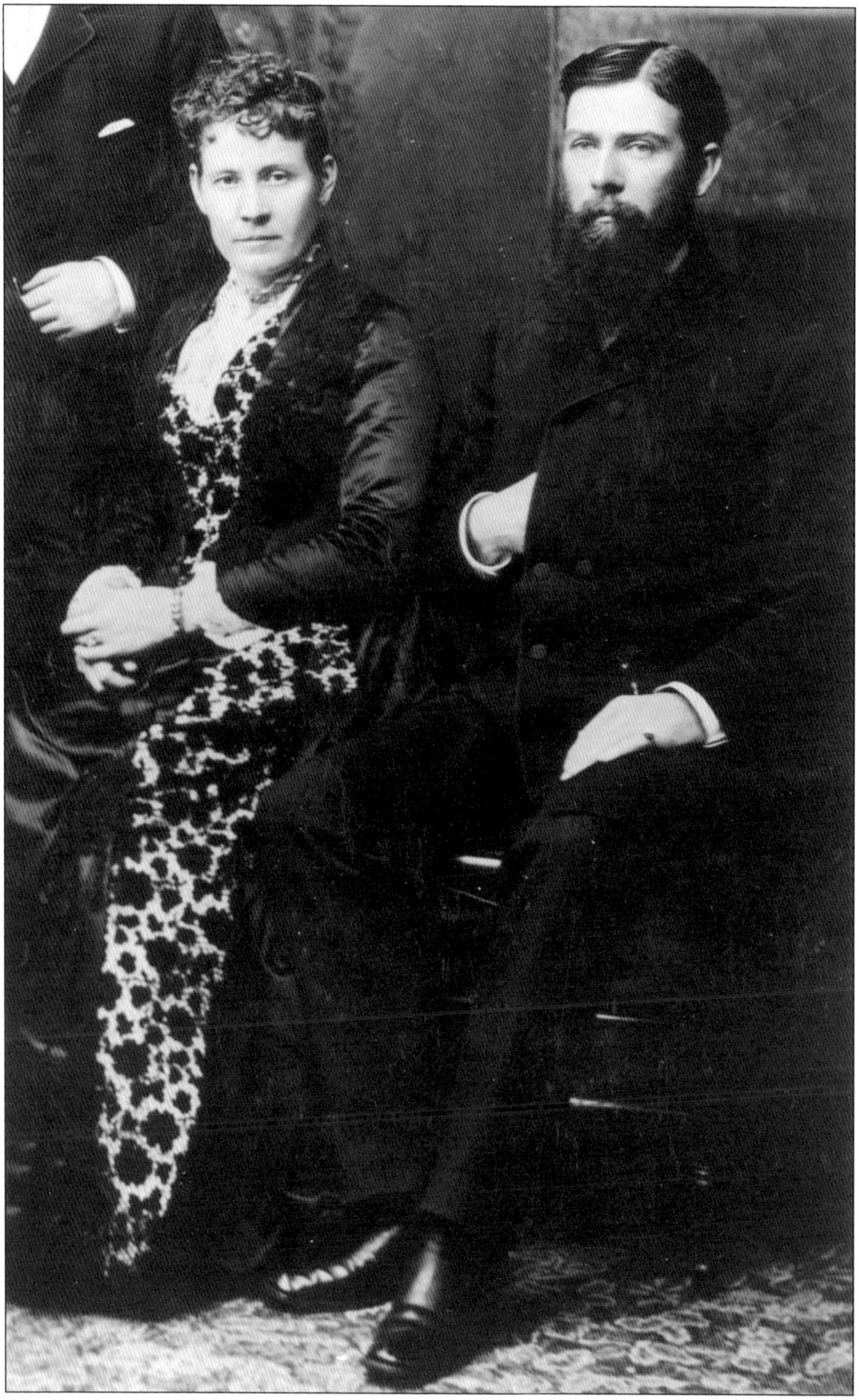

Franklin and Emily Richards resided at 175 A Street. Franklin Richards was a prominent attorney who served as the general counsel for the LDS Church for 50 years. He was a member of the Territorial Legislature and Utah Constitutional Convention. While in the legislature, he was an advocate for woman suffrage. Emily Richards took her advocacy for women's rights to national forums, representing Utah at several suffrage conventions.

Two

Mansions, Victorians, Bungalows, and Cottages

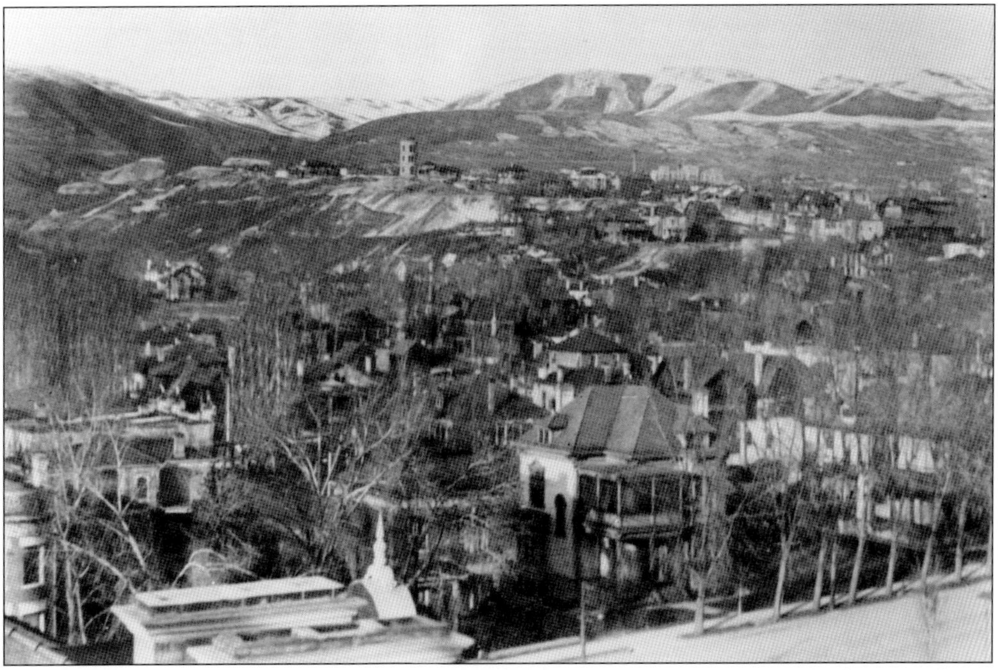

This view of the Avenues was taken from a rooftop on South Temple Street, looking northeast in early spring of 1909. Because the neighborhood was built up over a 70-year period, homes in the Avenues come in many different sizes and styles. This visual diversity gives the Avenues its unique character. While some homes were designed by prominent local architects, the majority came from popular pattern-book plans.

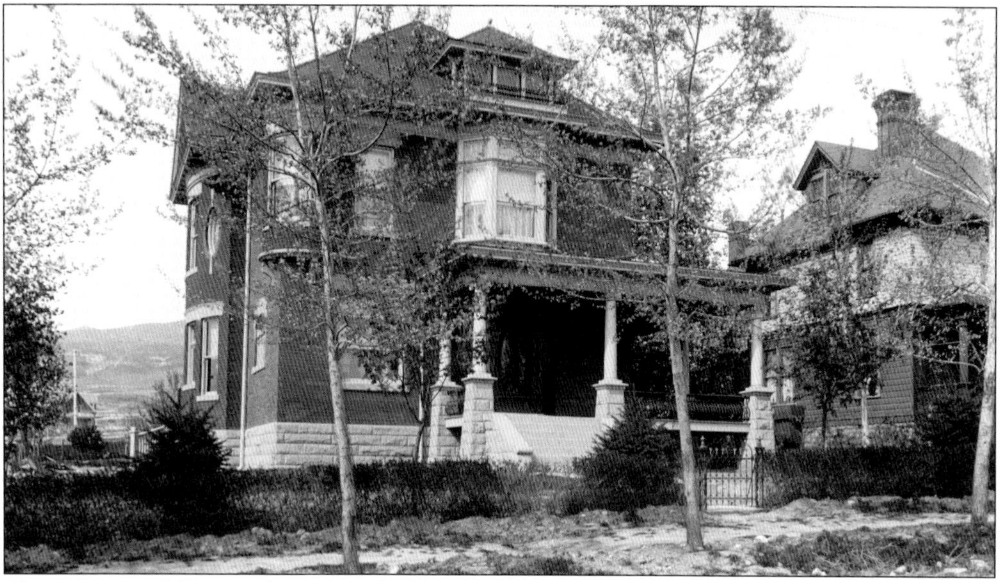

This two-story Victorian home was built on the east end of Second Avenue in 1903 for Earl T. Harvey, a real estate salesman. Later owners of the residence included Christopher B. Diehl, a corporate attorney for the Union Pacific Railroad, and Alexander E. Eberhardt, owner of the Salt Lake Mattress and Manufacturing Company. Turned Doric columns, a second-story rounded corner, and bay window are examples of some of the classical detailing found on the home's exterior. The photograph below shows the ornate woodwork in the entrance foyer and stairwell. To the right of the stairs is a nook with a built-in bench. The latticework in the colonnade is unique for late-period Victorian homes in Utah.

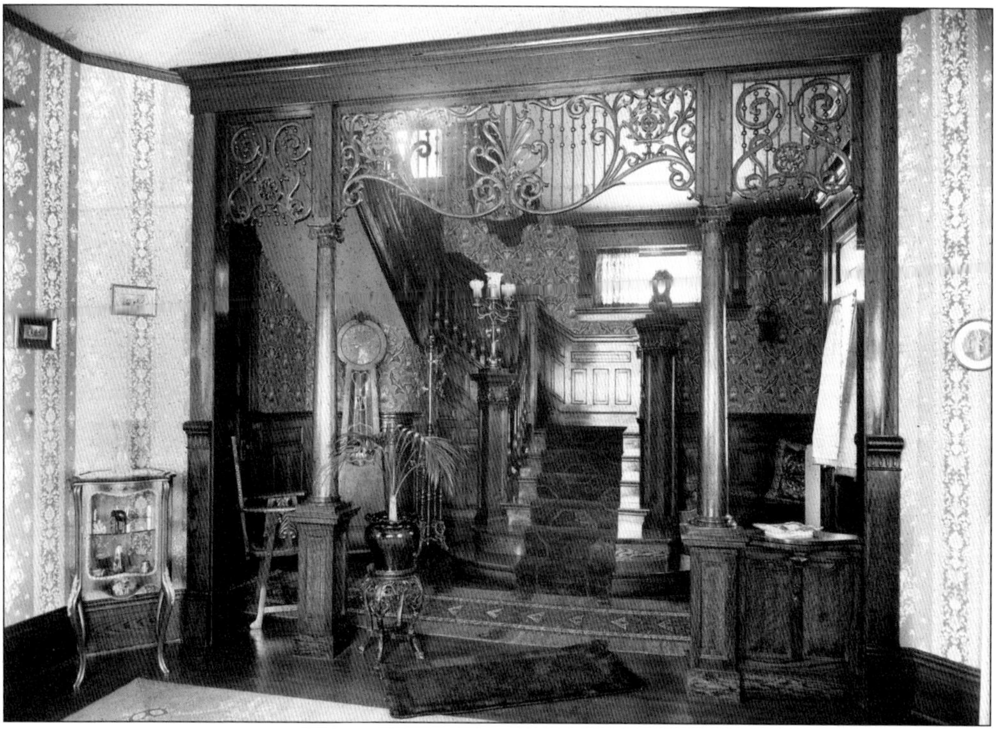

The photograph at right shows the parlor of the Earl T. Harvey home a 1225 First Avenue. A rustic stone fireplace contrasts with the ornate wood-trim detailing of the interior. In the image below, a colonnade separates the parlor from the dining room. Corinthian columns, leaded glass bookcases, and built-in lights make up the colonnade.

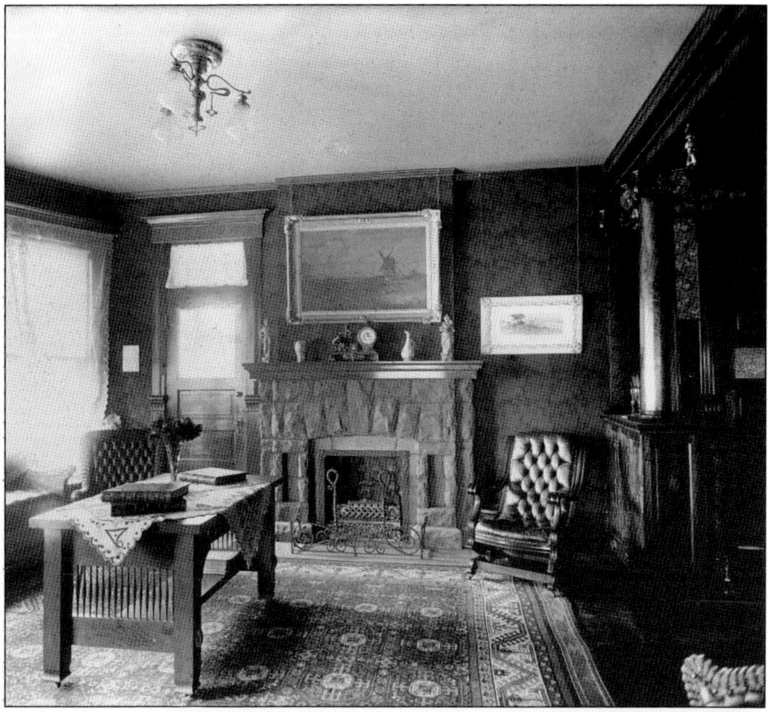

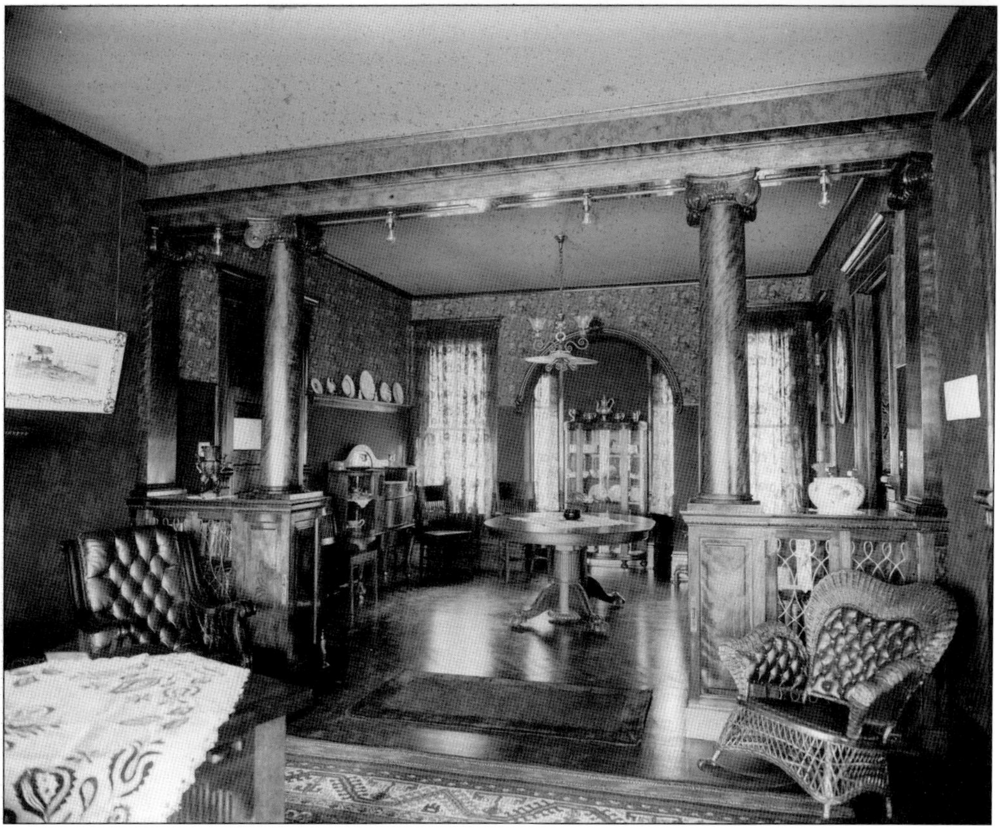

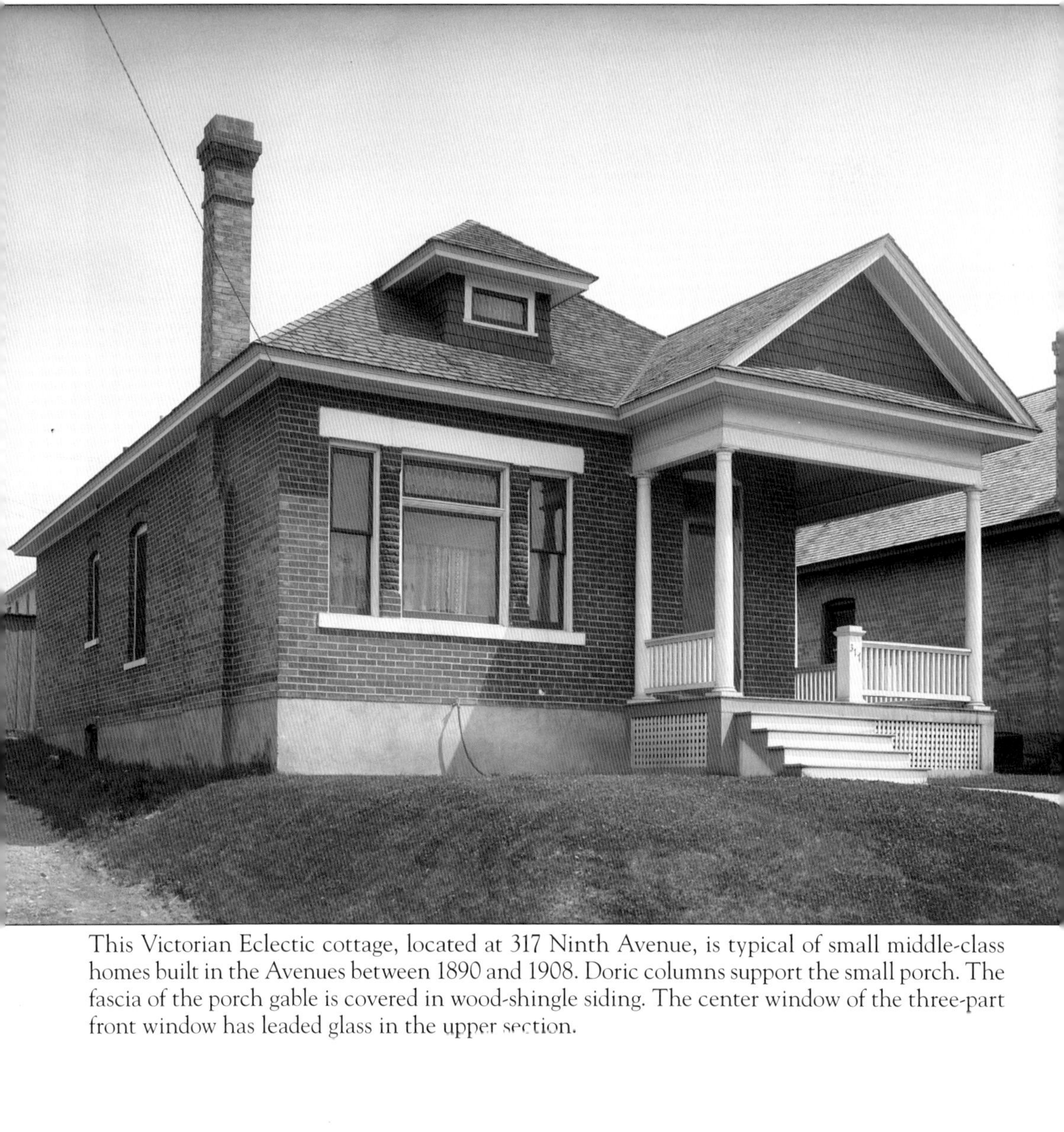

This Victorian Eclectic cottage, located at 317 Ninth Avenue, is typical of small middle-class homes built in the Avenues between 1890 and 1908. Doric columns support the small porch. The fascia of the porch gable is covered in wood-shingle siding. The center window of the three-part front window has leaded glass in the upper section.

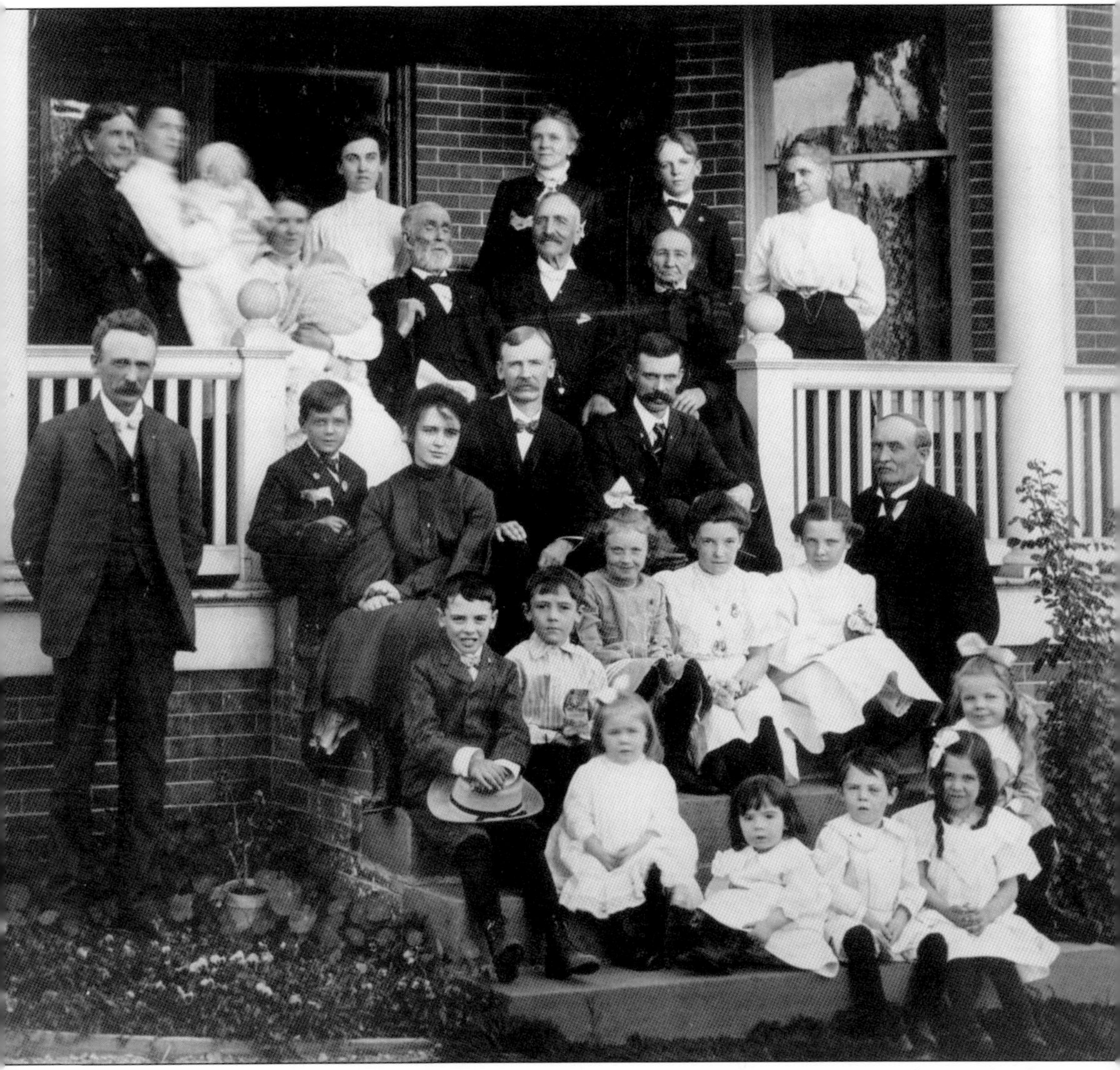

Multiple generations of the John Edward Callister family pose for this portrait on the porch of their home at 360 G Street during the summer of 1904. Callister had died before this photograph was taken. Original members of his family immigrated to Utah from England soon after members of the Mormon Church first settled Salt Lake Valley.

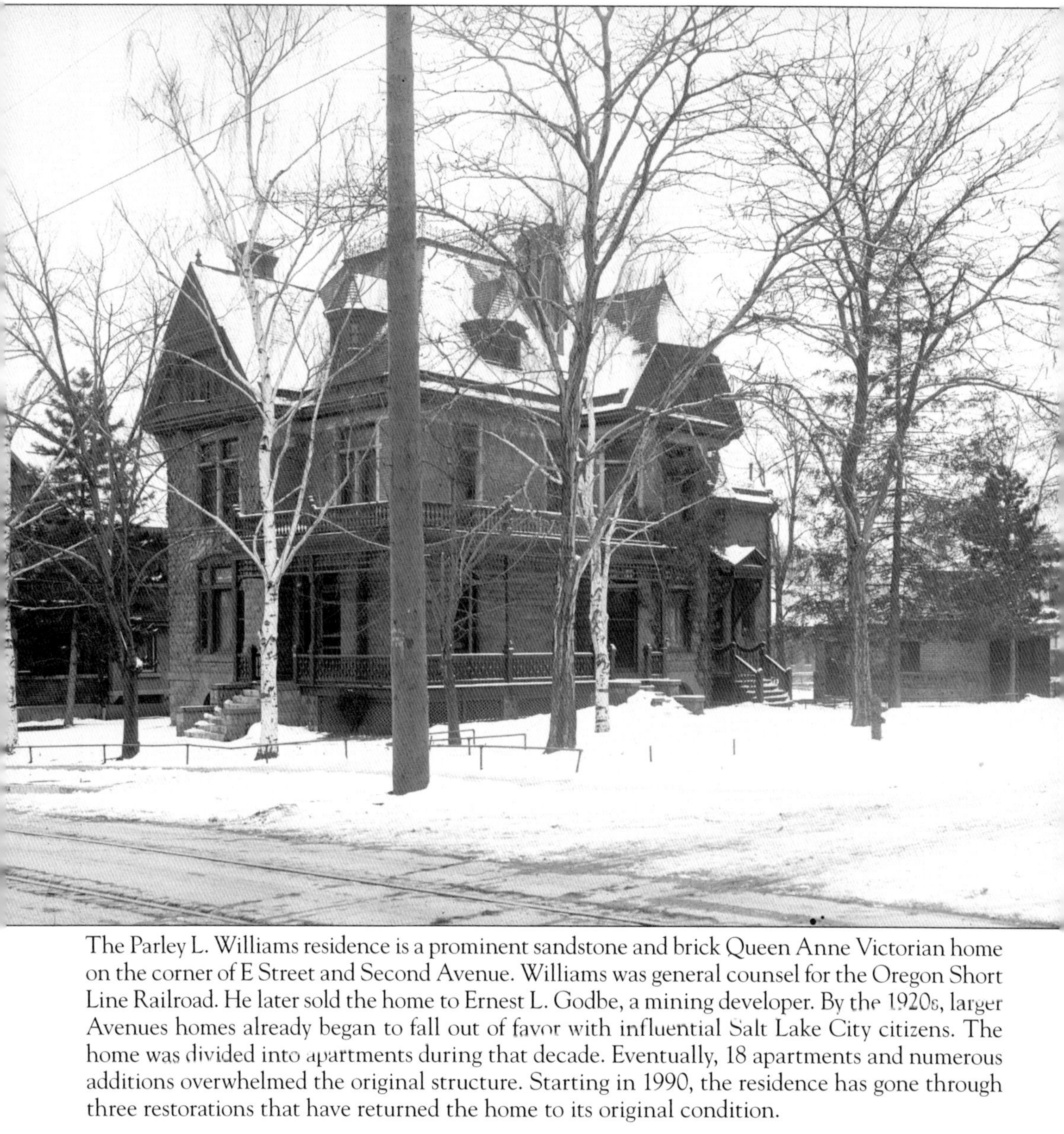

The Parley L. Williams residence is a prominent sandstone and brick Queen Anne Victorian home on the corner of E Street and Second Avenue. Williams was general counsel for the Oregon Short Line Railroad. He later sold the home to Ernest L. Godbe, a mining developer. By the 1920s, larger Avenues homes already began to fall out of favor with influential Salt Lake City citizens. The home was divided into apartments during that decade. Eventually, 18 apartments and numerous additions overwhelmed the original structure. Starting in 1990, the residence has gone through three restorations that have returned the home to its original condition.

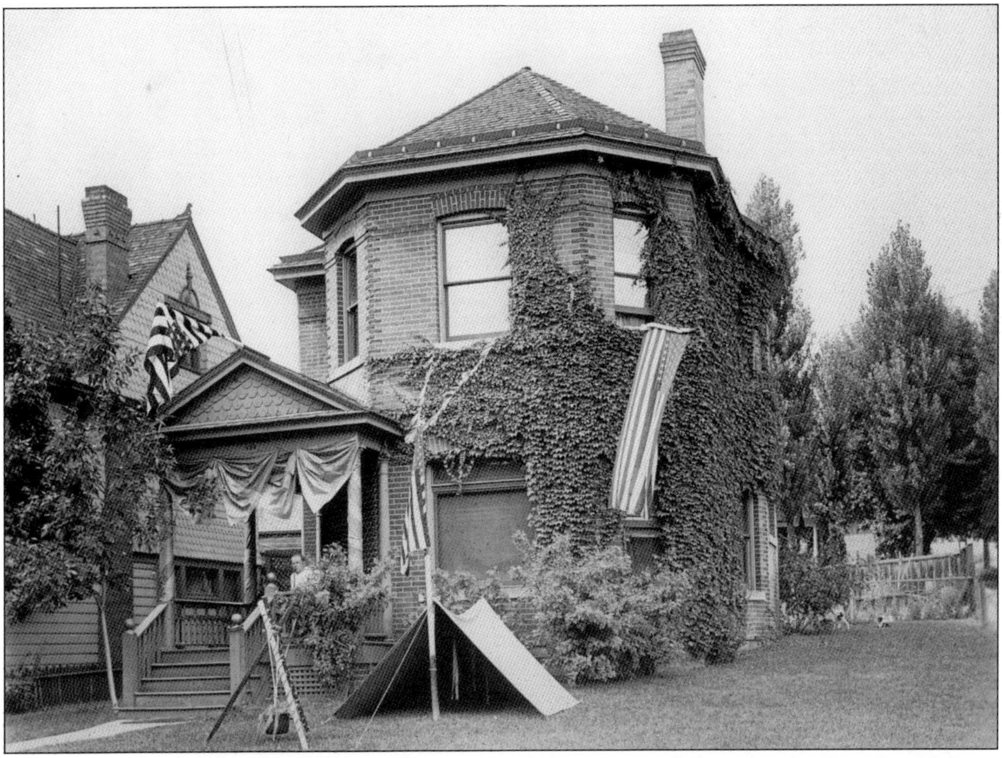

This home at 829 Third Avenue is decorated with bunting and flags for the Fourth of July in 1909. A pup tent camp and flagpole have been set up in the front yard.

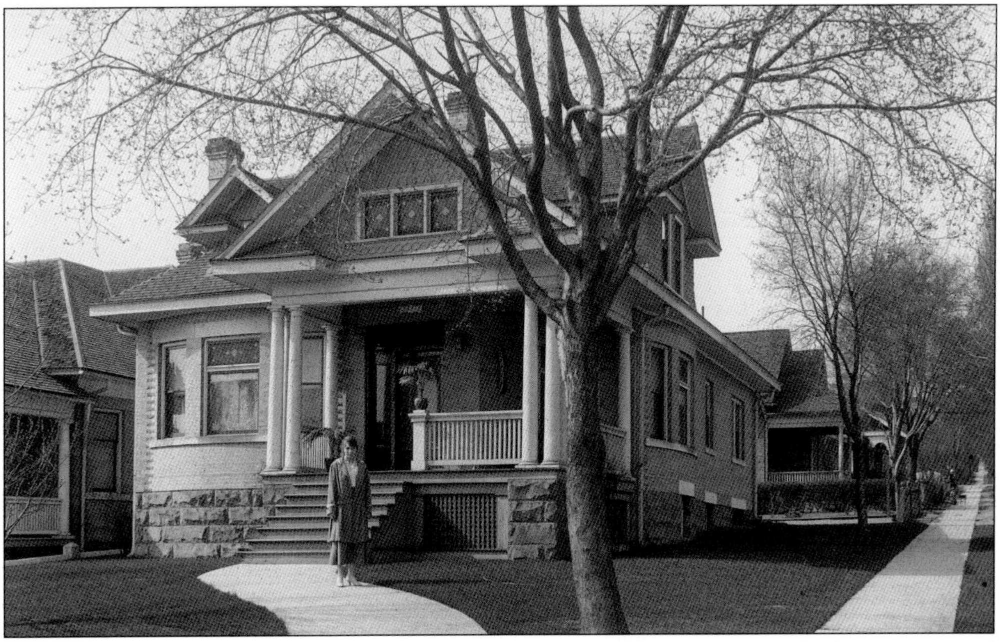

An unknown woman stands in front of this home at 637 Third Avenue. The house is a good example of a Victorian cottage design derived from a pattern book. Pattern-book Victorian homes are the most common type of residence located in the neighborhood.

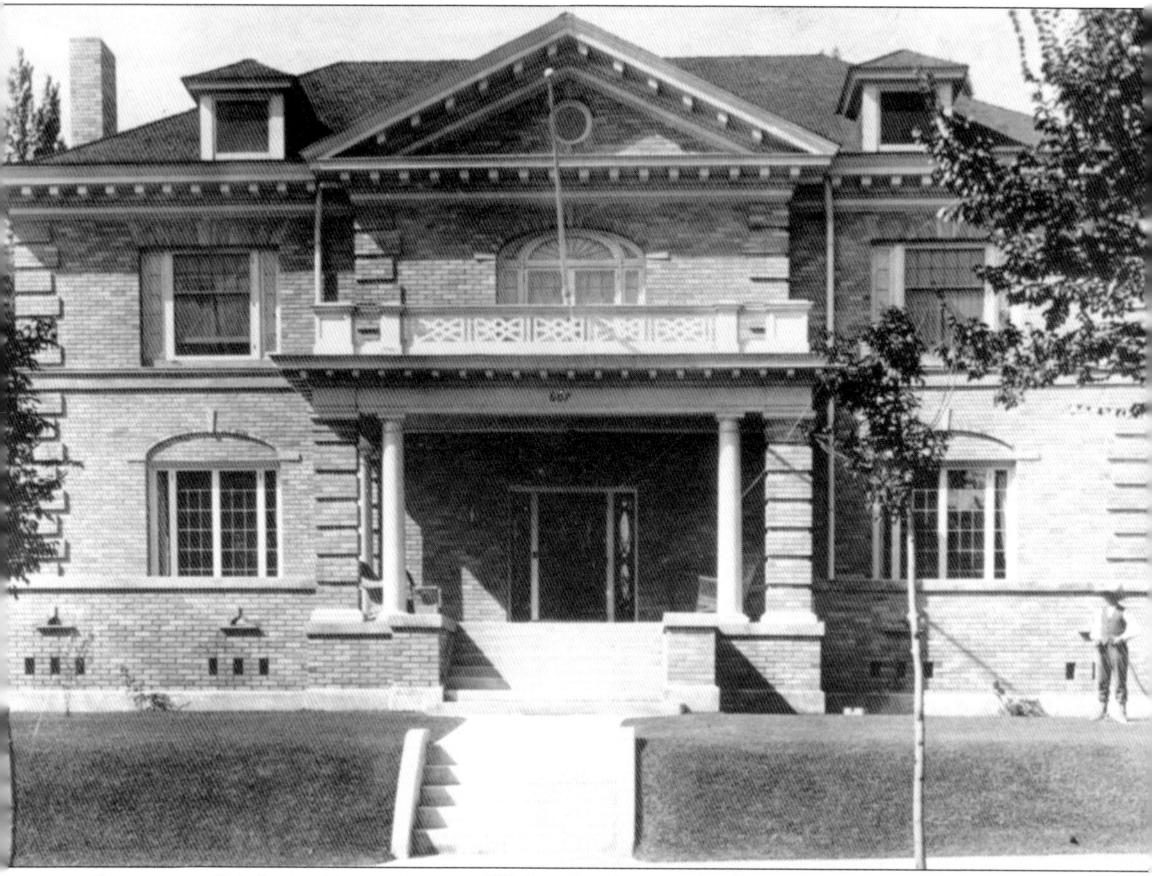

Prominent Salt Lake City architects Walter E. Ware and Alberto O. Treganza designed this Georgian Revival mansion for Adrian C. Ellis. This style is not common in the Avenues. Ellis was an attorney specializing in mining law and successfully invested in numerous mining properties. He served on the board of directors of several large Utah companies, including First Security Bank. The building was a rest home during the 1950s and 1960s.

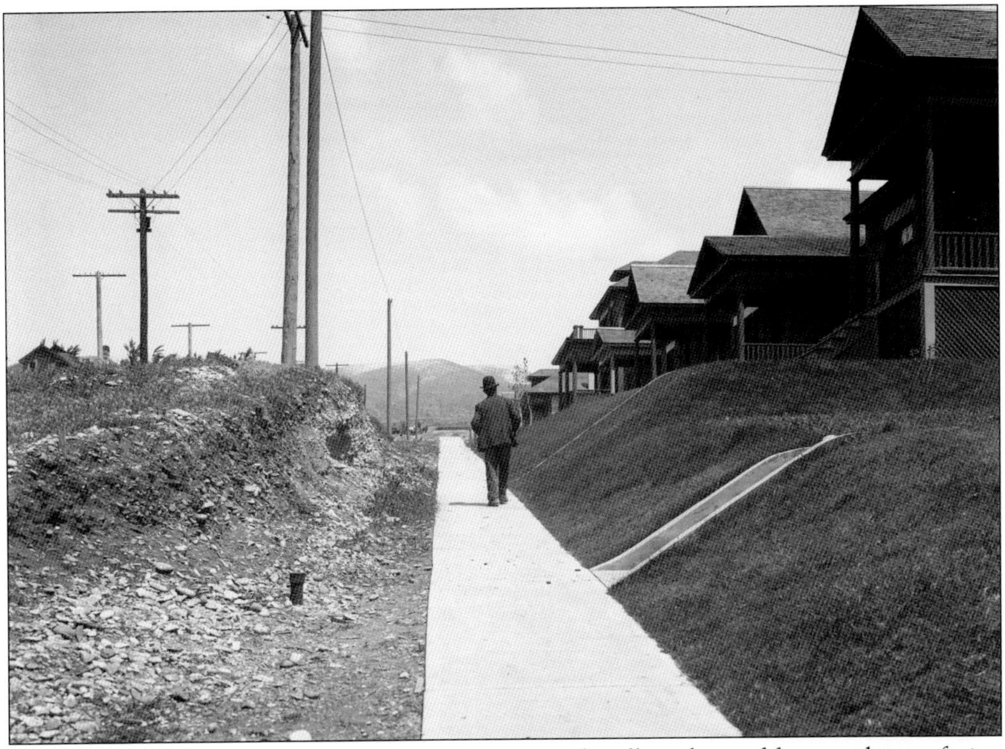

In the photograph above, a man walks up the steep sidewalk in front of five new homes facing C Street between Ninth and Tenth Avenues in 1908. The image below shows a front view of three Victorian cottages. These pre-bungalow homes were popular in the neighborhood. The residences were completed and occupied prior to the grading of C Street. The entire block is now occupied by the imposing LDS Hospital Physicians Tower and parking lot. Construction of the facility resulted in the demolition of nearly 30 homes in the mid-1970s. This project was one of many that galvanized the Avenues community to oppose further out-of-scale development and promote historic preservation.

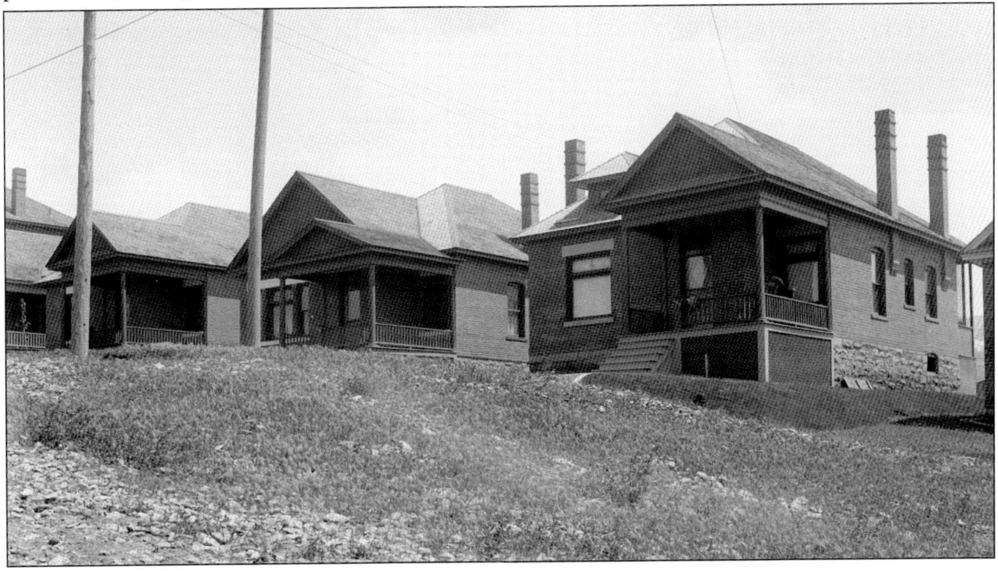

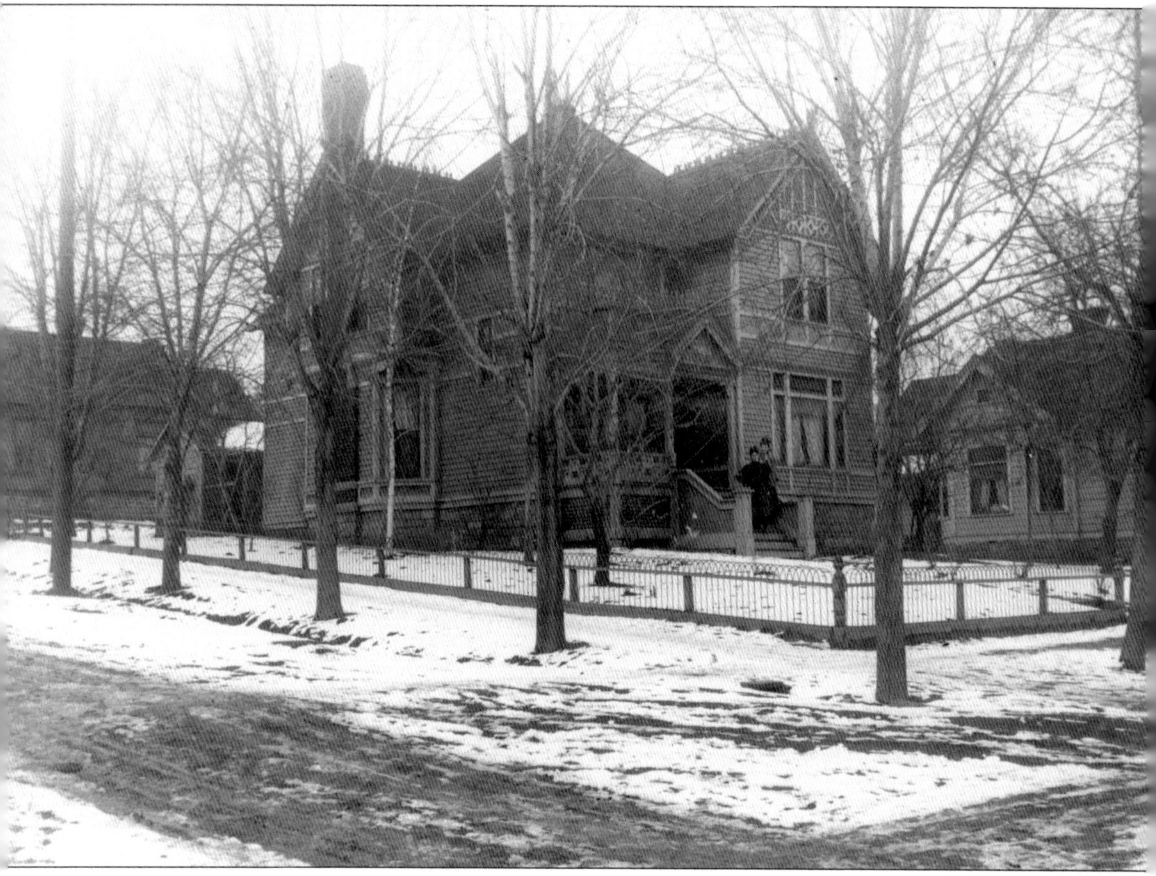

The Oliver and Georgia Jennings house was built on the corner of D Street and Sixth Avenue in 1890. Jennings, an executive with the Empire Laundry Company, maintained the home as a rental property for 20 years after it was constructed. The home is an early example of building a residence for rental purposes in the Avenues. The structure was encased in aluminum siding in the 1950s, hiding the ornate Victorian detailing. In 2001, the exterior was restored with the removal of the siding.

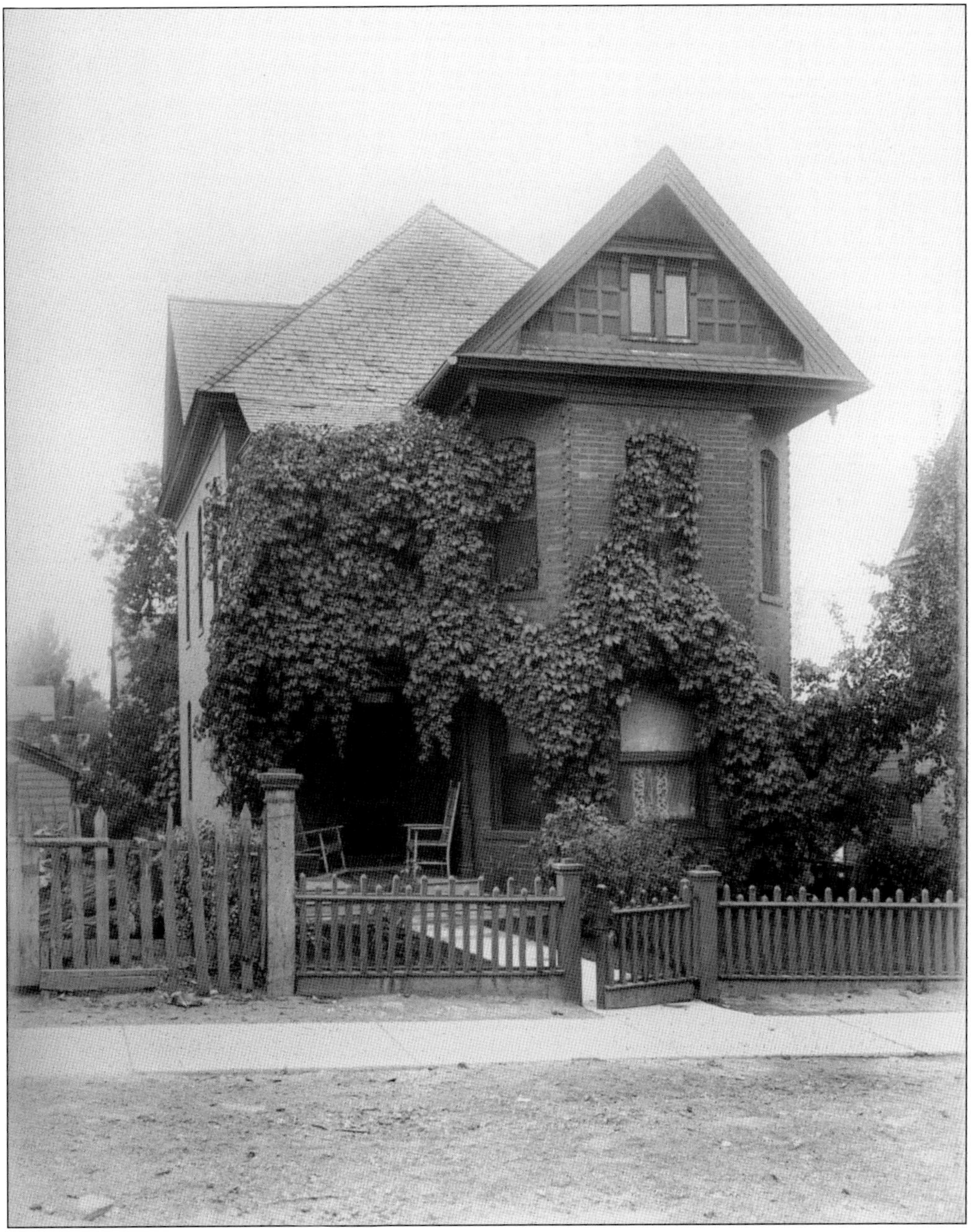

This vine-covered Victorian residence is located at 868 First Avenue. The home was built by E.G. Woodmansee for James Easton in 1895. Easton sold the home in 1899 to Milton E. Lipman, a Salt Lake City treasurer, founder of the Mercantile Investment Company, leader of the Salt Lake City Rotary Club, and an active Mason. The home was converted into apartments during the Great Depression. The residence was restored in the 1970s and is once again a single-family home.

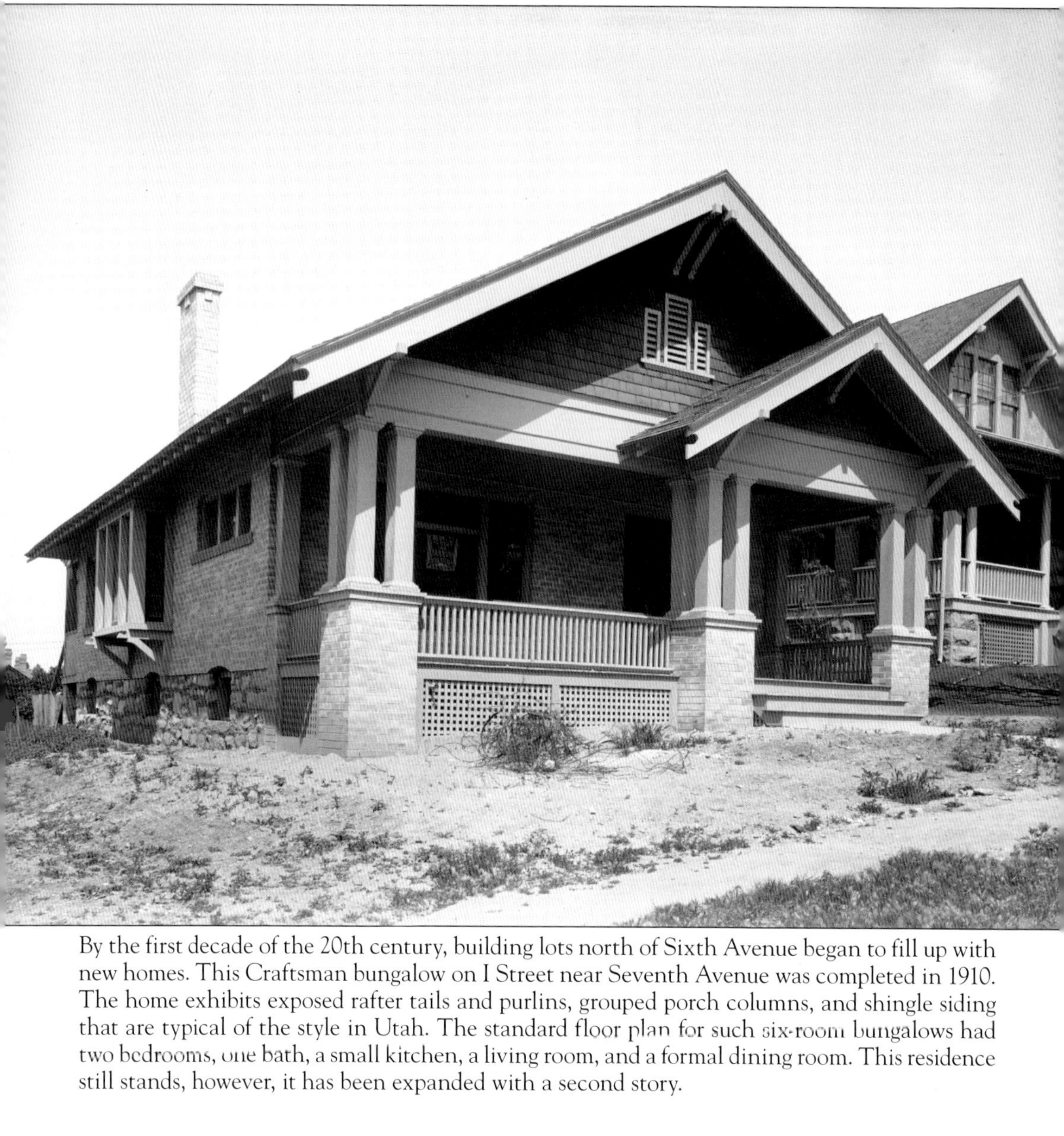

By the first decade of the 20th century, building lots north of Sixth Avenue began to fill up with new homes. This Craftsman bungalow on I Street near Seventh Avenue was completed in 1910. The home exhibits exposed rafter tails and purlins, grouped porch columns, and shingle siding that are typical of the style in Utah. The standard floor plan for such six-room bungalows had two bedrooms, one bath, a small kitchen, a living room, and a formal dining room. This residence still stands, however, it has been expanded with a second story.

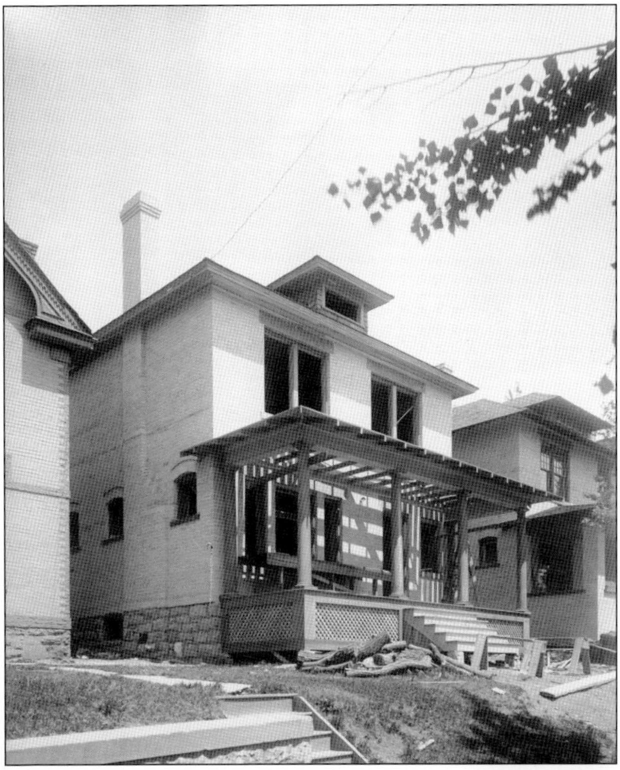

These two homes on First Avenue between O and P Streets were built in 1909 by the Salt Lake Security and Trust Company. The company was owned by Frank McGurrin, who had previously worked with Elmer E. Darling in the development of the nearby Darlington Place subdivision. The Salt Lake Security and Trust Company published a book entitled *Owning Your Own Home* in 1908. The publication was directed at the middle class, promoting the benefits of home ownership. McGurrin specifically promoted those homes and neighborhoods developed by his company. Three quarters of the homes featured in the book were located in the Avenues.

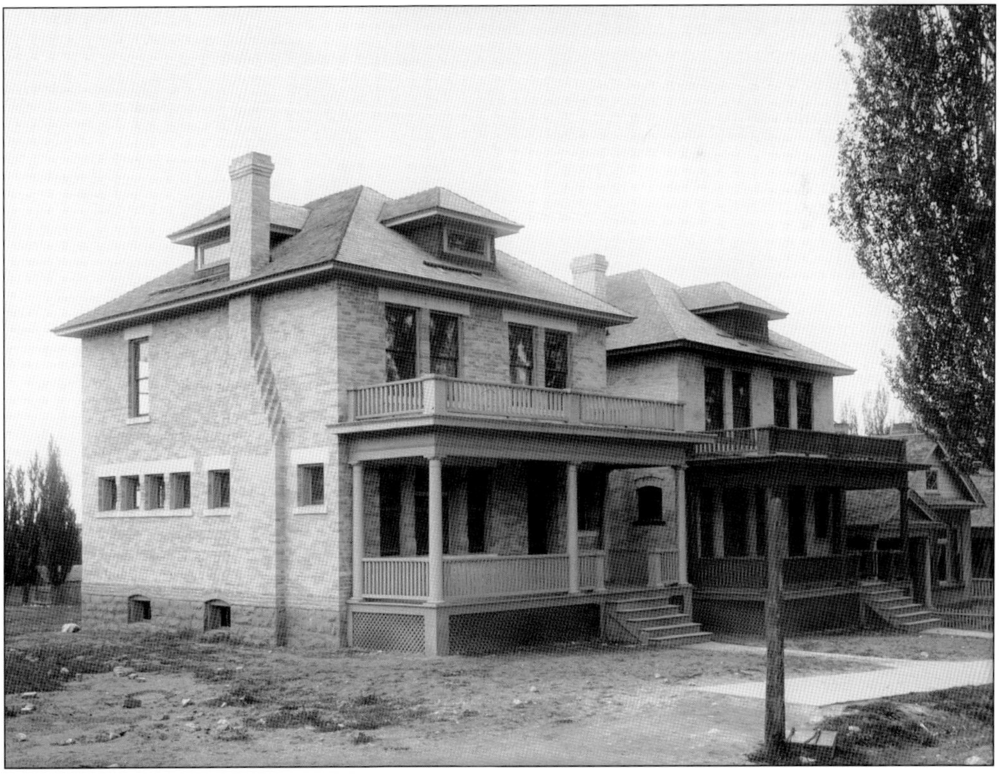

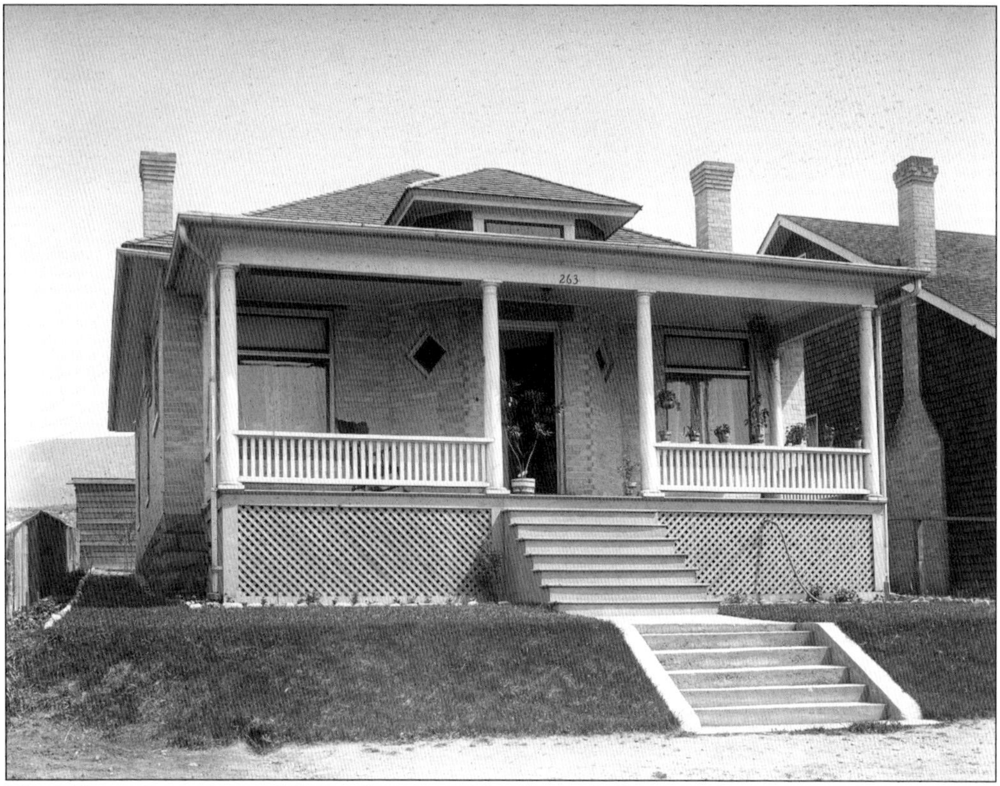

This Eclectic bungalow at 263 Tenth Avenue blends two different architectural styles. The Doric columns and diamond-shaped windows are more commonly found on Victorian cottages, while the full-width front porch is typical of the bungalow style. This home still stands, but the exterior was significantly altered in the 1950s.

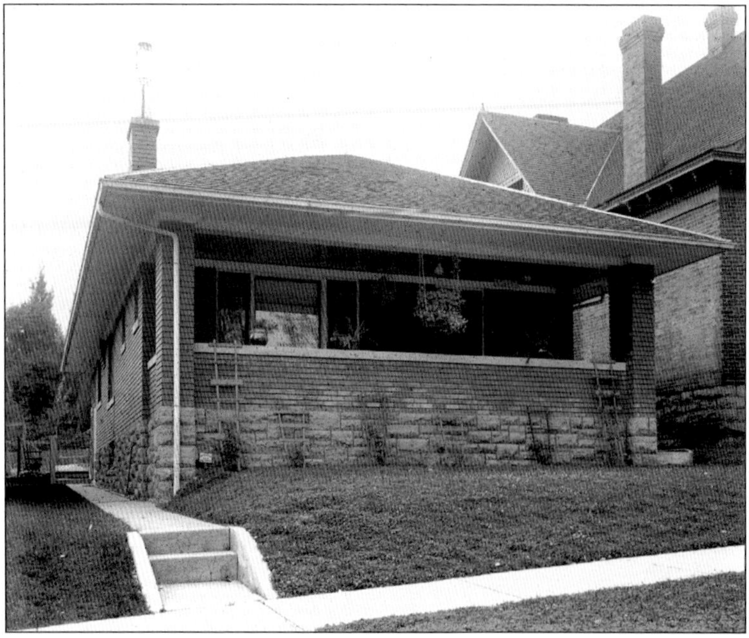

Charles A. Newton was the builder of numerous bungalows similar to this home throughout Salt Lake City in the second decade of the 20th century. This one-story, brick, Prairie-style bungalow located at 1083 First Avenue is an example of a popular design found throughout Utah. These homes were typically built out of brick with a full-face front porch, hip roof, and no dormer.

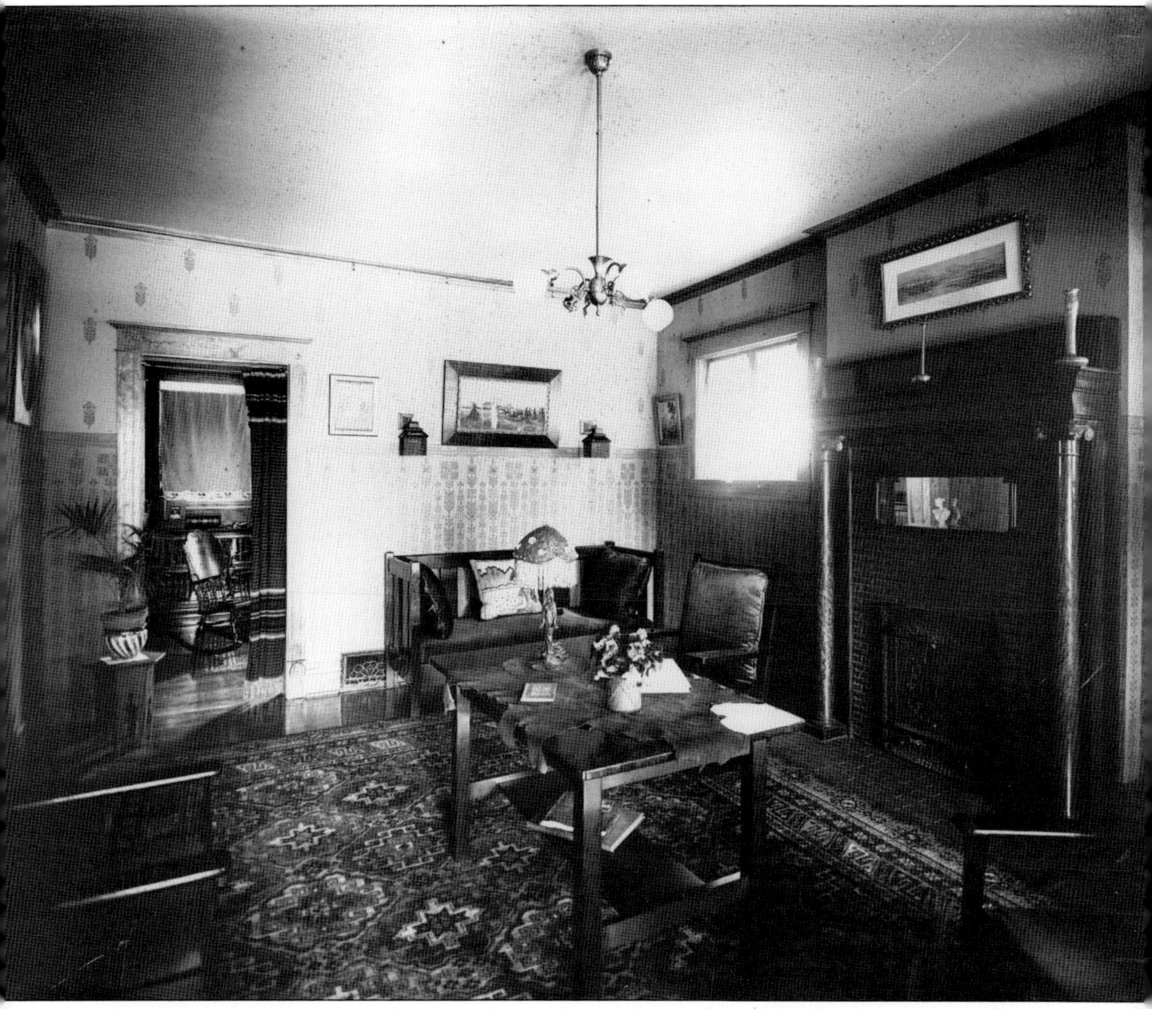

This is a rare, early interior photograph of a home located at 923 Third Avenue and built by developers Adolf and Lucy Richter in 1906. The exterior design was progressive for the year it was built, as it reflects a movement away from the common Victorian cottages. Prolific Avenues architect David C. Dart designed the home, and Joseph and Isabel Gates were the first residents. They initially rented the home before purchasing it from the Richters in 1911. Gates, a manager for the Mine and Smelter Supply Company, is best known for designing the first ski lift at the Alta Ski Area.

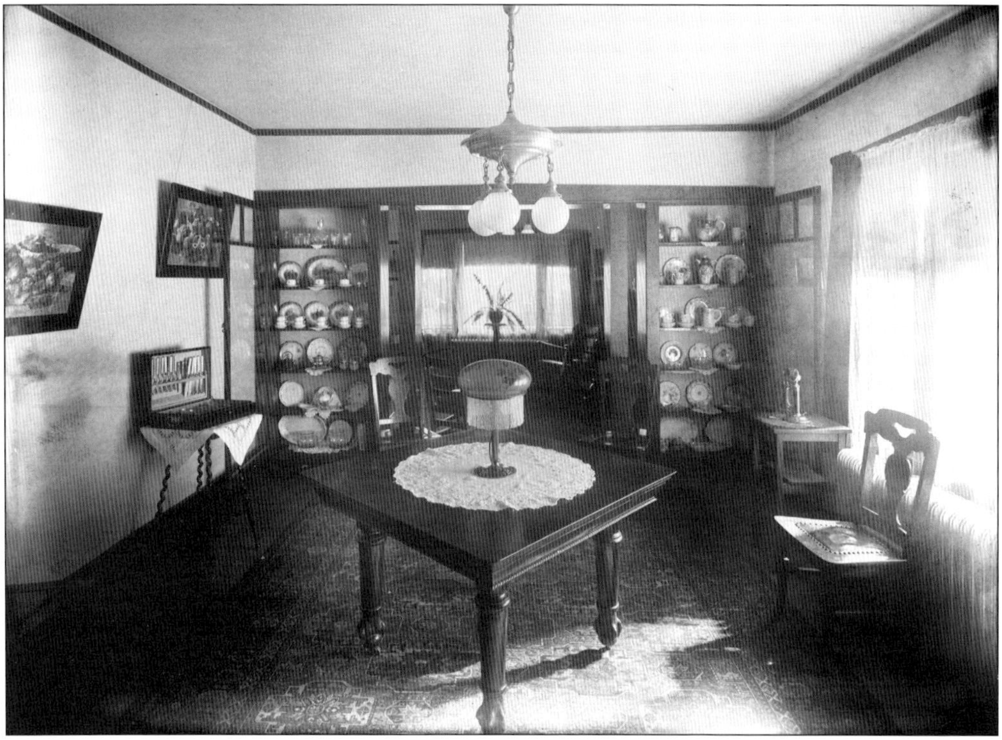

Herbert M. Chamberlain was the first resident of the bungalow at 1083 First Avenue. Chamberlain began working in the local banking industry at the age of 15, moving his way up from messenger boy to executive vice president of Walker Bank Corporation. He lived in this home until 1922. The interior photographs show a restrained interior with built-in shelves.

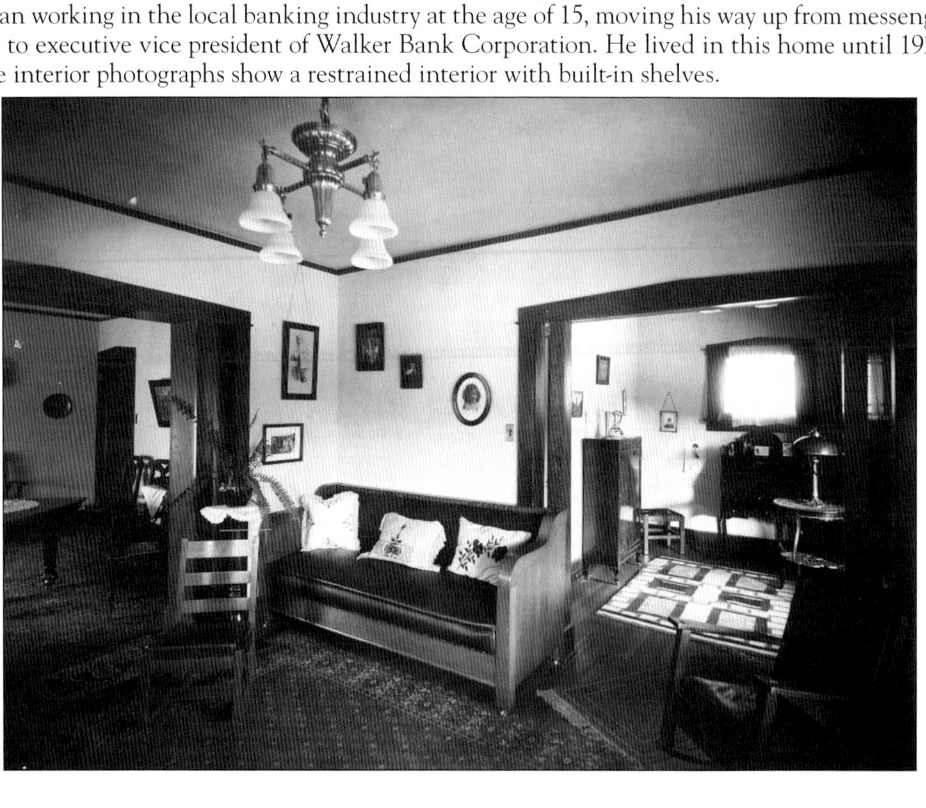

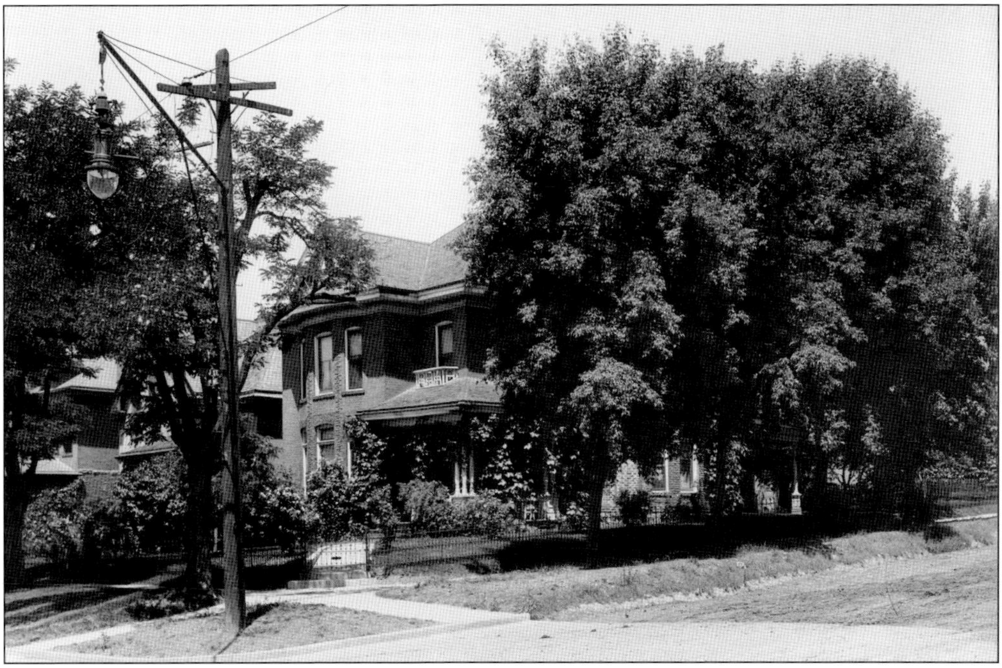

This two-story, late-Victorian home is located at 623 First Avenue. The residence still stands, however, the front porch was replaced by a Craftsman-style structure around 1915.

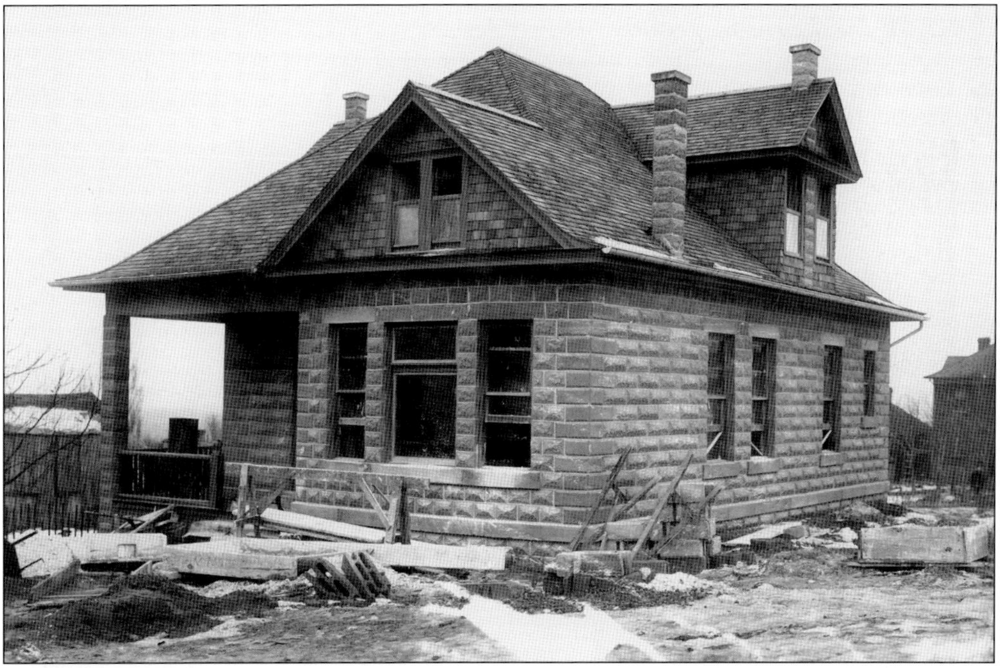

The address listed on this photograph is Seventh Avenue and K Street. However, there is no home exhibiting this unique pressed-stone exterior in that area today. The address may be incorrect, or the home was significantly altered or demolished. There are several other homes in the Avenues built from pressed stone. This technology was revolutionary at the time of this home's construction in 1905.

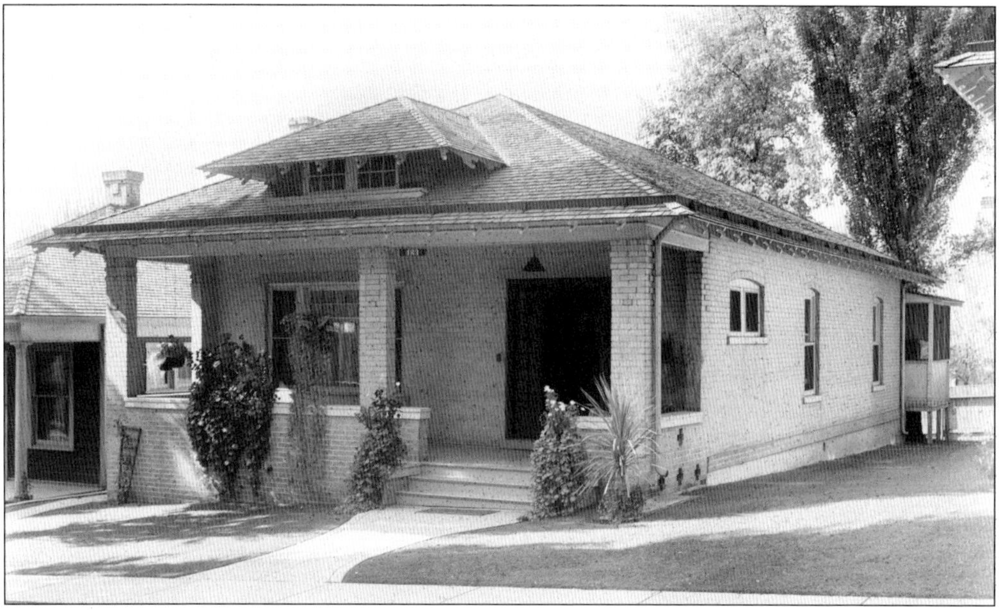

The house at 183 K Street is one of three nearly identical Craftsman-style bungalows built in a row by Dorius and Erickson Real Estate Company in 1908. The wide front porch is supported by brick columns with corbelled decorations. The rafter tails on the eaves are left exposed for decorative effect.

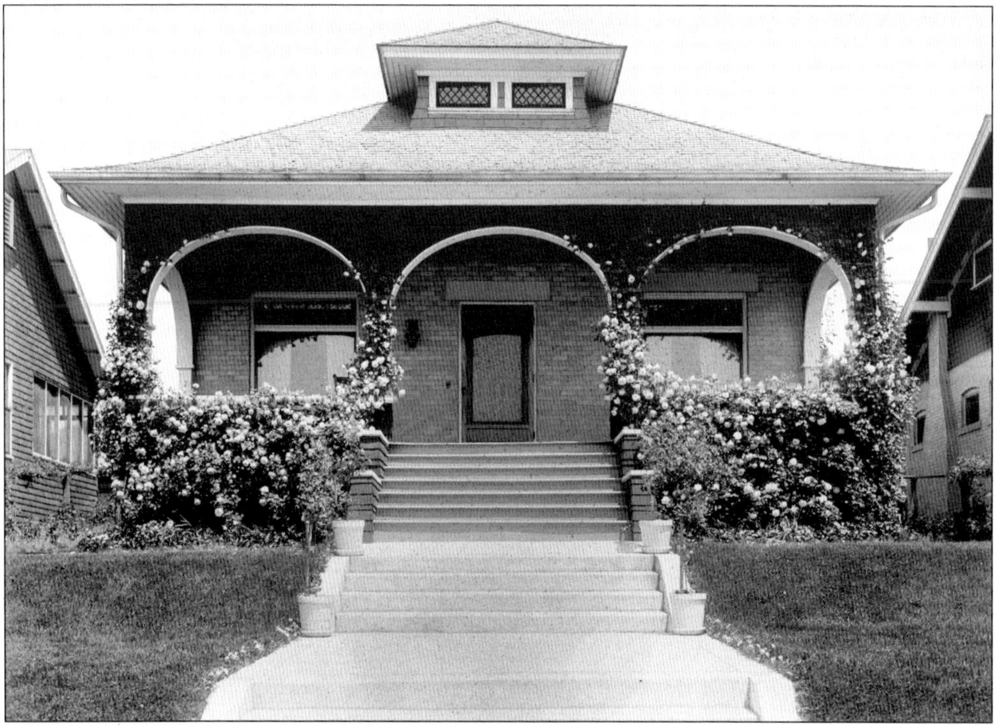

This is a 1912 photograph of a single-story bungalow located on the north side of 10th Avenue between B and C Streets. Rose bushes engulf the triple-arched front porch. The home still stands in its original location.

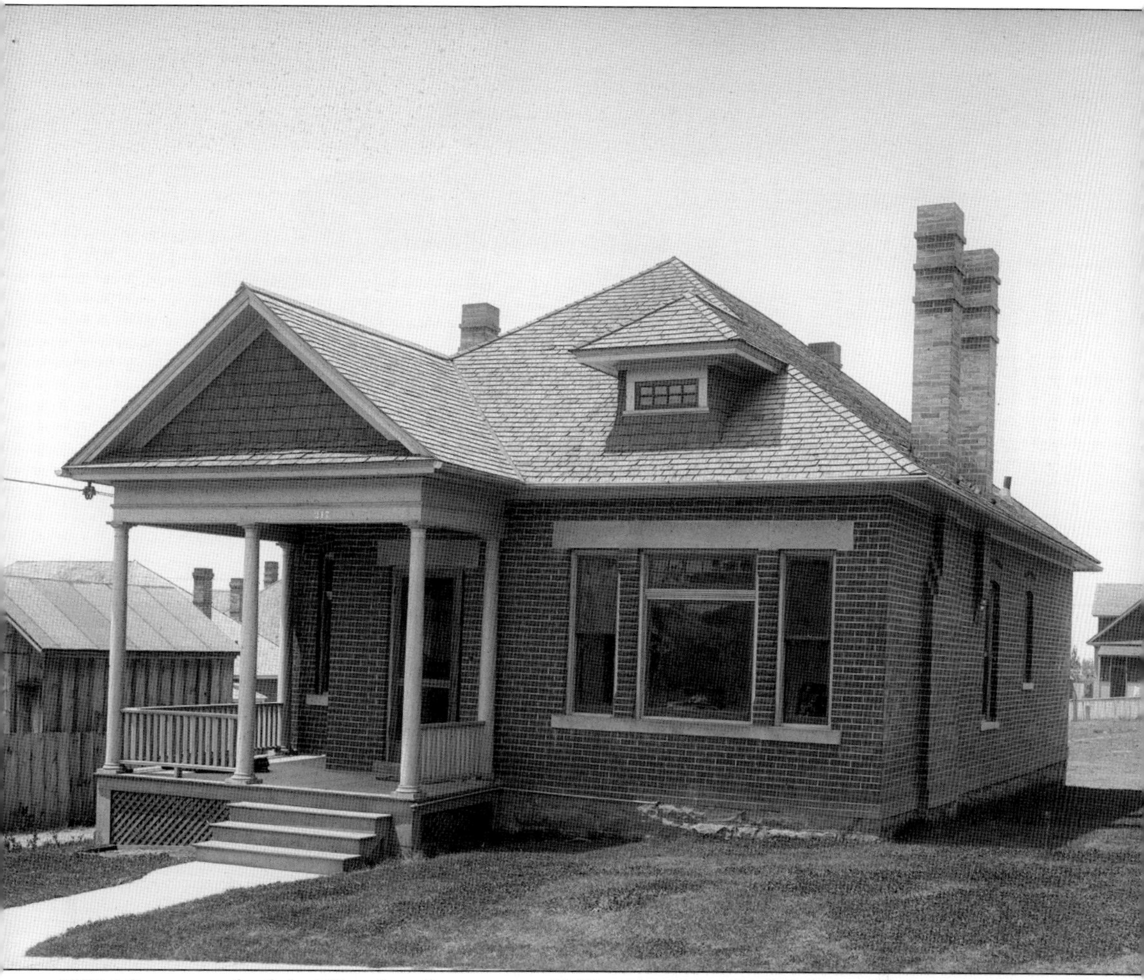

217 M Street was built by Theodore Bussman in 1907 and sold by the Salt Lake Security and Trust Company. Bussman built three homes adjacent to each other on M Street. He occupied 221 M Street and sold the other two. This late-Victorian cottage has a small front porch supported by Doric columns. The gables are covered in wood shingles.

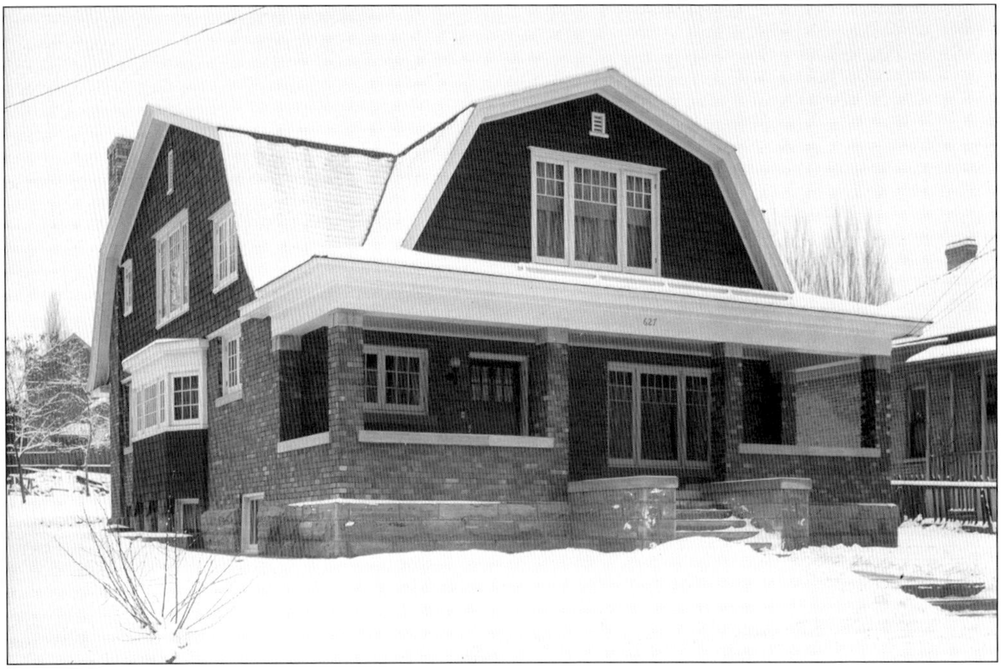

This cross-gabled Dutch Colonial Revival home is located at 627 Second Avenue. The gambrel roofs are typical of this architectural style. Joseph H. Weiner, manager of the Goodyear Tire and Rubber Company in Salt Lake City, purchased the home in 1920.

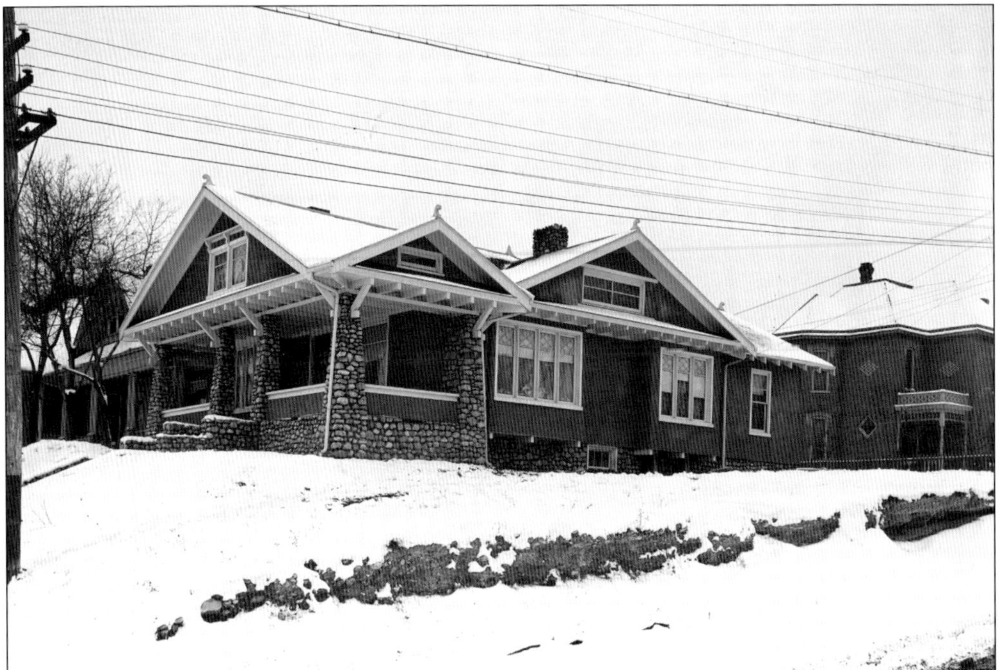

The Wimmer residence was located on the corner of C Street and Seventh Avenue. The home is a fine example of a one-story Craftsman bungalow. In the 1970s, nearly the entire block was demolished for the construction of a parking garage for the adjacent LDS Hospital.

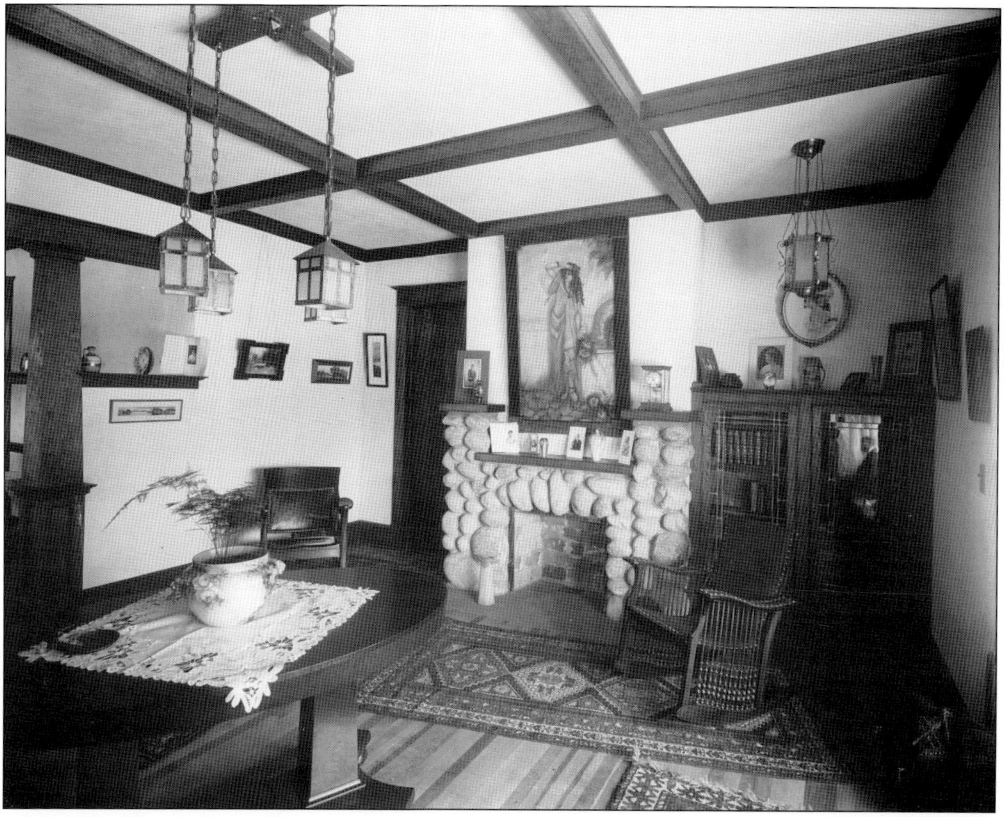

These two photographs show the interior of the former Wimmer residence. Both rooms have elements of classic Craftsman interior design. The small fireplace in the living room is constructed from cobblestones that match the home's front porch. Art glass is found on the doors of both the built-in china cabinet and bookcases. A colonnade, built from dark-stained Douglas fir, separates the dining room from the living room.

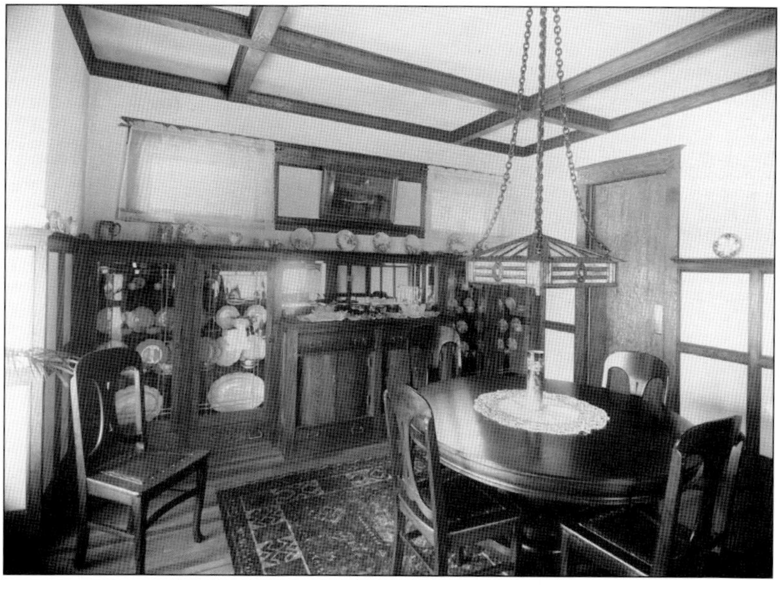

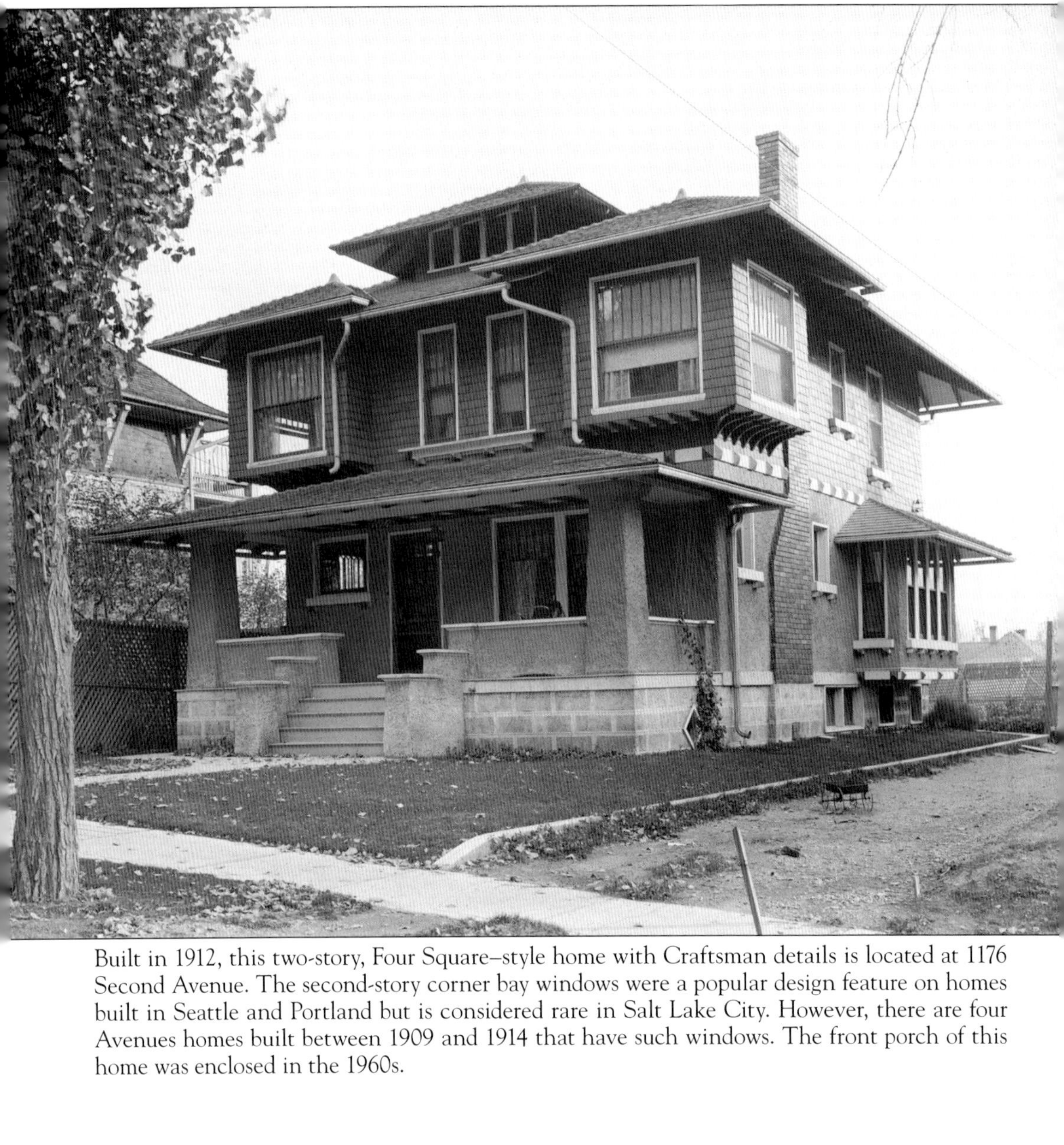

Built in 1912, this two-story, Four Square–style home with Craftsman details is located at 1176 Second Avenue. The second-story corner bay windows were a popular design feature on homes built in Seattle and Portland but is considered rare in Salt Lake City. However, there are four Avenues homes built between 1909 and 1914 that have such windows. The front porch of this home was enclosed in the 1960s.

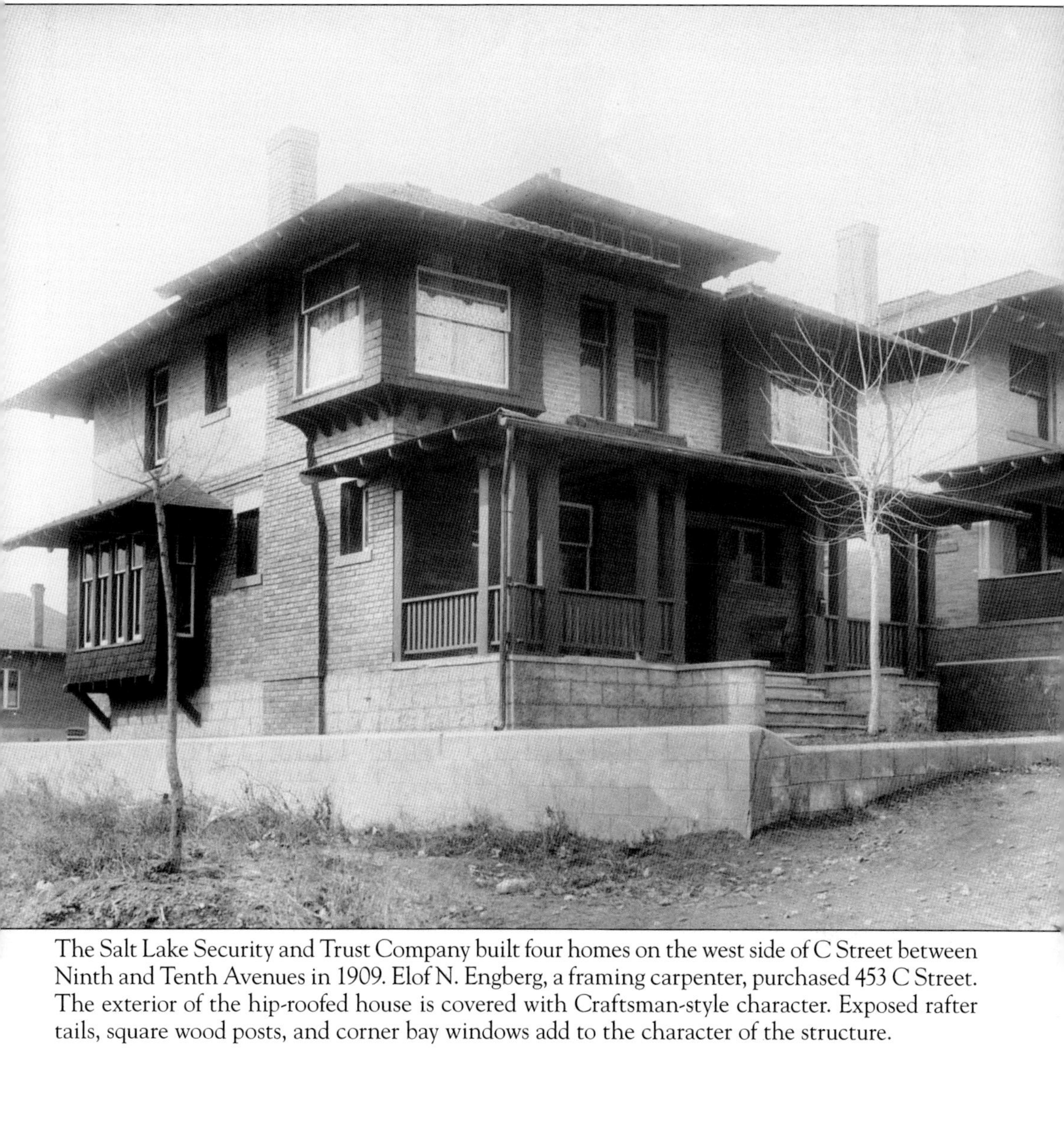

The Salt Lake Security and Trust Company built four homes on the west side of C Street between Ninth and Tenth Avenues in 1909. Elof N. Engberg, a framing carpenter, purchased 453 C Street. The exterior of the hip-roofed house is covered with Craftsman-style character. Exposed rafter tails, square wood posts, and corner bay windows add to the character of the structure.

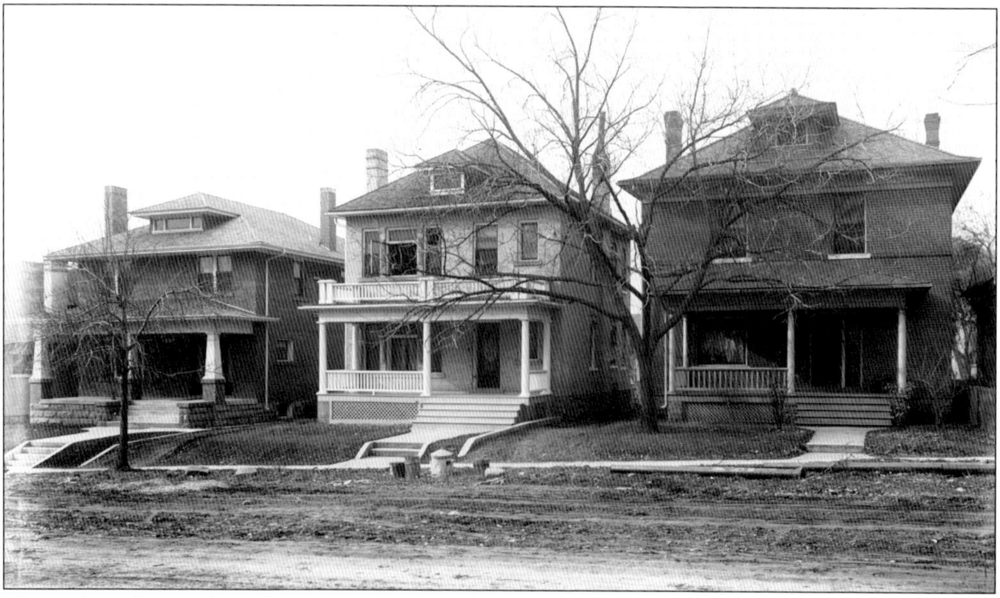

These three homes line the west side of H Street between First and Second Avenue. Longtime *Salt Lake Tribune* president Jack Gallivan grew up in the home on the right at 83 H Street. The residence was built by developer Aaron Keyser and sold to Sarah J. Wilson, the mother-in-law of mining magnate Thomas Kearns. Wilson sold the home to Gallivan's parents.

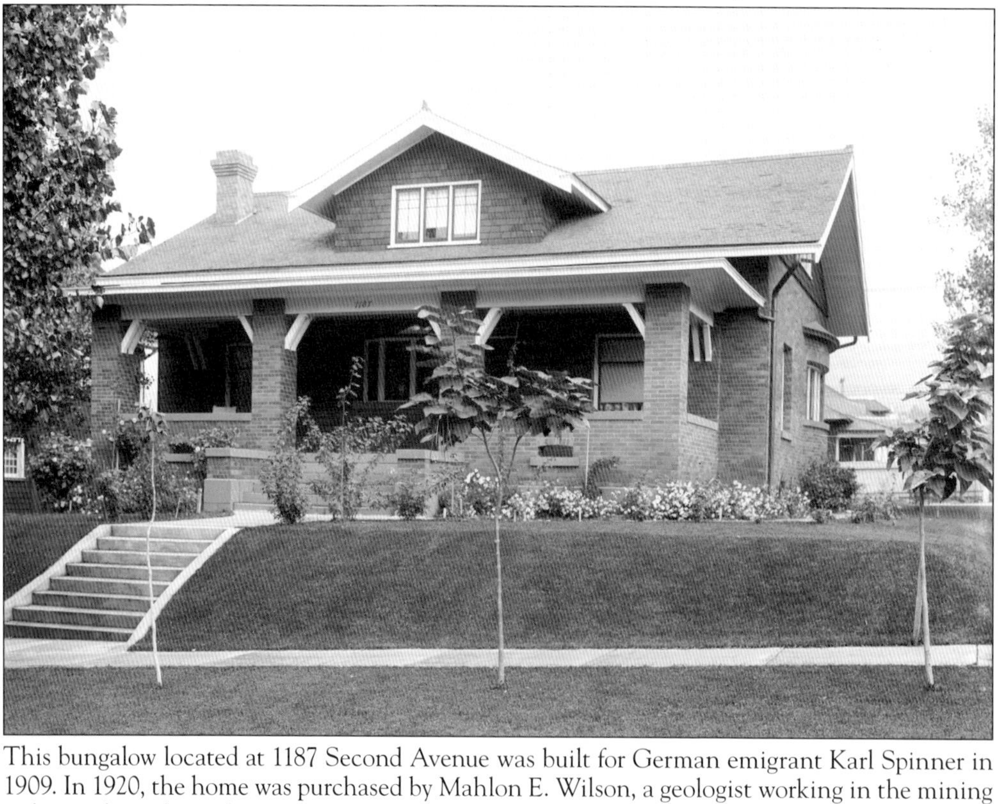

This bungalow located at 1187 Second Avenue was built for German emigrant Karl Spinner in 1909. In 1920, the home was purchased by Mahlon E. Wilson, a geologist working in the mining industry throughout the Intermountain West.

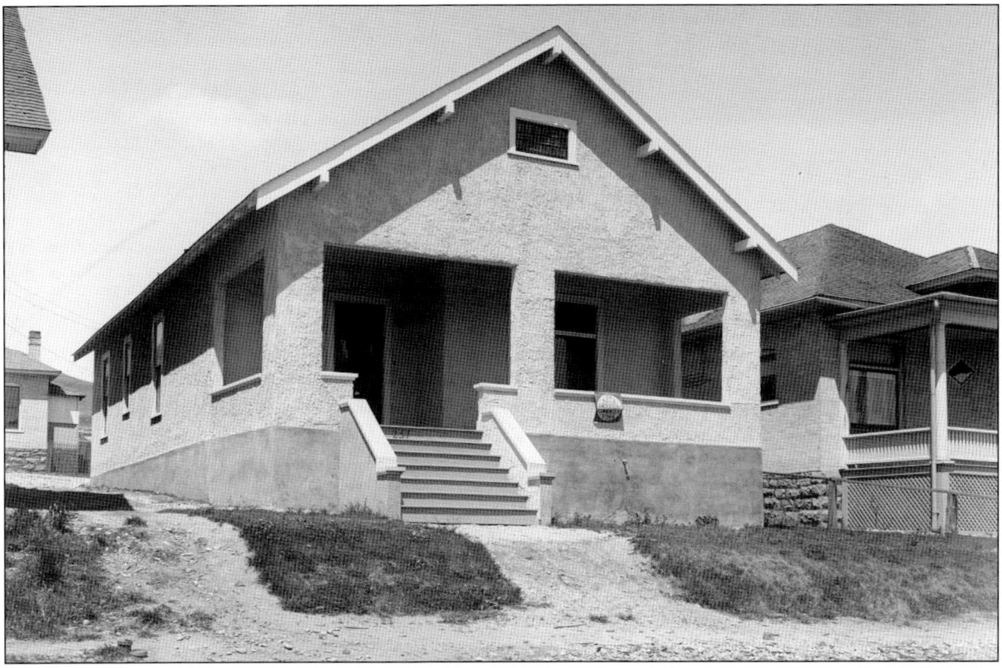

This rather plain, recently completed stucco-covered bungalow was built by the Salt Lake Security and Trust Company in 1909. The home is representative of the expansion of the Avenues neighborhood farther up the foothills to 10th Avenue. Municipal services had reached the area by that year. The home still stands but has been significantly altered.

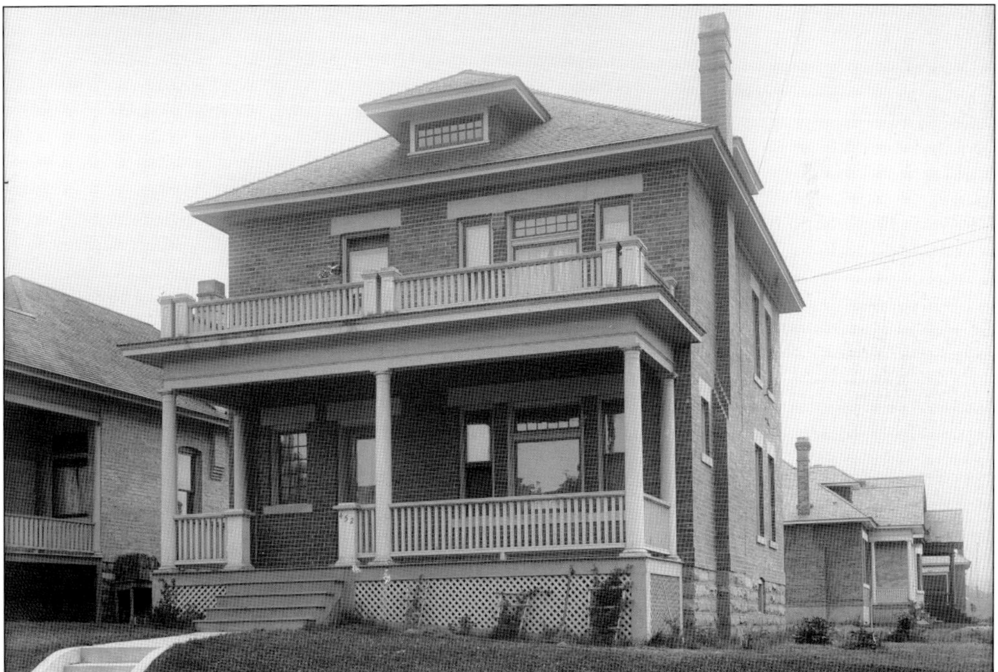

This Four Square–style home is another house built by the Salt Lake Security and Trust Company. Doric columns support the full-width front porch and second-story balcony.

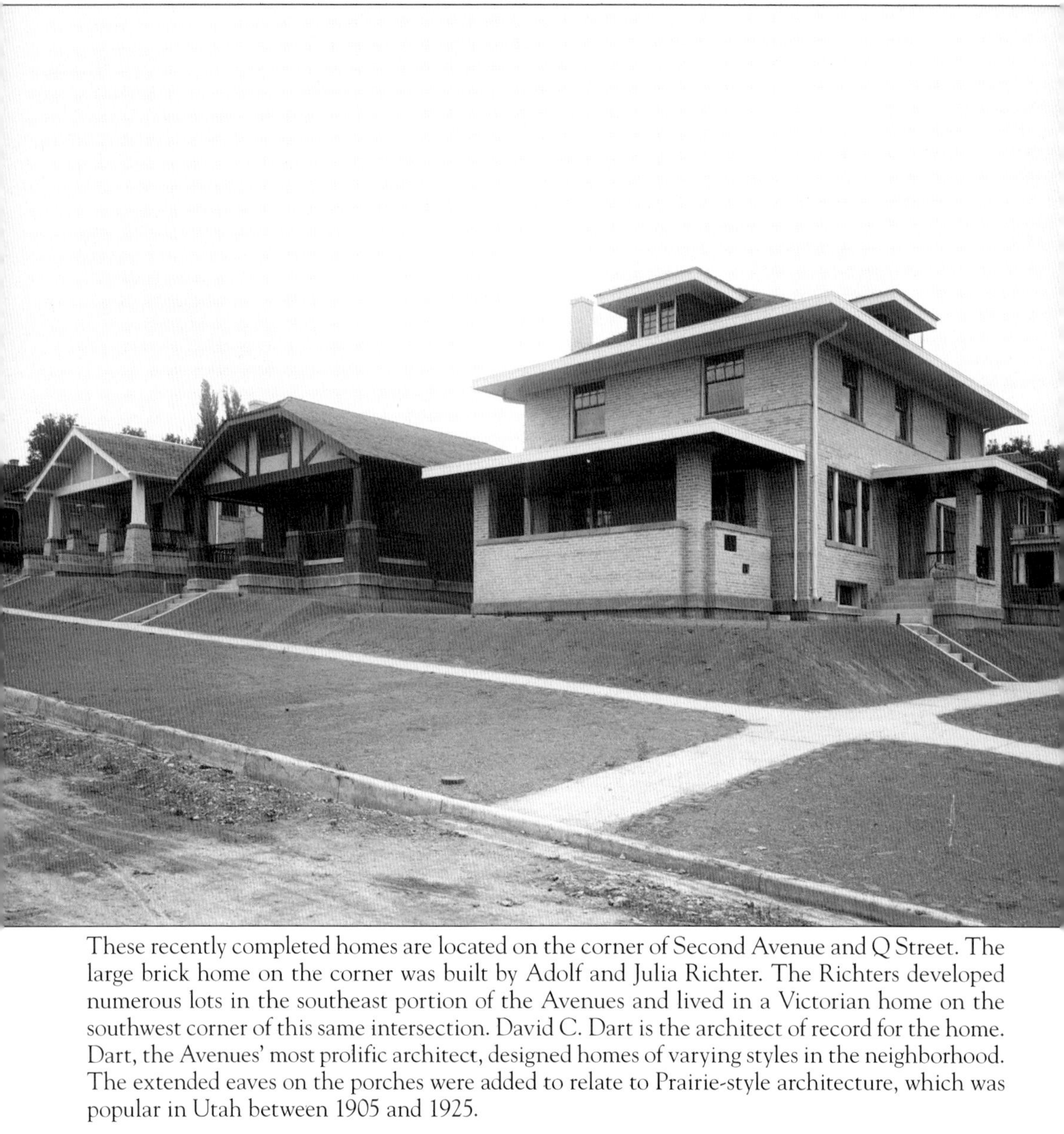

These recently completed homes are located on the corner of Second Avenue and Q Street. The large brick home on the corner was built by Adolf and Julia Richter. The Richters developed numerous lots in the southeast portion of the Avenues and lived in a Victorian home on the southwest corner of this same intersection. David C. Dart is the architect of record for the home. Dart, the Avenues' most prolific architect, designed homes of varying styles in the neighborhood. The extended eaves on the porches were added to relate to Prairie-style architecture, which was popular in Utah between 1905 and 1925.

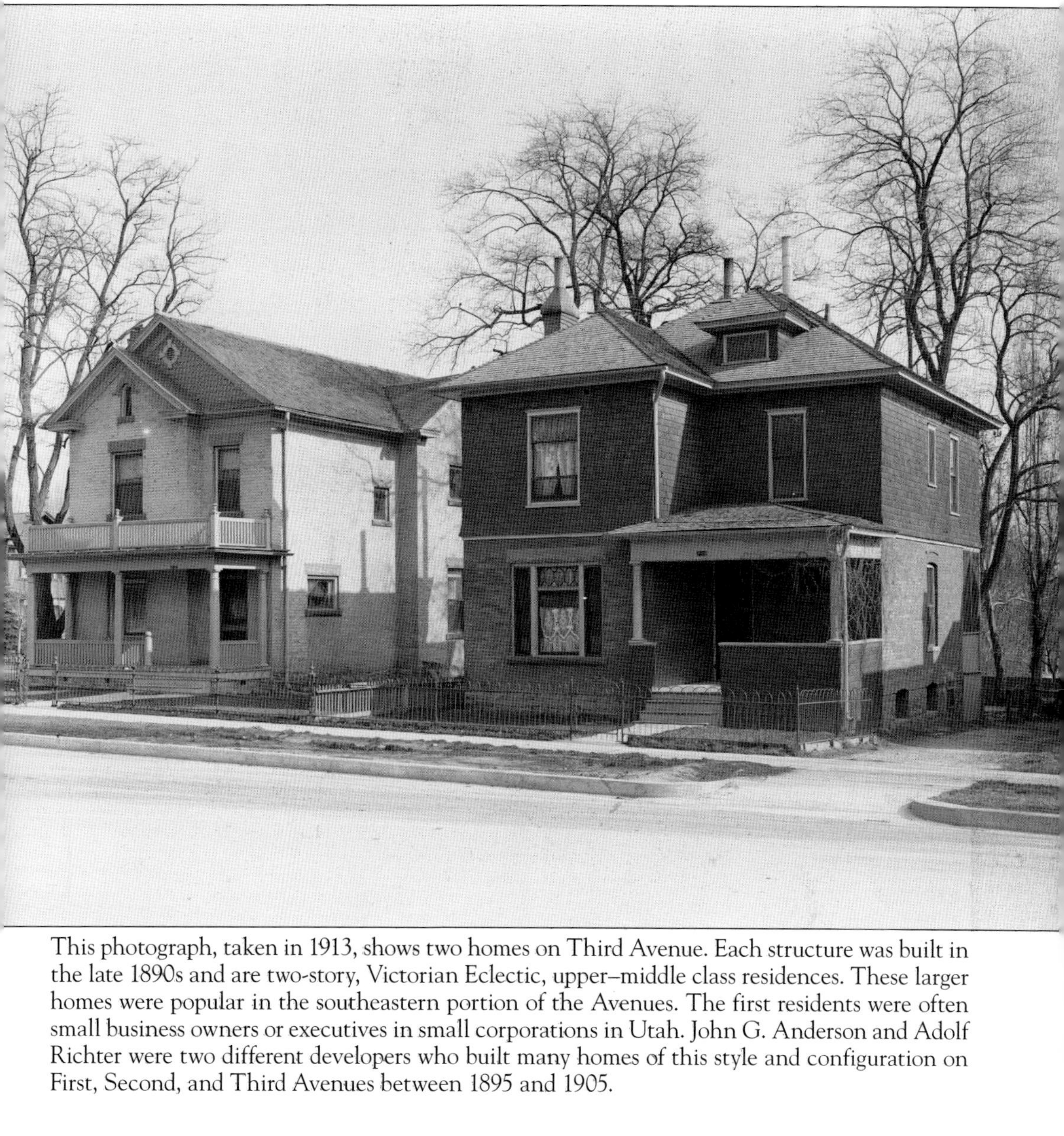

This photograph, taken in 1913, shows two homes on Third Avenue. Each structure was built in the late 1890s and are two-story, Victorian Eclectic, upper–middle class residences. These larger homes were popular in the southeastern portion of the Avenues. The first residents were often small business owners or executives in small corporations in Utah. John G. Anderson and Adolf Richter were two different developers who built many homes of this style and configuration on First, Second, and Third Avenues between 1895 and 1905.

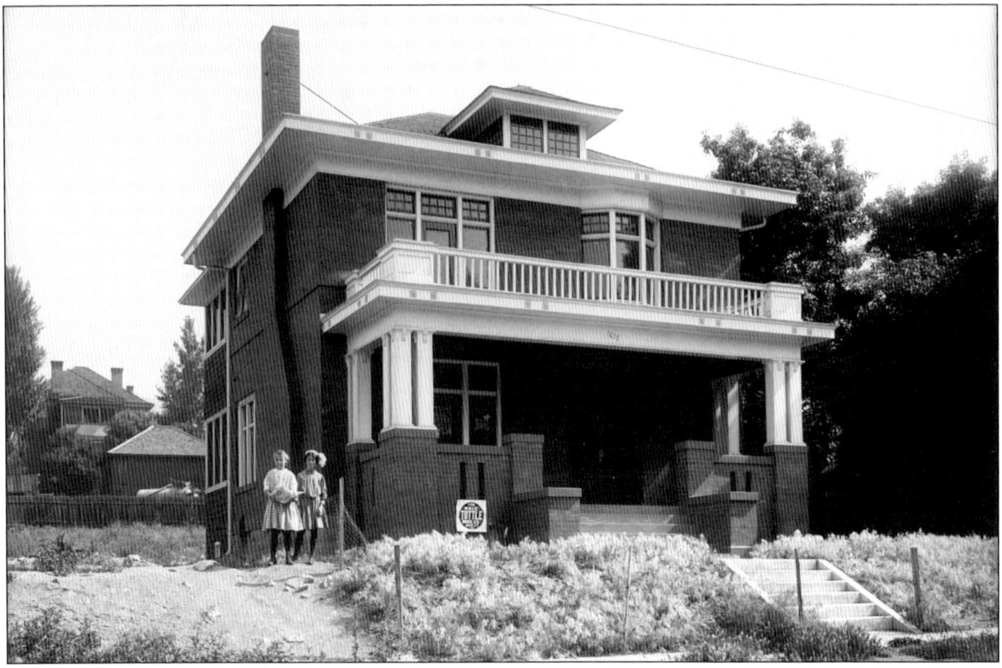

Two girls stand in front of the recently completed home at 1017 Second Avenue in 1911. Signs posted on the front window and front yard from the Tuttle Brothers Company advertise that the home is for sale. The house still stands, however, it has been altered and contains several apartments.

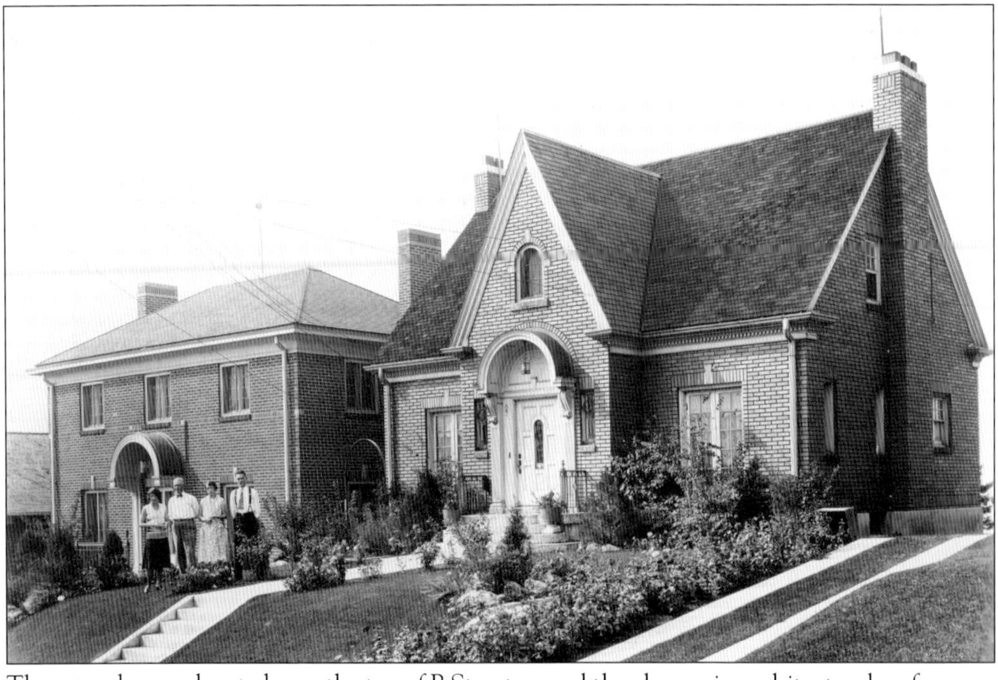

These two homes, located near the top of B Street, reveal the change in architectural preferences over time in the neighborhood. These residences were built in the late 1920s, as people preferred European historical styles instead of the bungalows and Craftsman homes built during the previous decade.

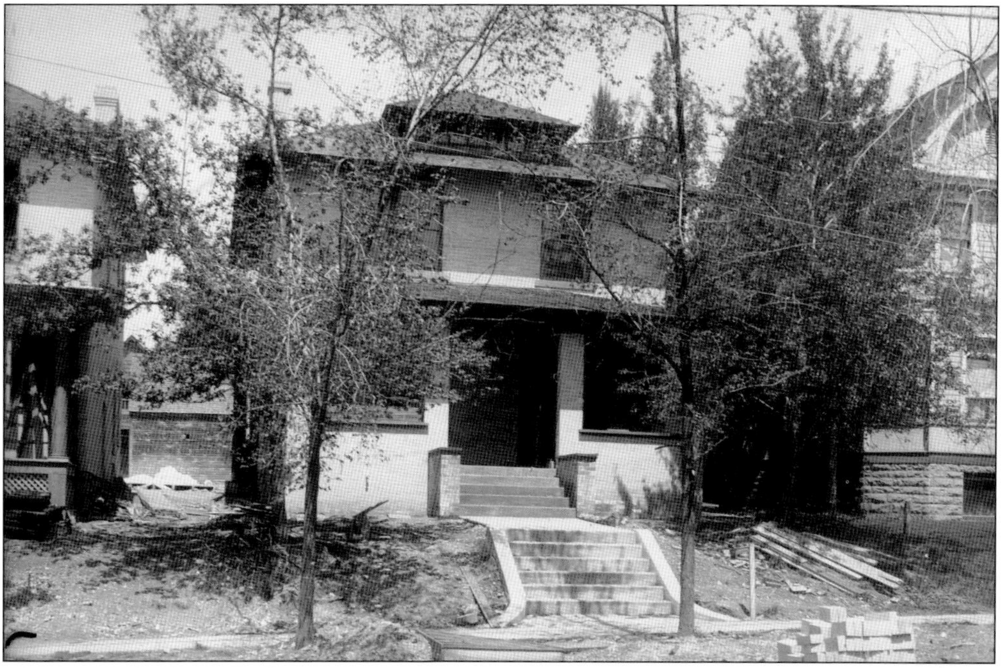

This is another home built by the Salt Lake Security and Trust Company on the north side of First Avenue between P and Q Streets. The American Four Square type of home was popular around the United States between 1890 and 1930. Typically, the second floor was large enough to hold three or four bedrooms. The first floor was reserved for large living and dining rooms. This type of home can be found in many styles, including Victorian and Craftsman.

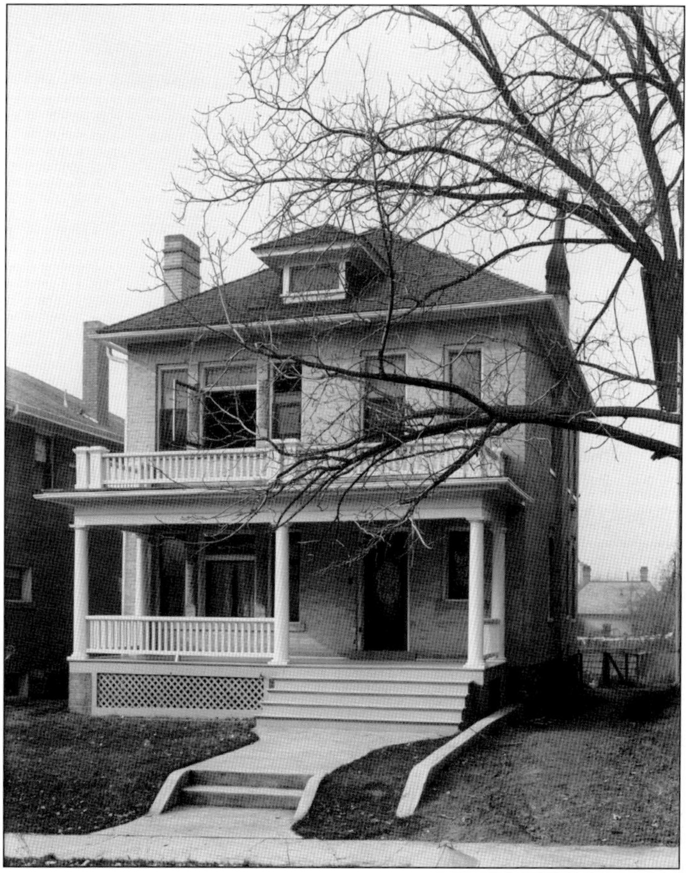

This Four Square–style home located at 75 H Street was built in 1903 and used as a rectory for the First Methodist Church in the 1920s.

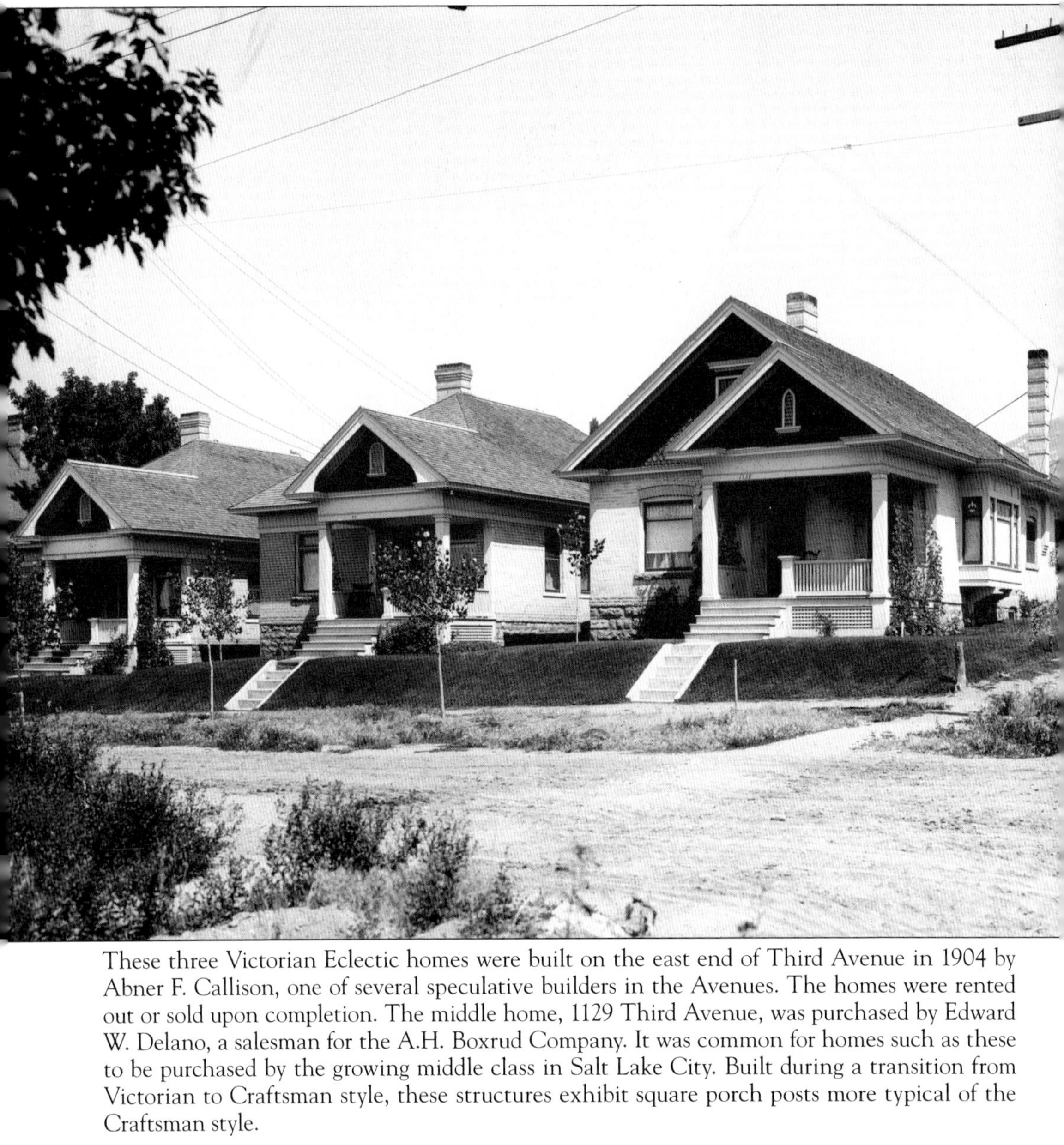

These three Victorian Eclectic homes were built on the east end of Third Avenue in 1904 by Abner F. Callison, one of several speculative builders in the Avenues. The homes were rented out or sold upon completion. The middle home, 1129 Third Avenue, was purchased by Edward W. Delano, a salesman for the A.H. Boxrud Company. It was common for homes such as these to be purchased by the growing middle class in Salt Lake City. Built during a transition from Victorian to Craftsman style, these structures exhibit square porch posts more typical of the Craftsman style.

Three

Building a Neighborhood

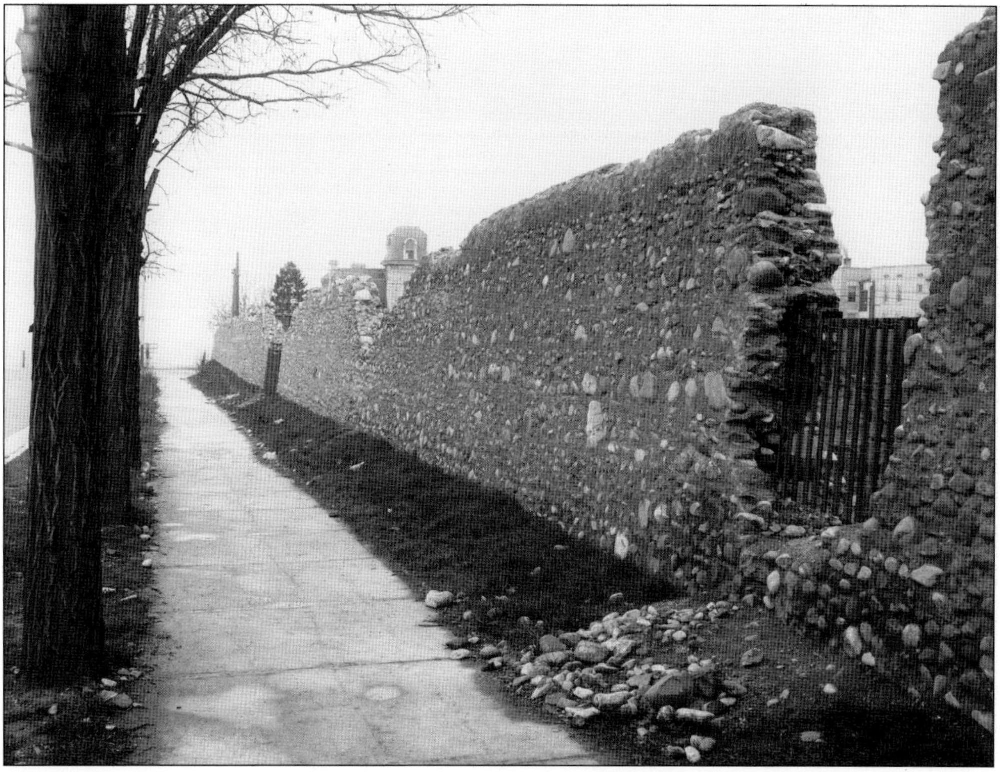

The remains of the city wall runs along A Street in 1911. Early development of the Avenues was influenced by the poor infrastructure serving the area. Salt Lake City's first settlers referred to the area as the Dry Bench due to the lack of irrigation. As the city's first true residential neighborhood, community leaders concentrated funding for the latest innovations in water supply, paving, and public landscaping early in the 20th century.

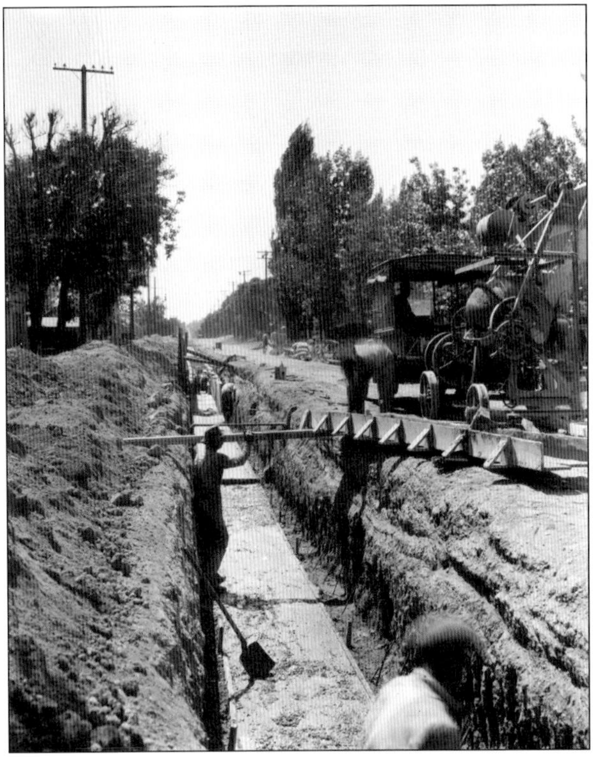

Salt Lake City Engineering Department workers build a new sewer line along Fourth Avenue near N Street in 1922. In the 1920s, significant improvements were made to the infrastructure of the Avenues neighborhood.

An employee of the P.J. Moran Construction Company uses survey equipment during the construction of the City Creek aqueduct in 1906 near Third Avenue and Canyon Road. The Salt Lake LDS Temple is seen in the background. Today, this portion of the creek remains buried in piping under Canyon Road.

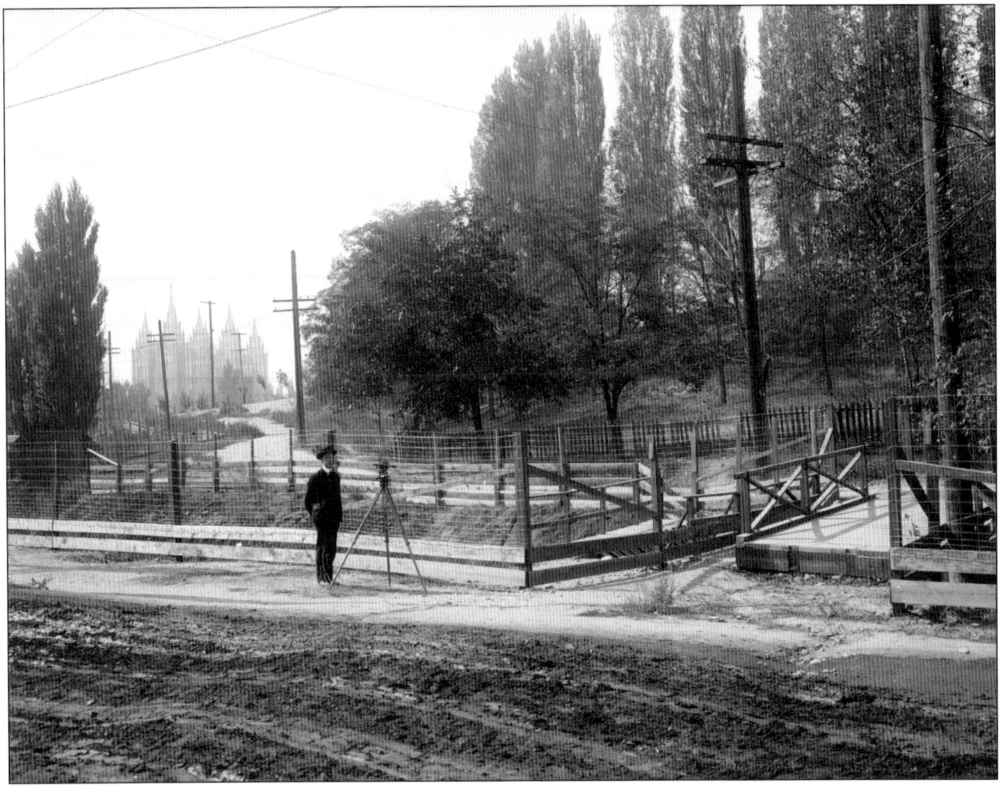

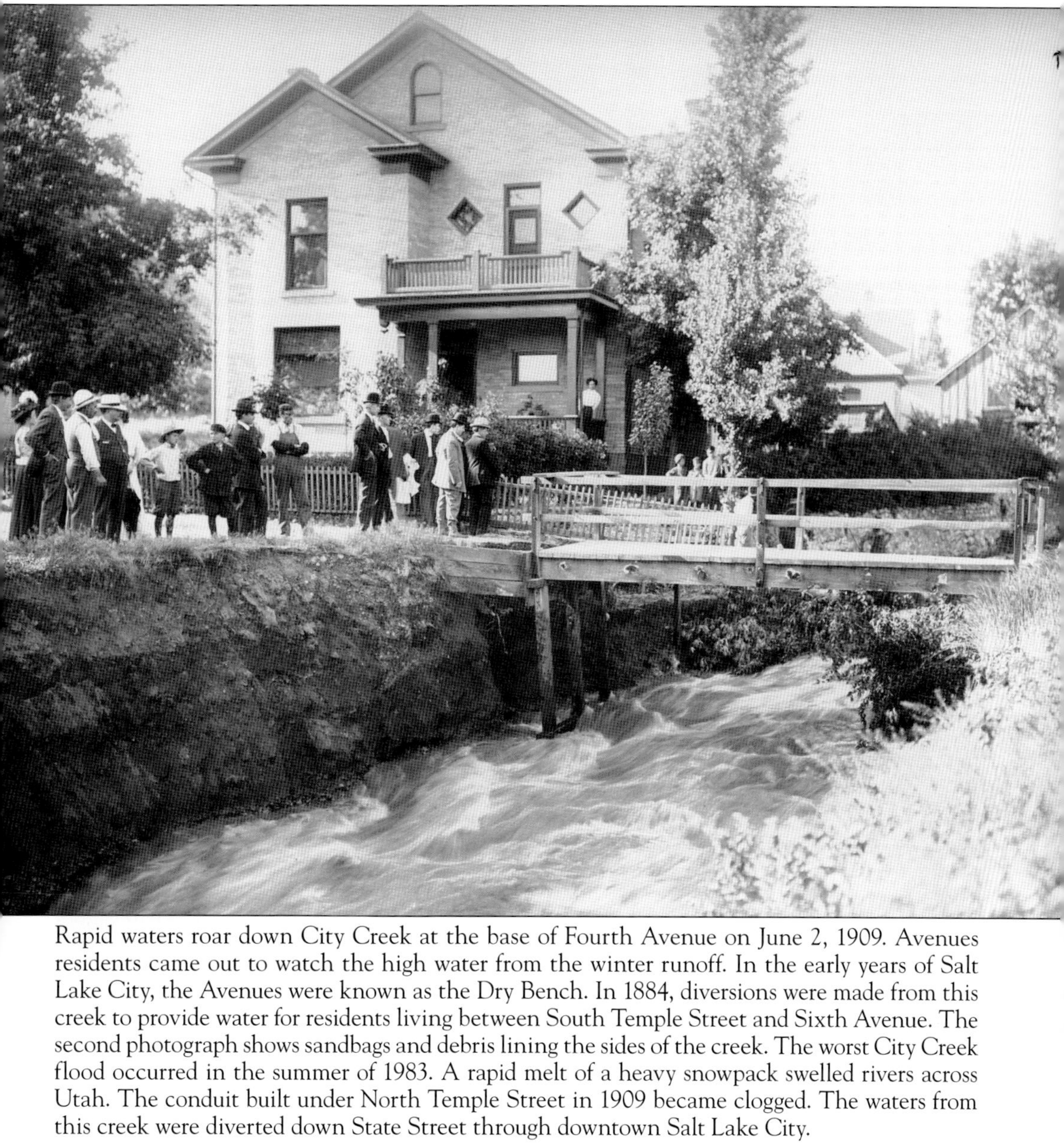

Rapid waters roar down City Creek at the base of Fourth Avenue on June 2, 1909. Avenues residents came out to watch the high water from the winter runoff. In the early years of Salt Lake City, the Avenues were known as the Dry Bench. In 1884, diversions were made from this creek to provide water for residents living between South Temple Street and Sixth Avenue. The second photograph shows sandbags and debris lining the sides of the creek. The worst City Creek flood occurred in the summer of 1983. A rapid melt of a heavy snowpack swelled rivers across Utah. The conduit built under North Temple Street in 1909 became clogged. The waters from this creek were diverted down State Street through downtown Salt Lake City.

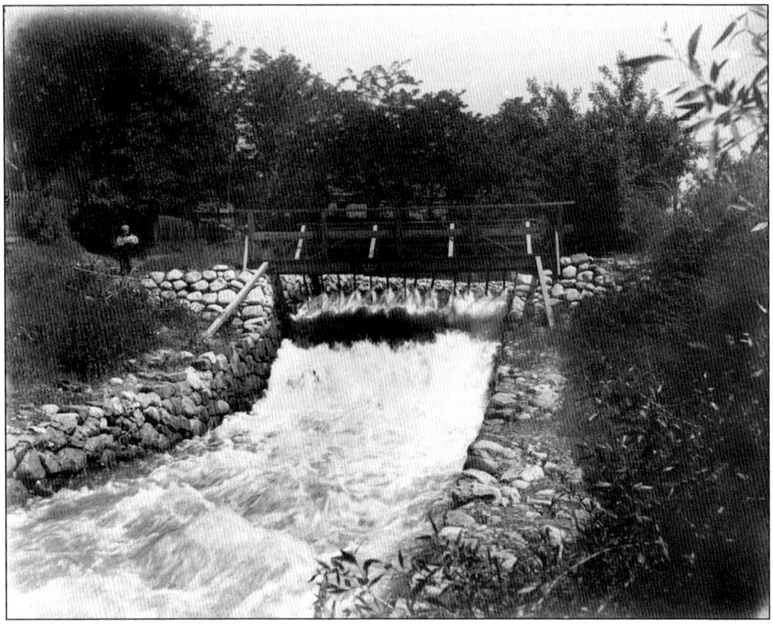

A boy stands near the raging waters of City Creek during the spring runoff period in 1907. The bridge over the water was known as the Goat Bridge. It is not known how it acquired this name.

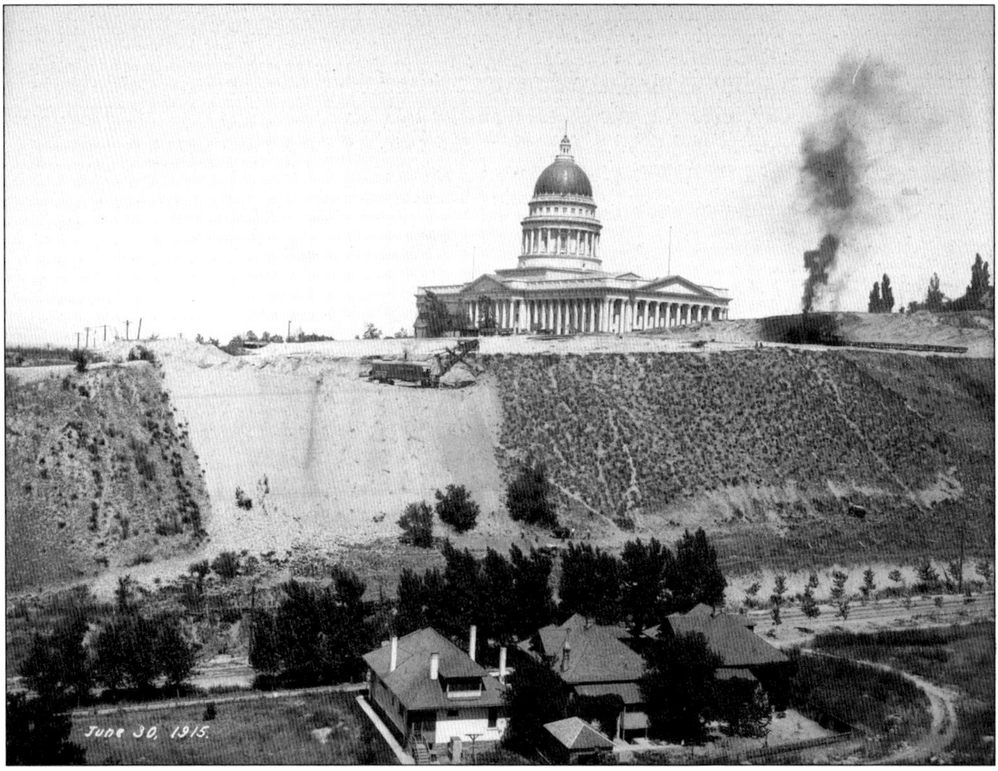

Although not part of the Avenues neighborhood, the development of the area has been influenced by its proximity to City Creek Canyon and Capitol Hill. Steam shovels and graders were used to build the road that connects City Creek Canyon and the Avenues to the recently completed state capitol. A few years after this photograph was taken, Memory Grove Park was developed on the property north of the three homes located at the canyon bottom.

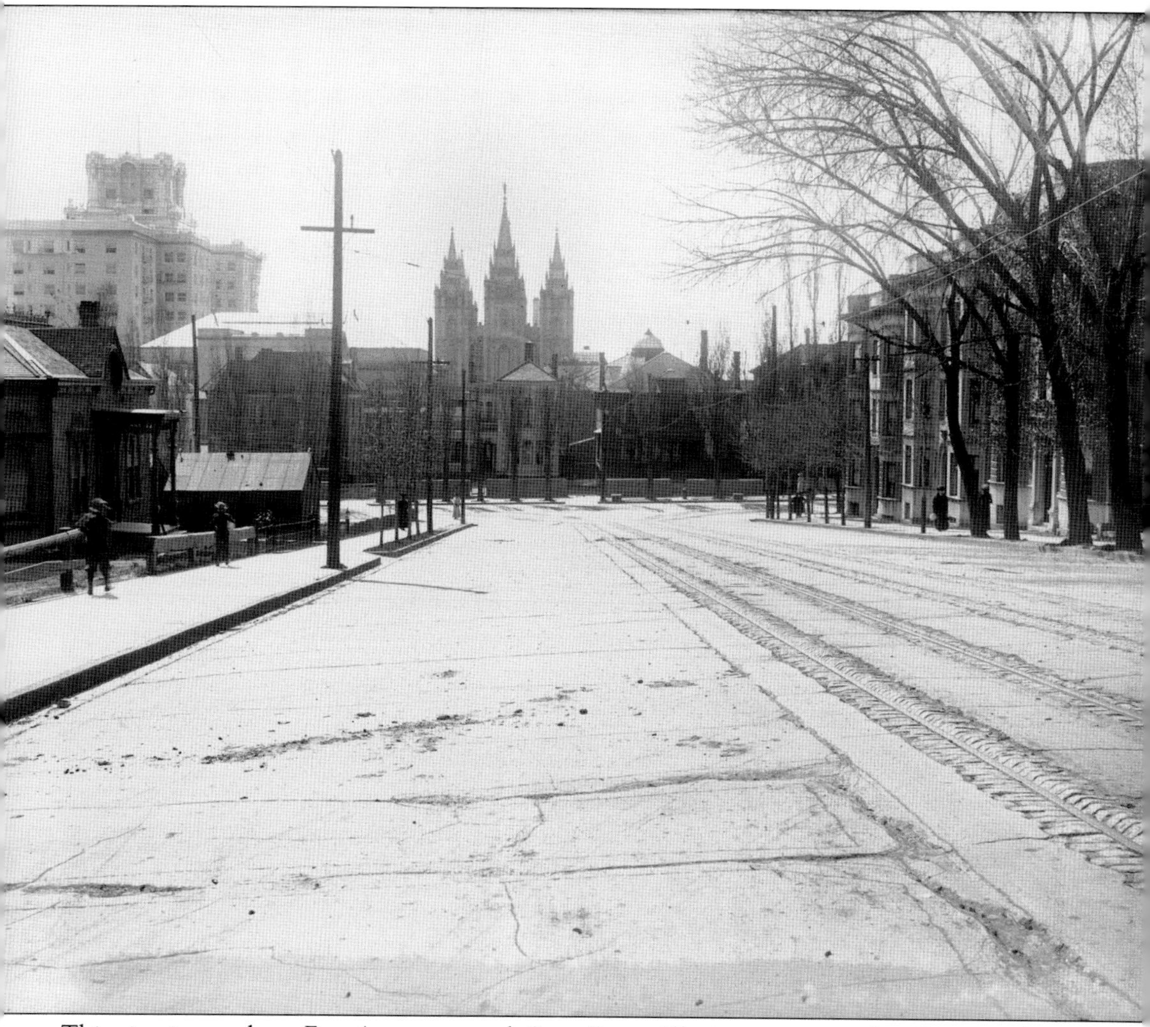

This view is west down First Avenue towards State Street. The image, captured in 1911, reveals a recently paved street. The first asphalt paving of Avenues streets by the Salt Lake City Engineering Department took place in 1910. The Grace Louise Emery Apartments are seen on the right. The Eagle Gate Apartments have yet to be built across the street. All of the buildings in this photograph, except the Salt Lake City LDS Temple and Hotel Utah, have been demolished.

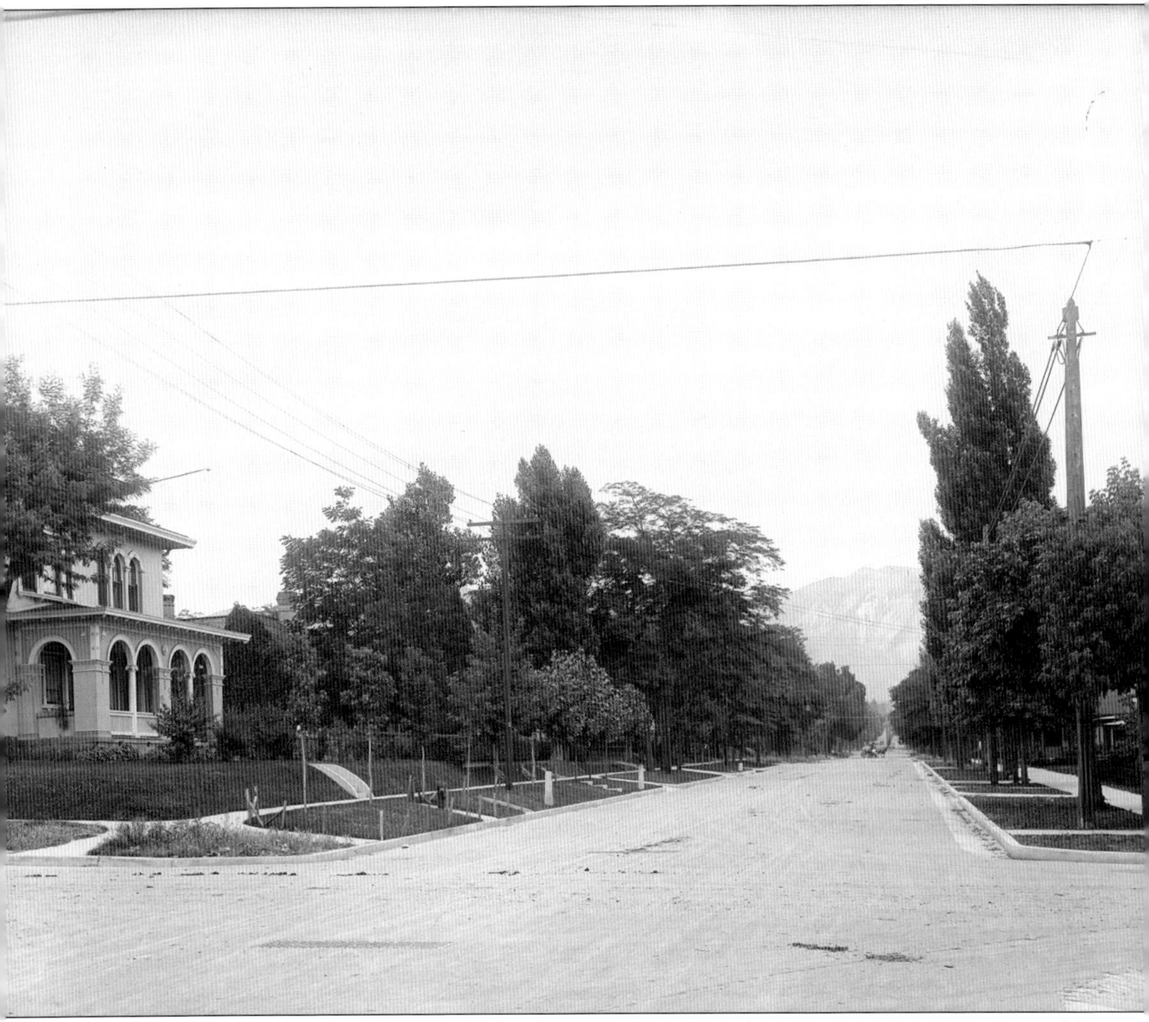

Progress with the Salt Lake City Public Works is evident in this image of First Avenue and F Street. The street has been paved, and a fire hydrant has been installed. Concrete hitching posts stand on the curb in front of the first two homes on the left of the photograph.

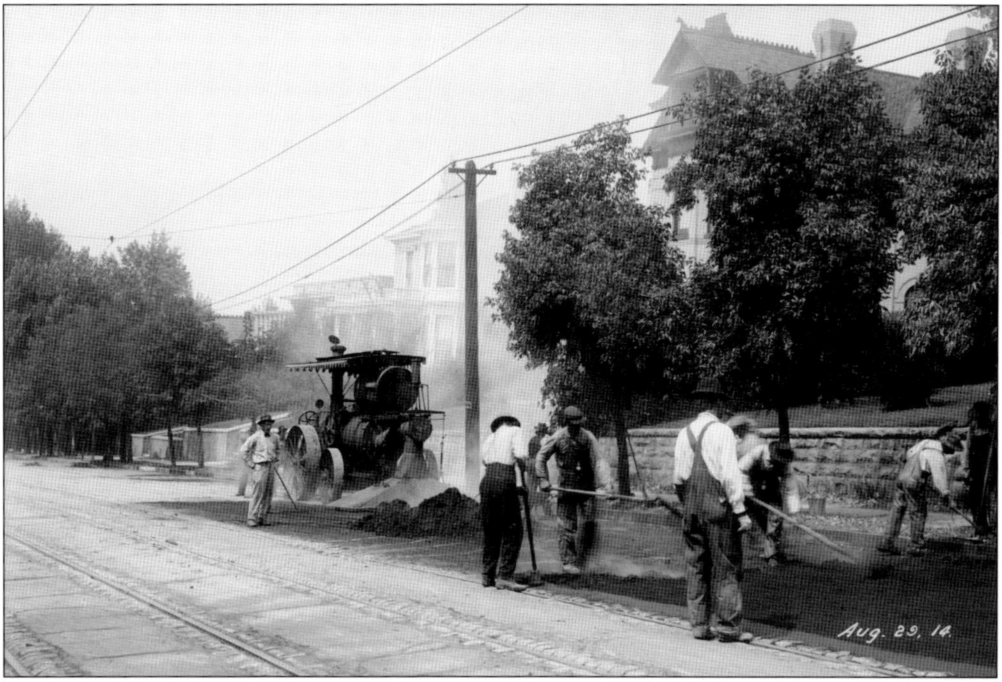

A crew from the P.J. Moran Company resurfaces the north side of First Avenue with steam-powered equipment on August 29, 1914. None of the homes in this picture remain standing.

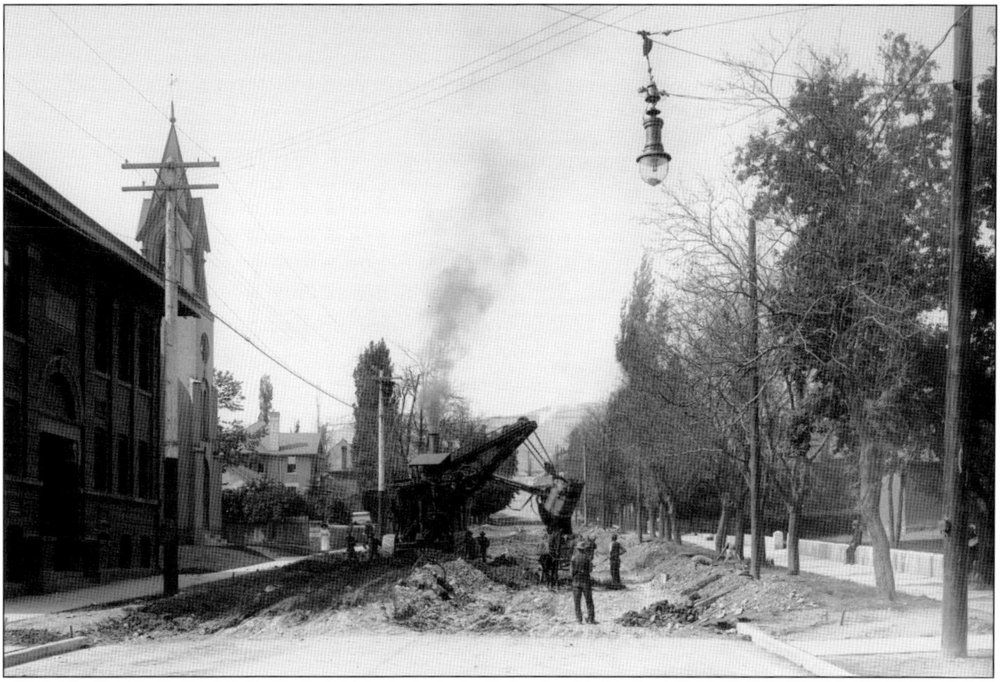
A steam shovel from the P.J. Moran Company digs up an unpaved A Street in 1909. Whitney Hall and the 18th Ward chapel are seen on the left. One of Salt Lake City's early streetlights hangs over the intersection. Salt Lake City was one of the first municipalities in the United States to add lights to its streets.

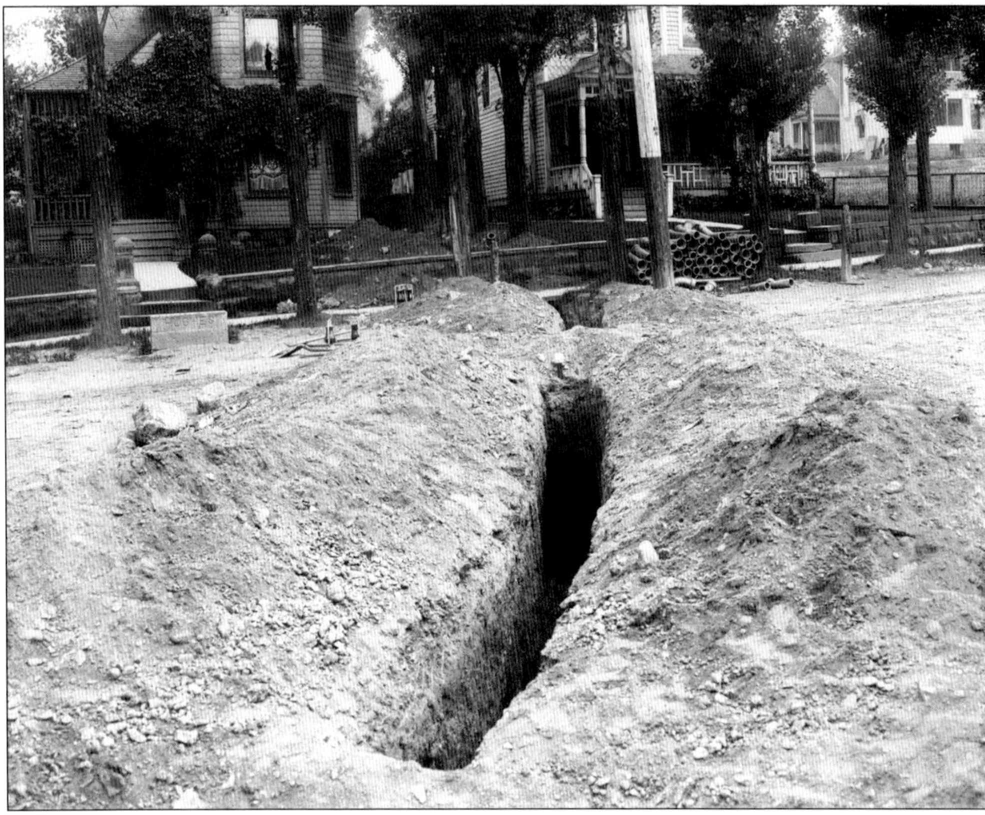

Work crews dig trenches across First Avenue as part of a massive effort to modernize Salt Lake City's sewer system in 1910. The stone on the curb in front of the home on the left reads "Hughes." These stones were used as steps for persons climbing out of a carriage or off of a horse.

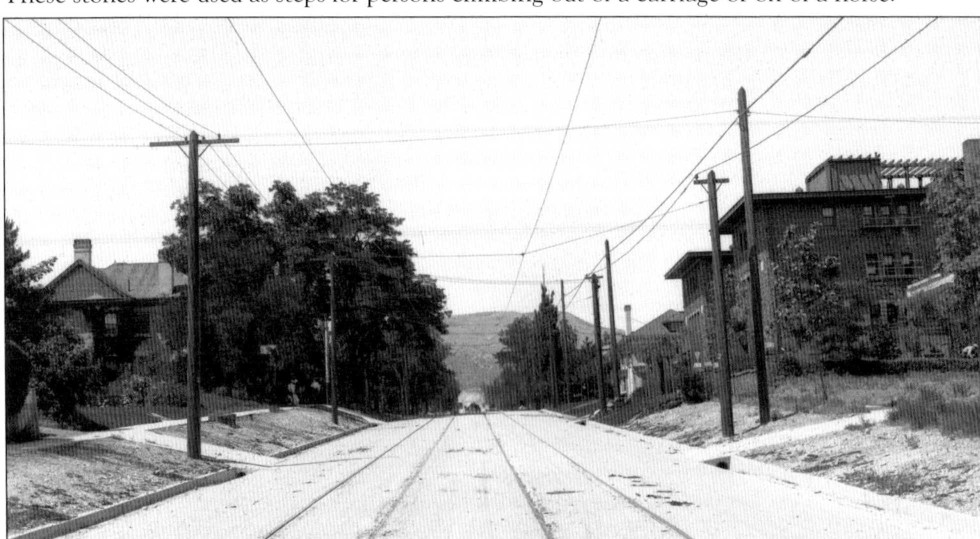

This is a view up B Street from First Avenue in 1912. The Salt Lake City Municipal Railway had built a route up B Street to Ninth Avenue to serve Avenues residents. The Caithness-Riter Apartment building is seen on the right.

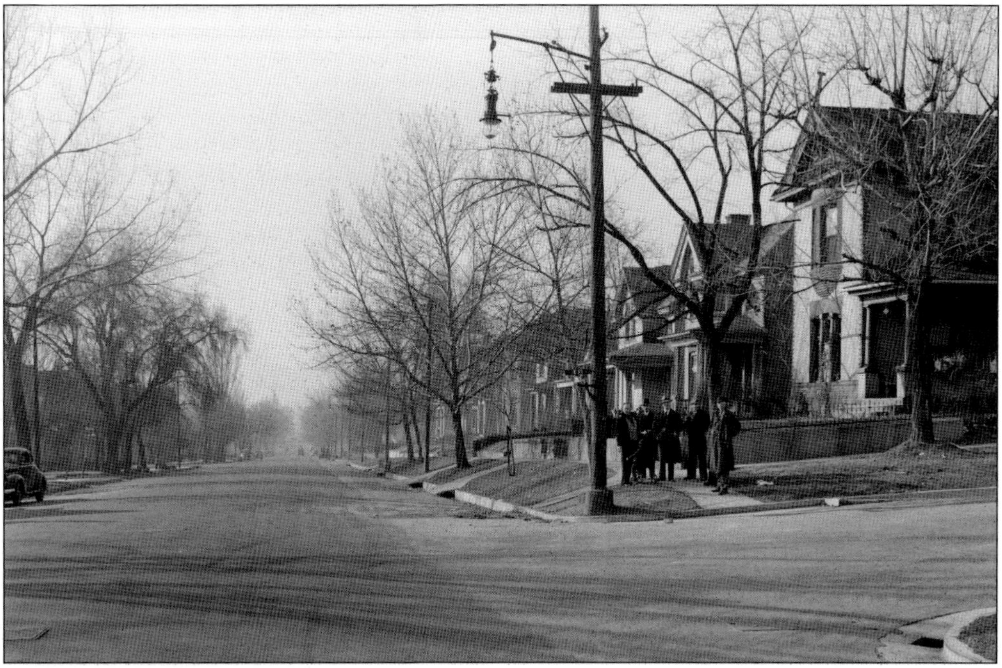

A group of men stand on the corner of K Street and Third Avenue on January 27, 1938, after a car accident in the intersection. One-way streets and an inconsistent pattern of stop signs continue to cause vehicle accidents in the neighborhood.

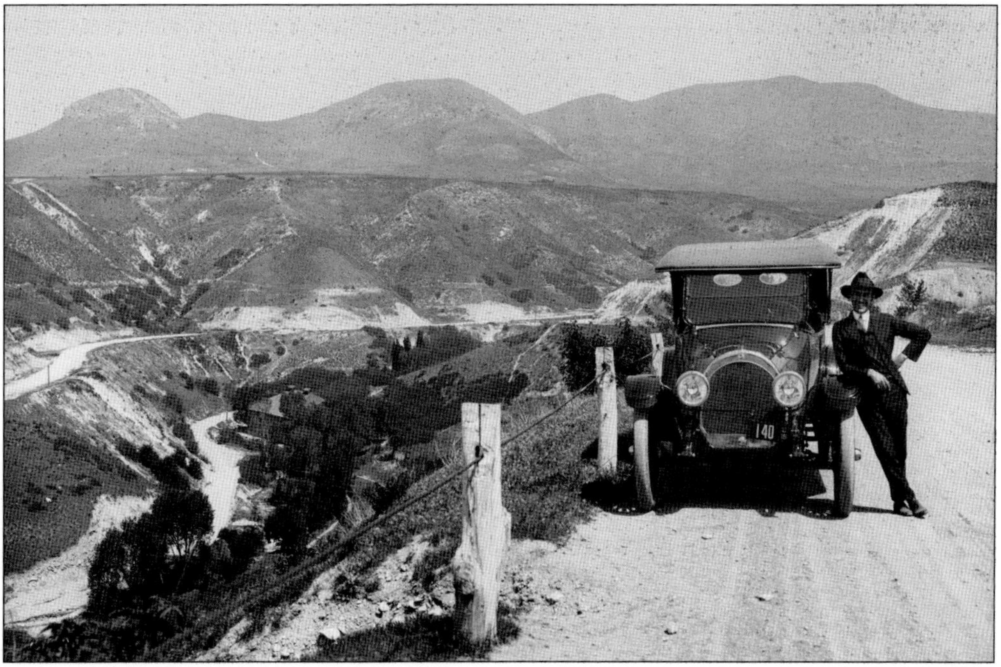

A gentleman stands next to his Oldsmobile car at the top of B Street near 11th Avenue in 1919. The unpaved road drops down into City Creek Canyon. The canyon has always been a valuable source of water and recreation for the neighborhood's residents. Today, this road is a popular route for bikers and hikers to access the canyon and creek.

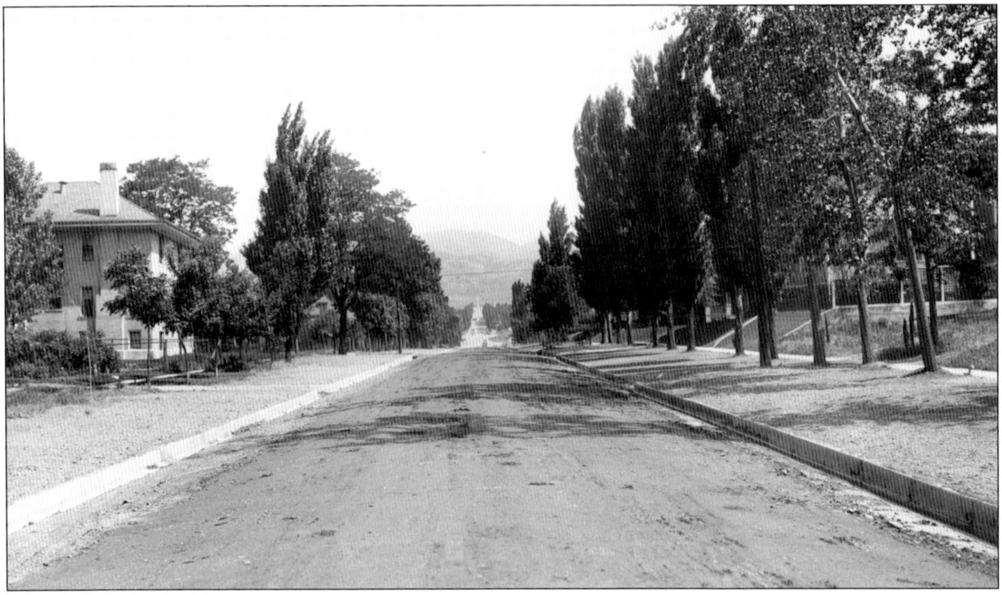

T Street is viewed from First Avenue, looking north towards the Salt Lake City Cemetery. A large cross is seen at the end of the street, marking the Catholic Cemetery. The road is being prepared for paving in this June 1913 photograph.

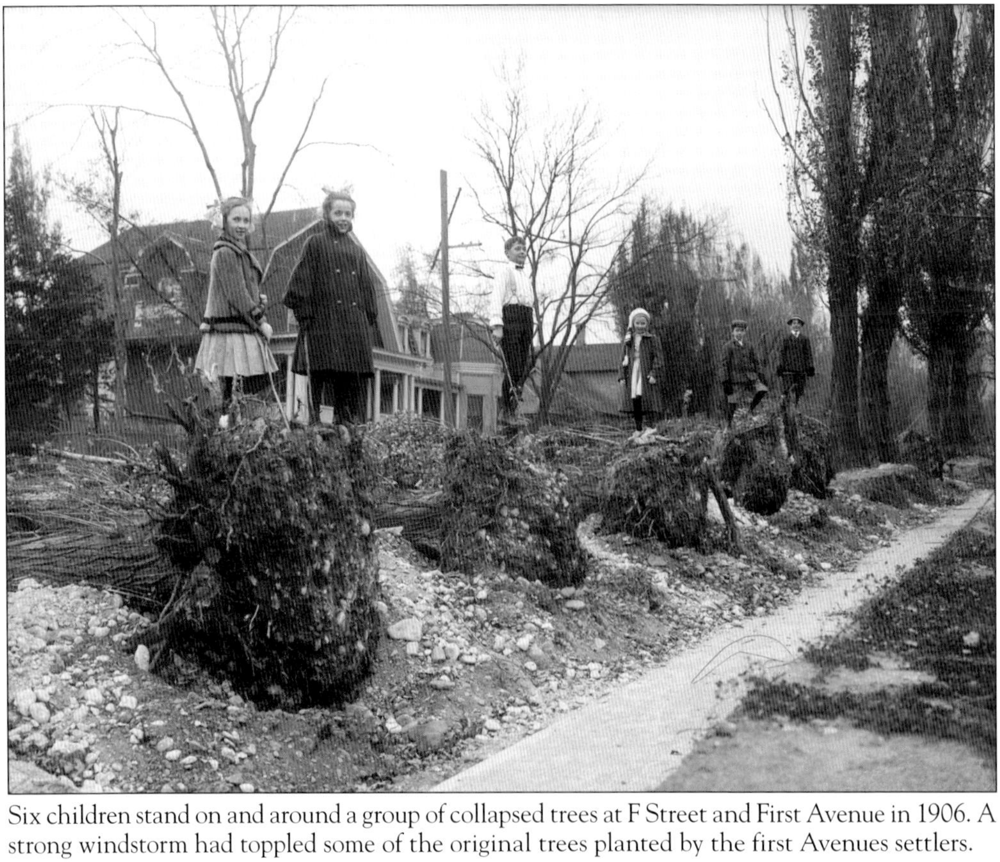

Six children stand on and around a group of collapsed trees at F Street and First Avenue in 1906. A strong windstorm had toppled some of the original trees planted by the first Avenues settlers.

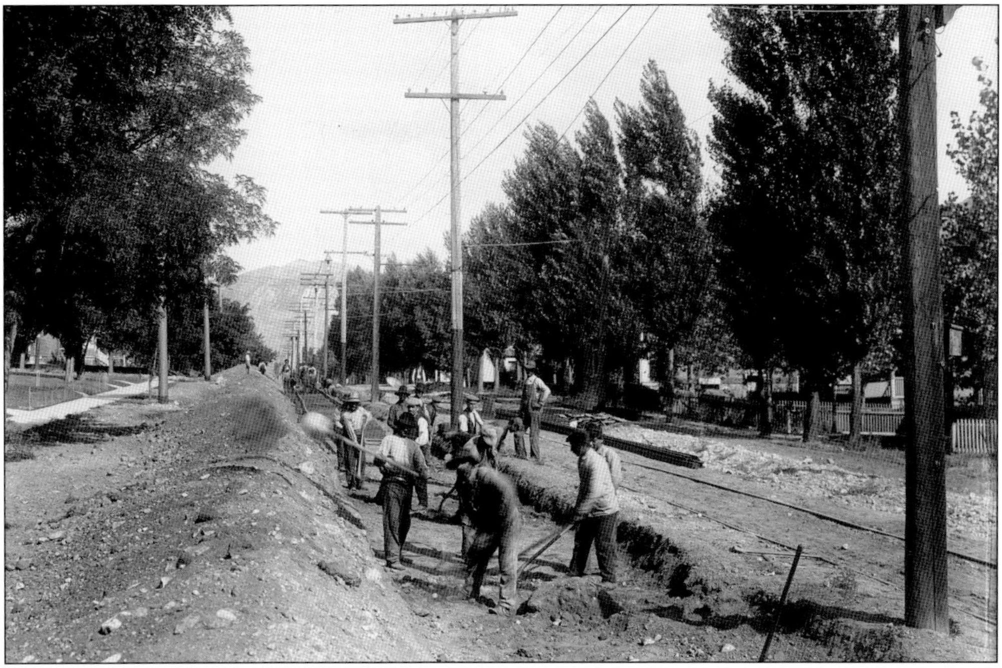

Construction is under way on Third Avenue for the new streetcar tracks in 1907. Sections of this route were first built in 1875 and used by horse-drawn cars. The tracks, which ran nearly the entire length of Third Avenue, linked the Federal Heights neighborhood near the University of Utah to downtown Salt Lake City. Easy access to public transportation added to the desirability of the Avenues as a place to live.

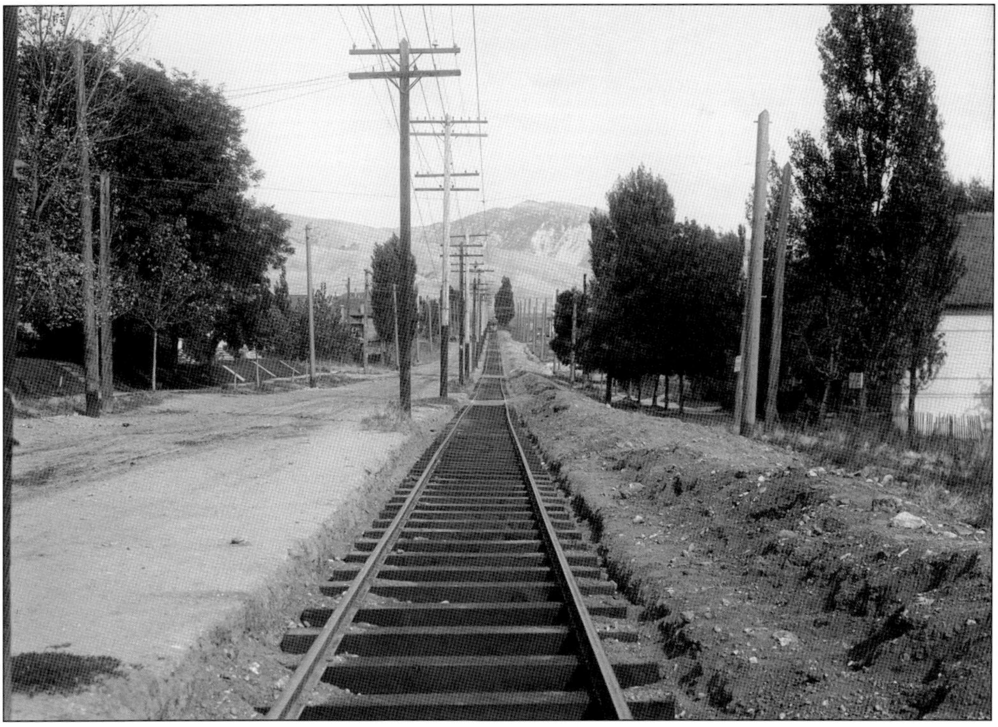

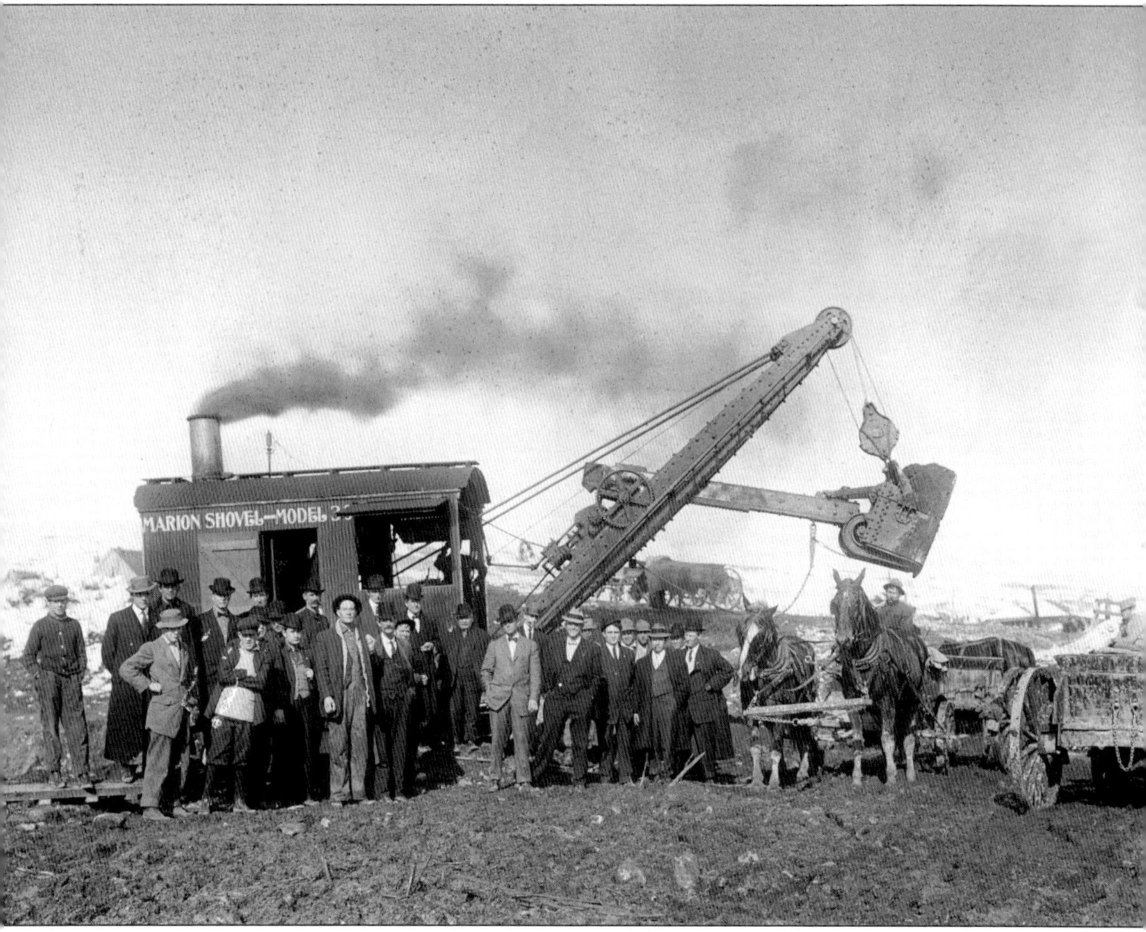

A group of workers, horses, and a steam shovel are pictured on the corner of Ninth Avenue and A Street as the two streets are joined in 1912.

Four

Places of Worship and Learning

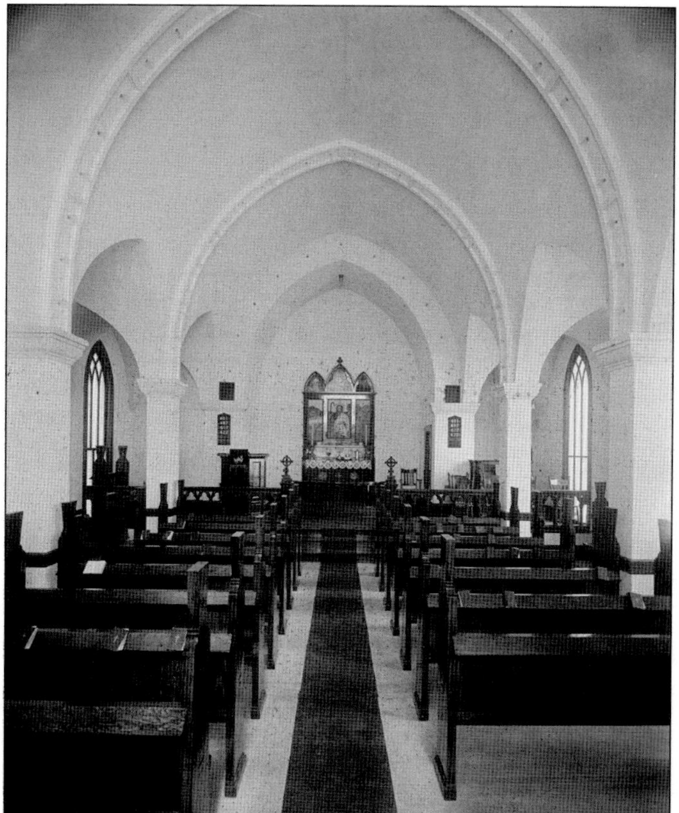

As the neighborhood grew during the early 20th century, four public schools, one private school, five LDS churches, and one Lutheran church served the Avenues. The vaulted Gothic ceiling and quarter-sawn oak pews in this photograph are found in the interior of the Danish Evangelical Lutheran Church in 1911. By the 1970s, schools and churches closed, leaving their legacy on the community as the neighborhood's population changed.

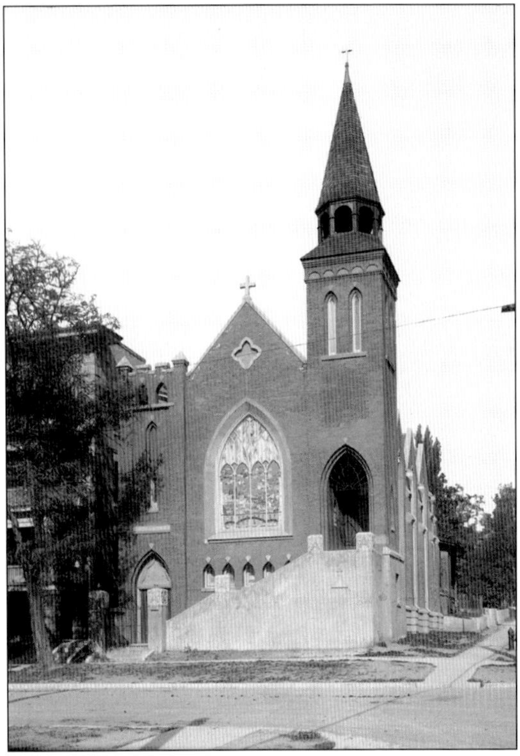

These two views are of the Danish Evangelical Lutheran Church located at 389 First Avenue. This is the only non–Latter-day Saints church in the Avenues proper. The Gothic Revival structure was built between 1907 and 1911 by members of the Danish congregation. The United Danish Evangelical Lutheran Church wanted to convert Mormon Danes back to their native religion. They sent missionaries to Salt Lake City in 1902 to start a congregation. They met at various locations in the neighborhood, including the home at 760 First Avenue. Pastor Harold Jensen built a home at the rear of the church. Theodor Lauridsen, a member of the congregation, designed the church and home. The congregation later became known as the Tabor Lutheran Church and continued to meet in the building until 1963. That same year, they moved to their current location on Second South and Seventh East Streets. The Central Baptist Church used the facility until it was converted into an office in 1987.

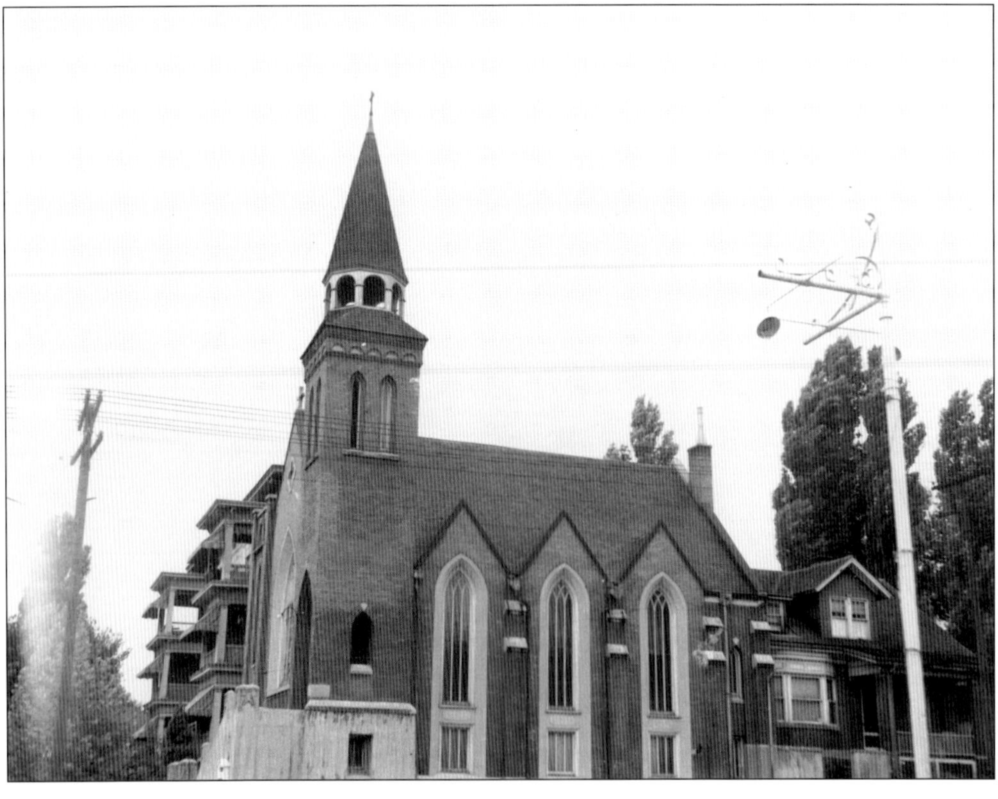

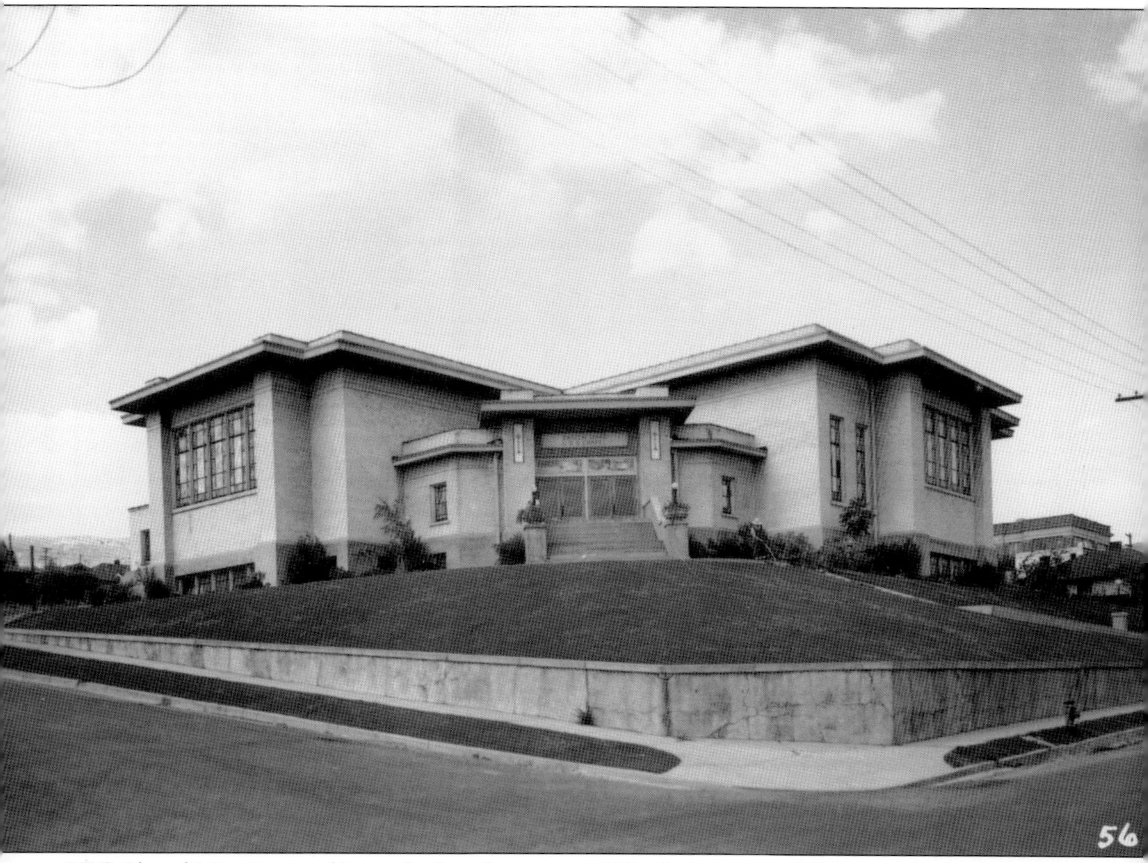

LDS Church's Ensign ward is perched on the corner of Ninth Avenue and D Street. As the Avenues expanded north up the bench, additional wards were added to the neighborhood. Prairie-style architecture was popular with church architects early in the 20th century. The exterior of this building was hidden by an addition in the 1950s. A townhouse development replaced this building and the original Ensign school located on an adjacent block in the late 1980s. The concrete retaining wall and stairs are all that remain of this church.

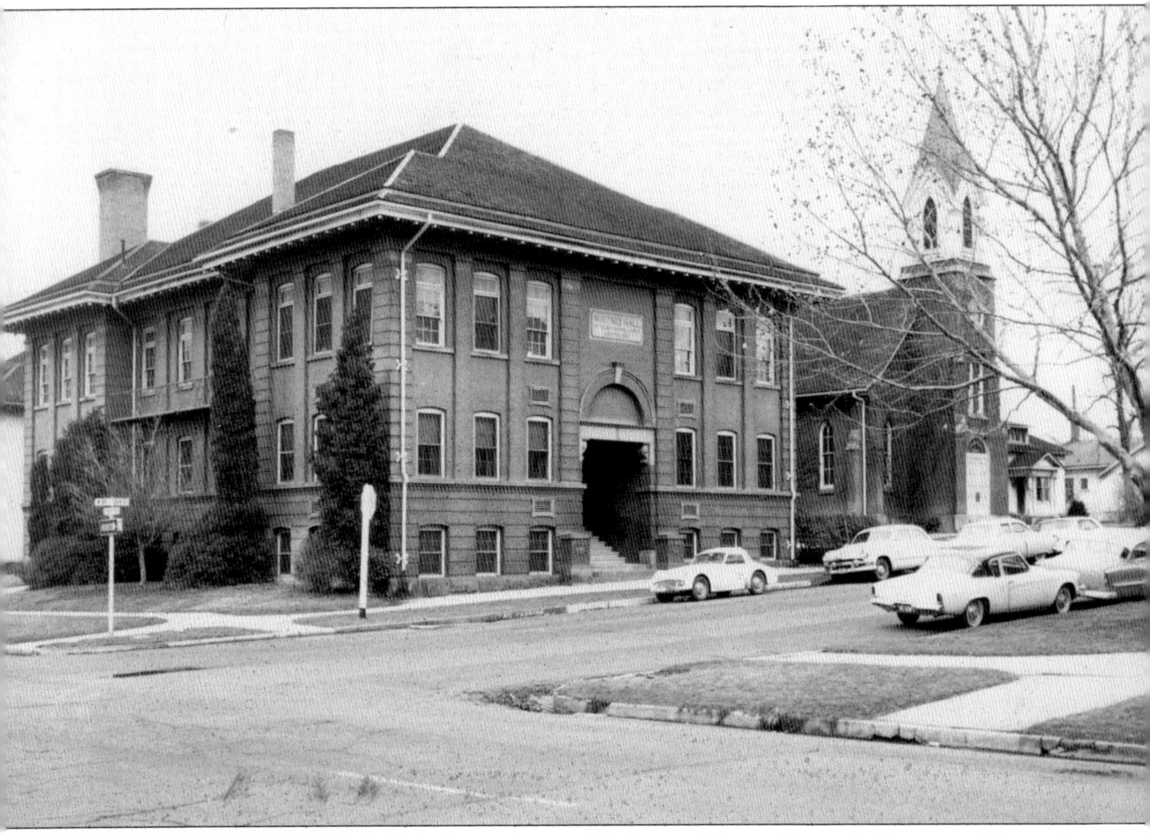

The old city wall once ran along this portion of A Street. The wall was built as a public works project to employ incoming immigrants for the LDS Church. It also was used to control the flow of livestock in and out of the city. The wall was completed just seven years after the first pioneers entered the Great Salt Lake valley. It was made of a mixture of mud, rocks, and straw. The construction of Whitney Hall in 1907 furthered the demolition of the wall. Noted Salt Lake City architect David C. Dart designed the building for the LDS Church. Whitney Hall and the homes north of the chapel were demolished prior to the construction of a new church in the 1970s. Pieces of the old original 18th Ward chapel were moved to a lot across from the Utah State Capitol to build a replica structure.

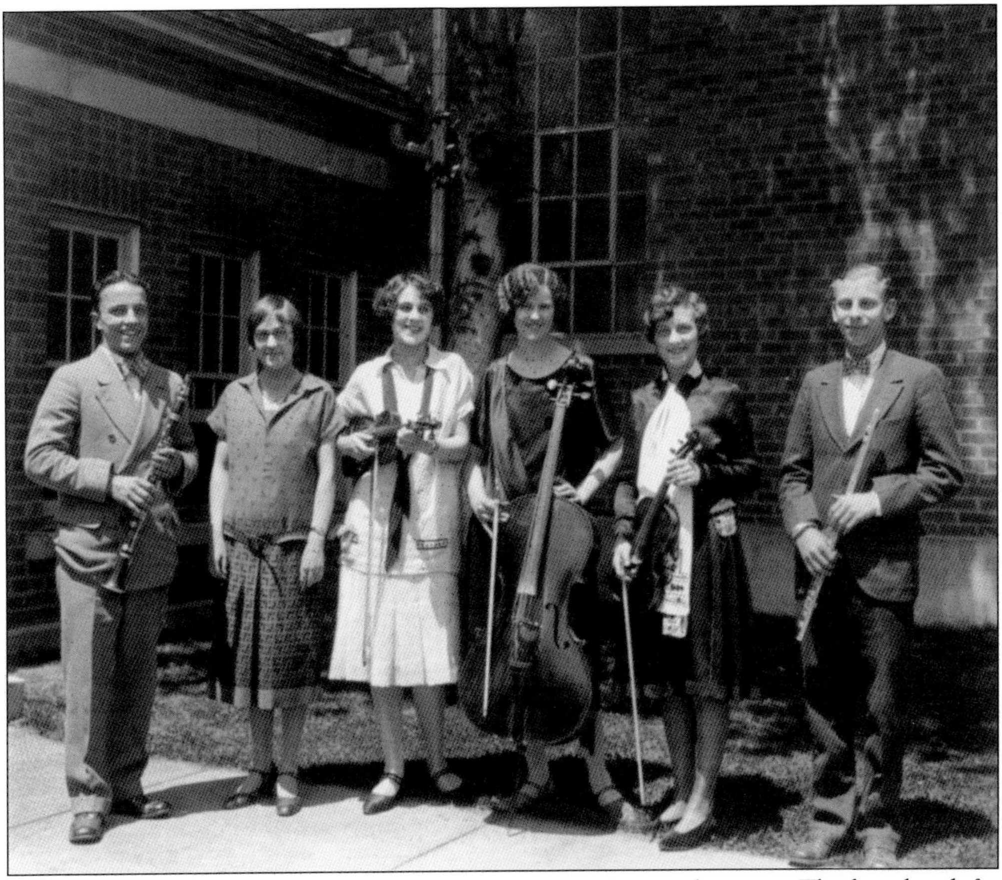

The 20th Ward chapel stood on the corner of D Street and Second Avenue. The first church for the congregation was built in 1856. It was the first LDS chapel in the Avenues neighborhood. The building was placed on land deeded to John C. Sharp by Brigham Young. Sharp became the first bishop for the ward. In 1884, this structure replaced the original church. Lowell Elementary School was built adjacent to the church. The congregation moved to a new building on Second Avenue and G Street in 1923. This building remained and was used as part of the elementary school until it was demolished in the 1960s. In the photograph above, musicians from the 20th Ward chapel youth group are pictured in front of their new chapel in the 1920s.

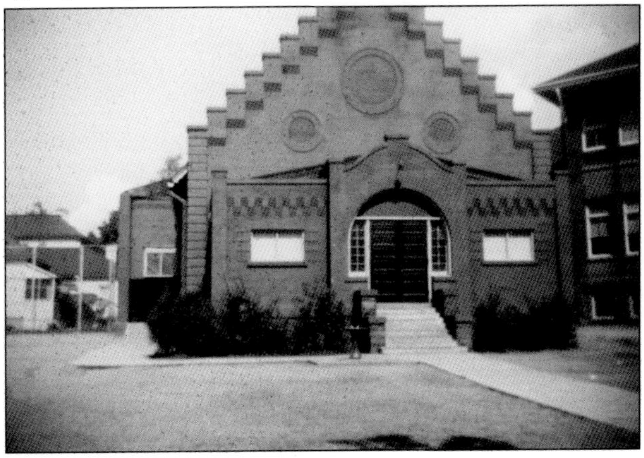

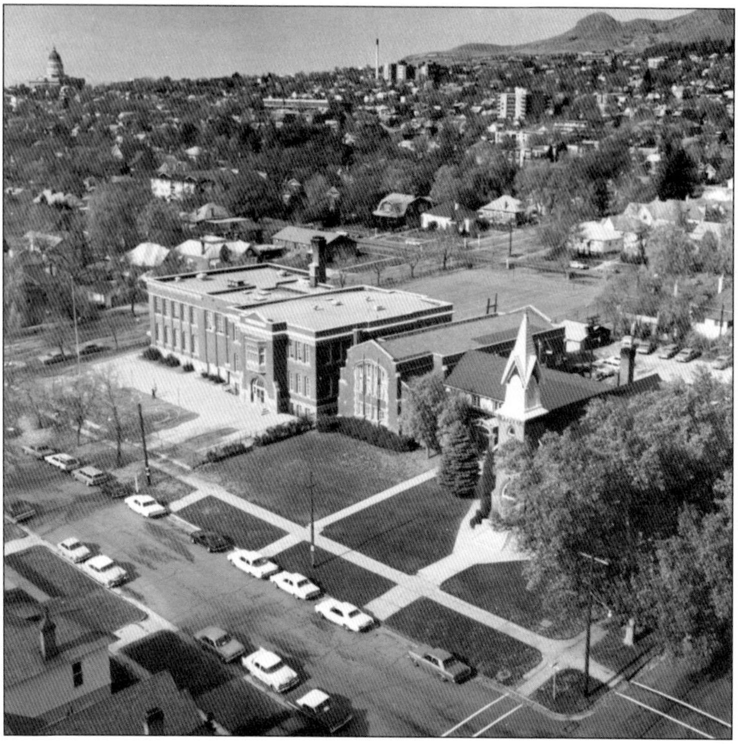

This 1960s aerial view of the block between First Avenue, Second Avenue, and J and K Streets shows both the 21st Ward chapel and Longfellow Elementary school. Both buildings have been demolished. A new church building occupies the northeast corner of this block. Grass and a parking lot occupy the site of the school and original church.

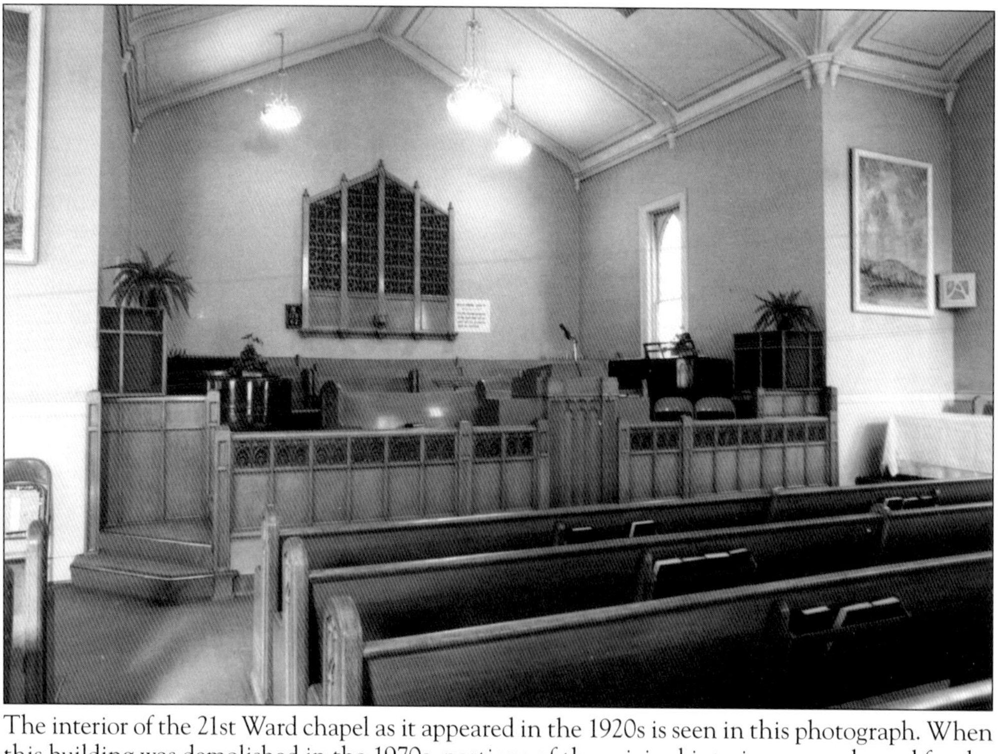

The interior of the 21st Ward chapel as it appeared in the 1920s is seen in this photograph. When this building was demolished in the 1970s, portions of the original interior were salvaged for the new church building.

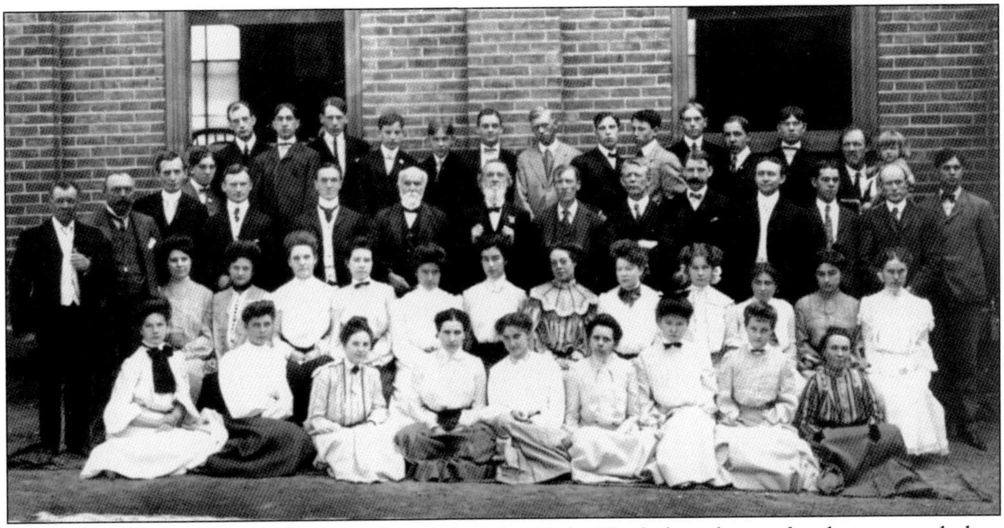

Junior and adult Sunday school students from the 20th Ward chapel pose for their annual class photograph in August 1904. The large open windows provide cool air to the church on a hot summer day.

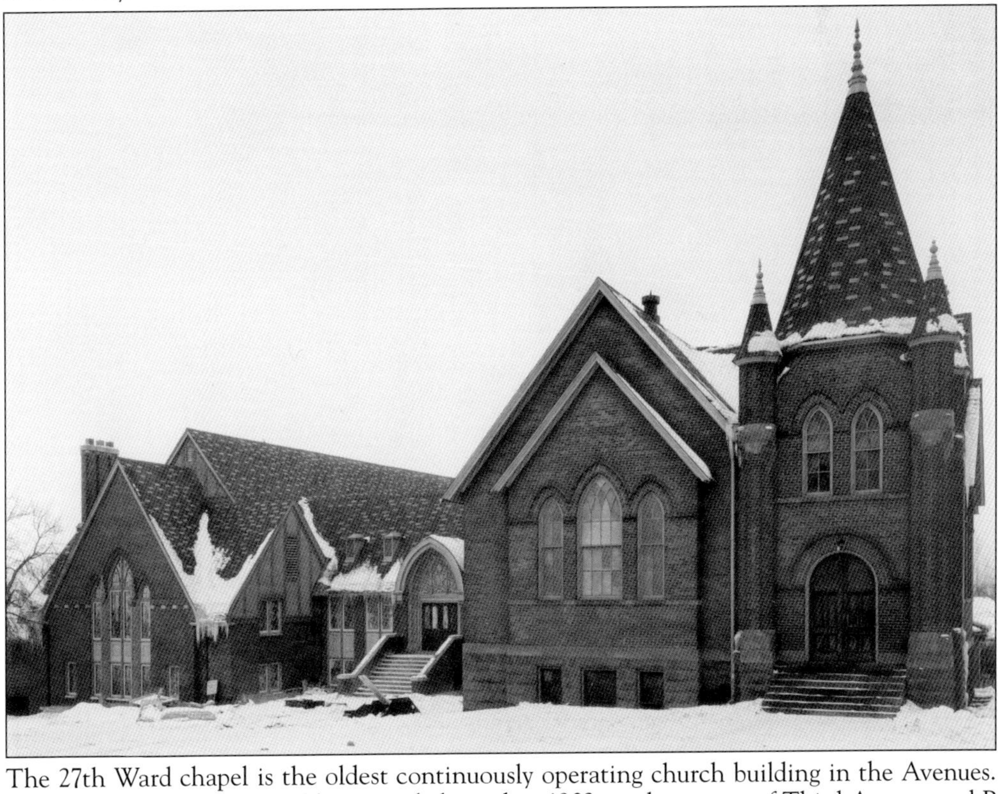

The 27th Ward chapel is the oldest continuously operating church building in the Avenues. The Gothic-style chapel building was dedicated in 1903 on the corner of Third Avenue and P Street. The design of the church is dominated by the square tower with an octagonal roof on the northeast corner of the building. A compatible recreation hall annex was added in 1927. The Tudor Revival half-timbering found on the annex was a popular design feature in Salt Lake City homes and churches during the 1920s.

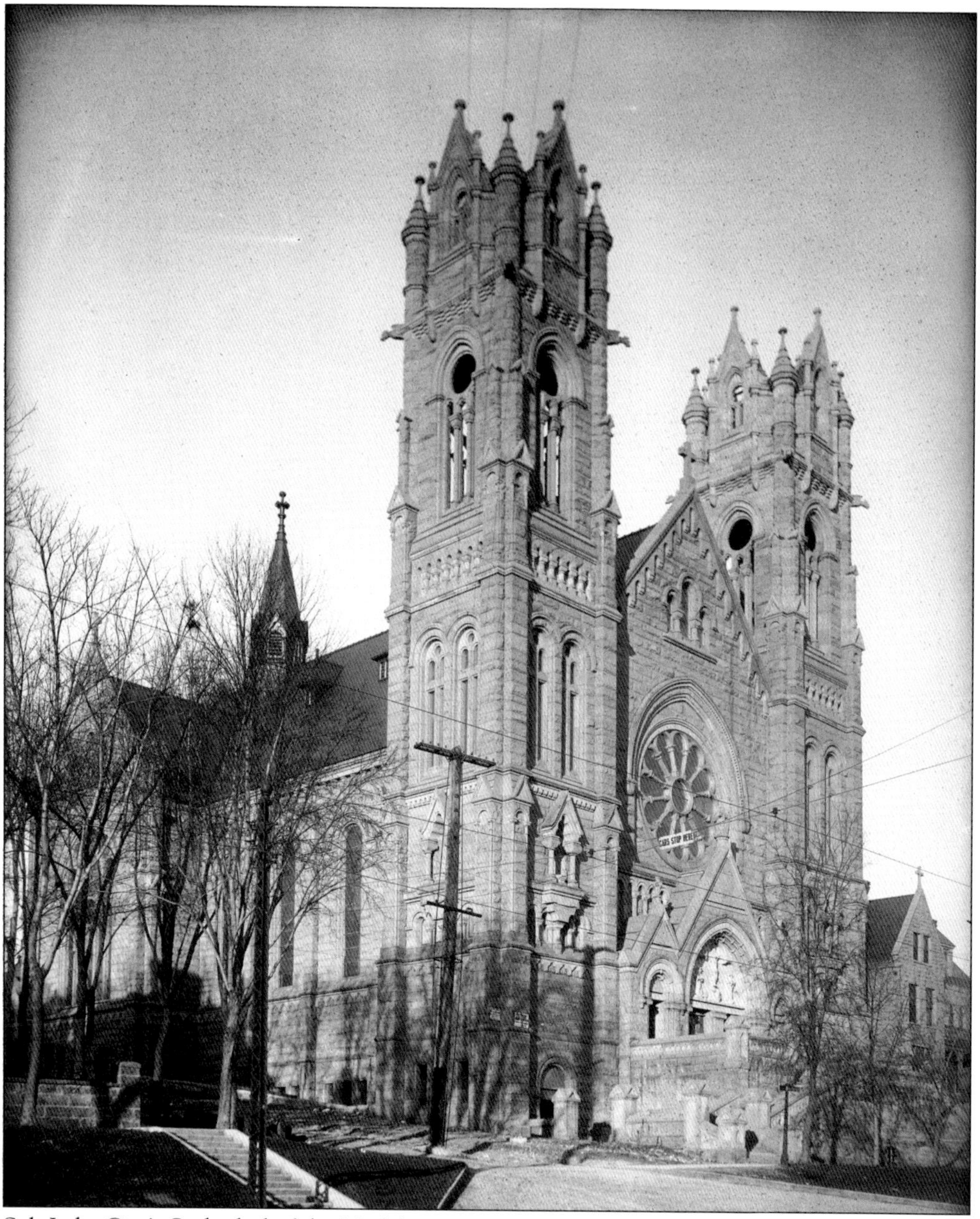

Salt Lake City's Cathedral of the Madeleine sits at the foot of the Avenues along South Temple Street. The building's exterior is neo-Romanesque style, while its interior is Gothic. The structure was designed by Bernard O. Mecklenburg and Carl M. Neuhausen. Mecklenburg designed several homes in the Avenues, while Neuhausen resided in the neighborhood early in his architectural career. Construction of the building began in 1900 and was completed in 1909. The cathedral served the Avenues' Catholic residents.

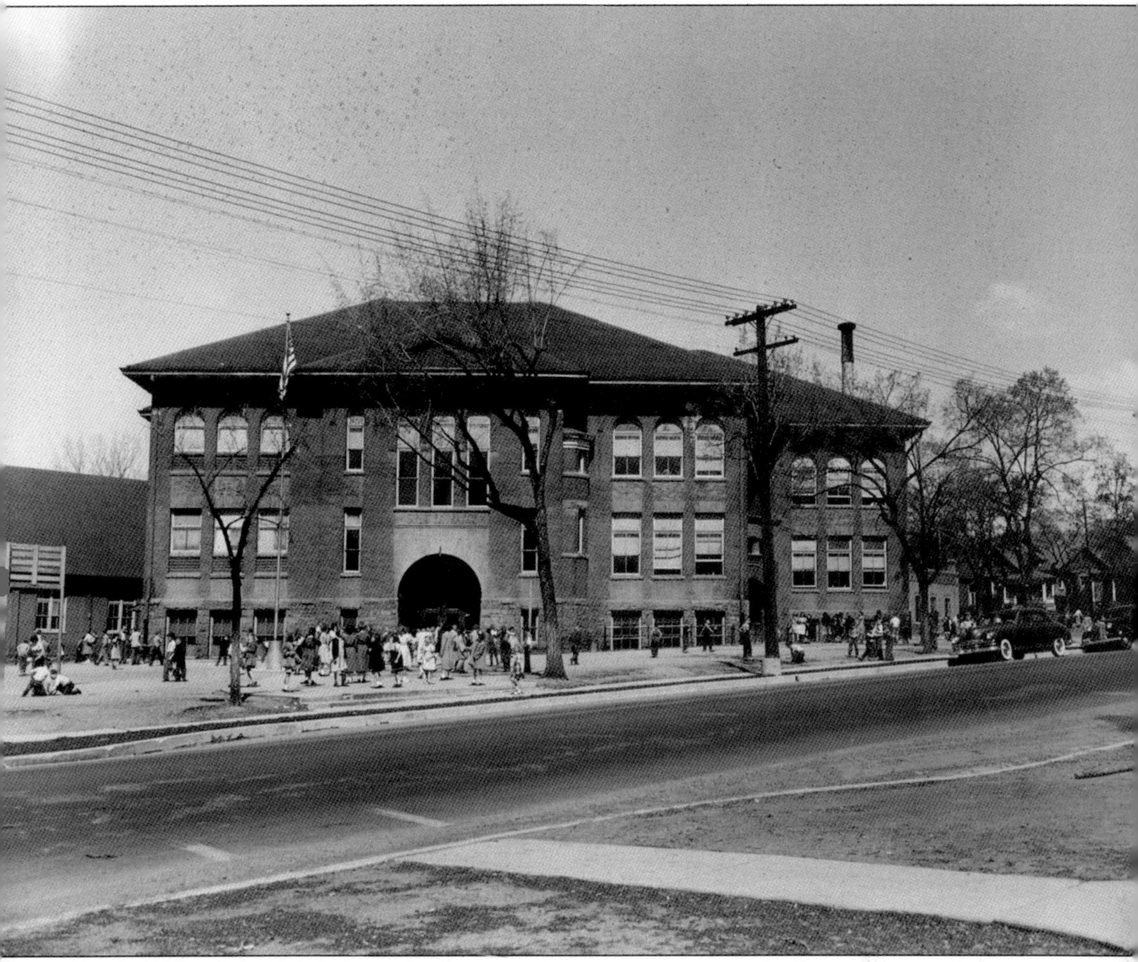

The original Lowell Elementary school is pictured from E Street in 1949. Above the east entrance are the words "Girls Entrance." The old 20th Ward church is located on the left side of the photograph. It was being used by the school district as an annex to the school. The home on the far right edge at the corner of E Street and Third Avenue was demolished in the 1950s for construction of an apartment building. The original Lowell school was replaced in the late 1960s by a plain single-story structure. Today, that building is occupied by a charter school.

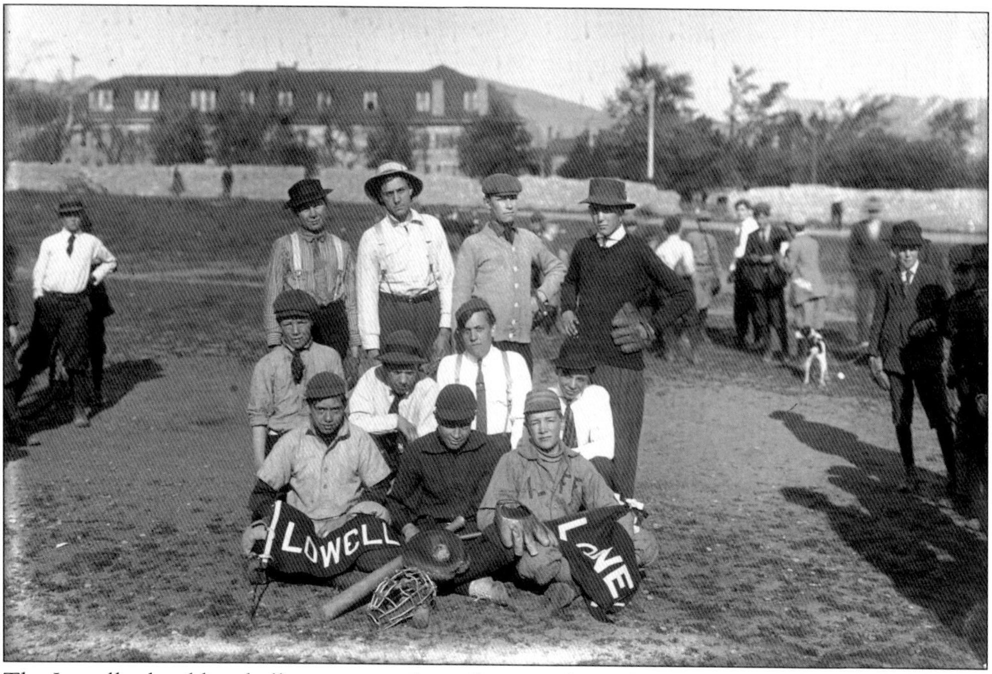

The Lowell school baseball team poses for a photograph in 1909. Interestingly, most of the boys are wearing neckties for the game. The old city wall is seen in the background, and the building behind the wall is part of Rowland Hall school.

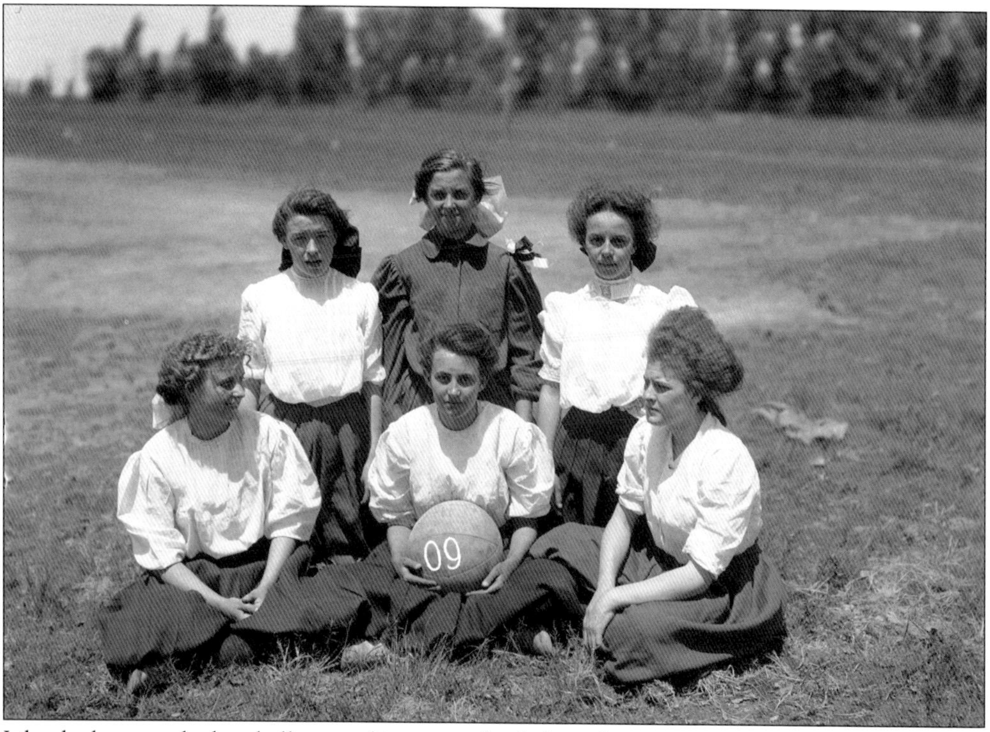

Like the boys on the baseball team, this group of girls from the 1909 Lowell school girls' basketball team is well dressed for the photograph.

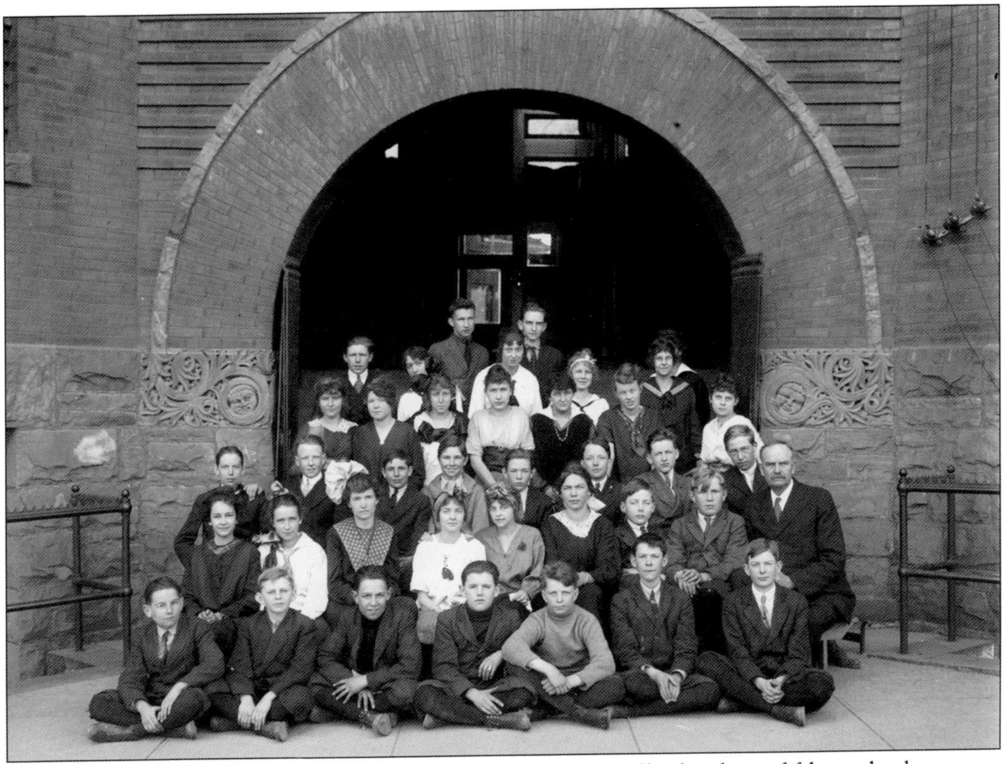

A Sullivesque-style arch stretches over the entrance to Lowell school as a fifth-grade class poses for a class portrait in 1915. Most of the girls are dressed in sailor outfits.

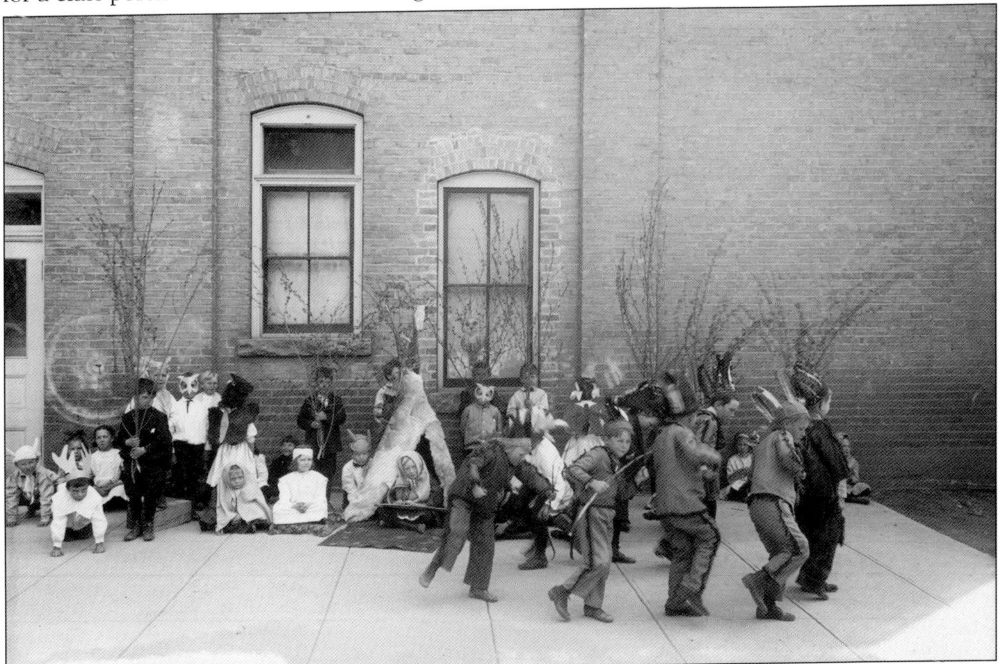

A group of schoolchildren perform in an outdoor play at Longfellow school in 1911. A closer look at the image reveals students dressed up as a moose, Native Americans, a butterfly, and owls.

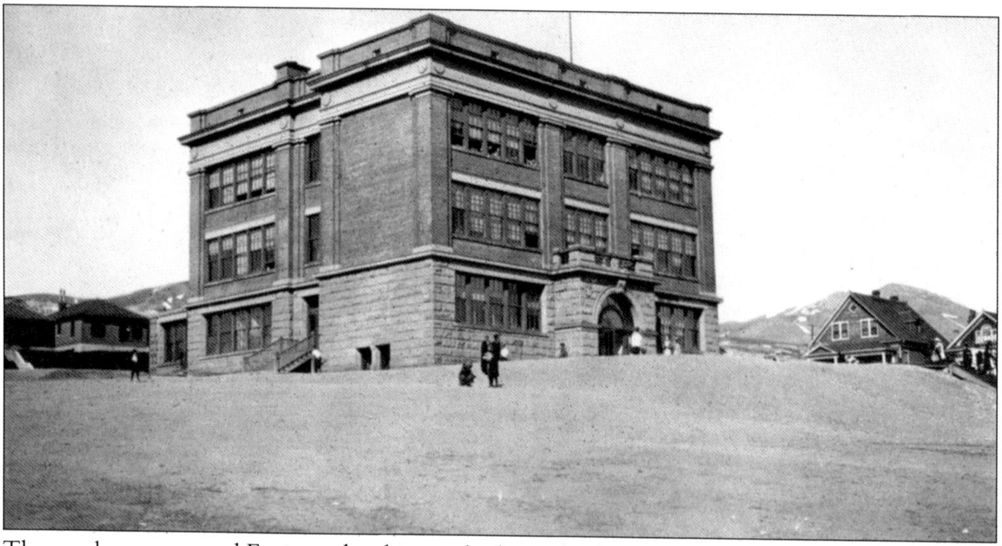

The newly constructed Ensign school is perched on a lot located at F Street and Ninth Avenue. Construction of the building was needed as new homes expanded north up the Avenues bench. The school was designed by Utah State Capitol architect and Avenues resident Richard K.A. Kletting. In the 1970s, a new Ensign school was constructed even higher up in the Avenues. This building was eventually demolished and replaced by condominium townhomes and a library.

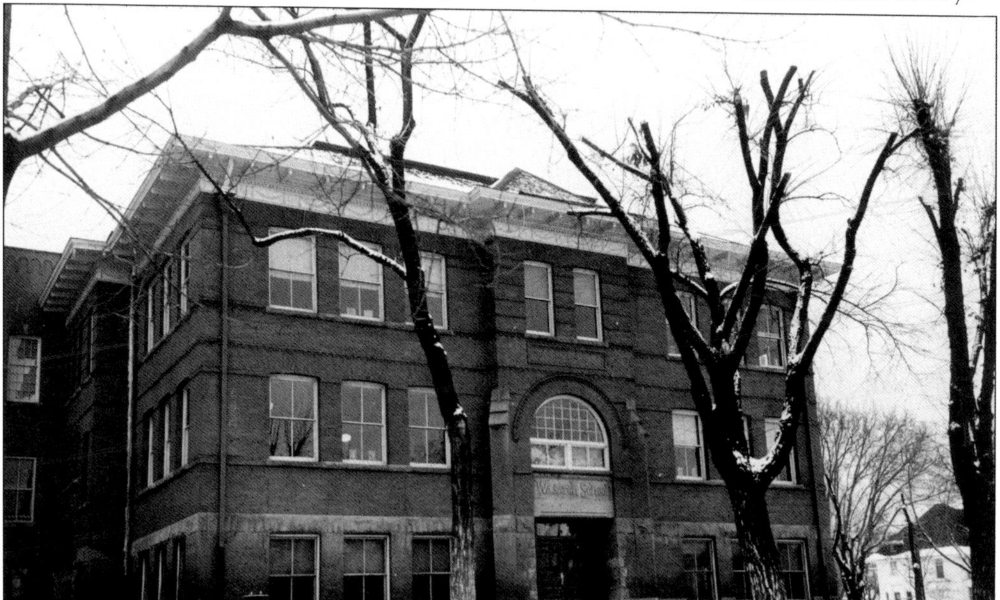

The original school building for Wasatch Elementary school, constructed about 1895, is pictured on a winter day in 1948. Additions to the structure filled the block between South Temple Street, First Avenue, and R and S Streets. They were all demolished in the mid-1970s and replaced by the existing structure at the same location.

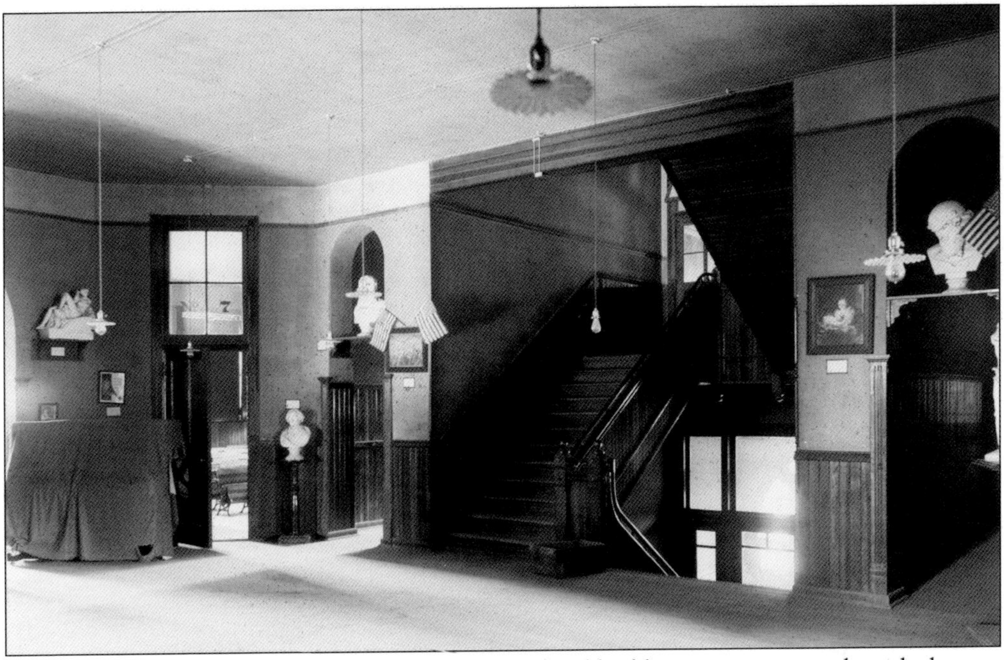

The corridor of the original Wasatch Elementary school building contrasts greatly with the way schools are built today. The central corridor with rooms off the sides and corners was a typical design feature for school buildings constructed during the late 19th century around Utah. In the photograph below, an eighth-grade class poses for a portrait in front of the South Temple Street entrance to the main school building in 1916.

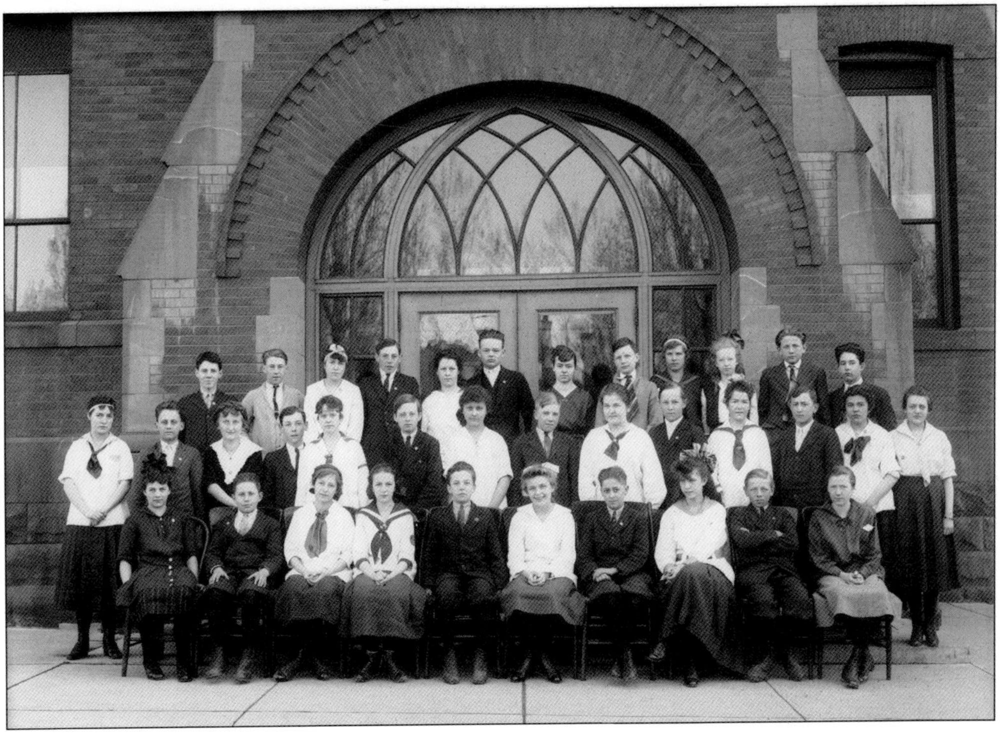

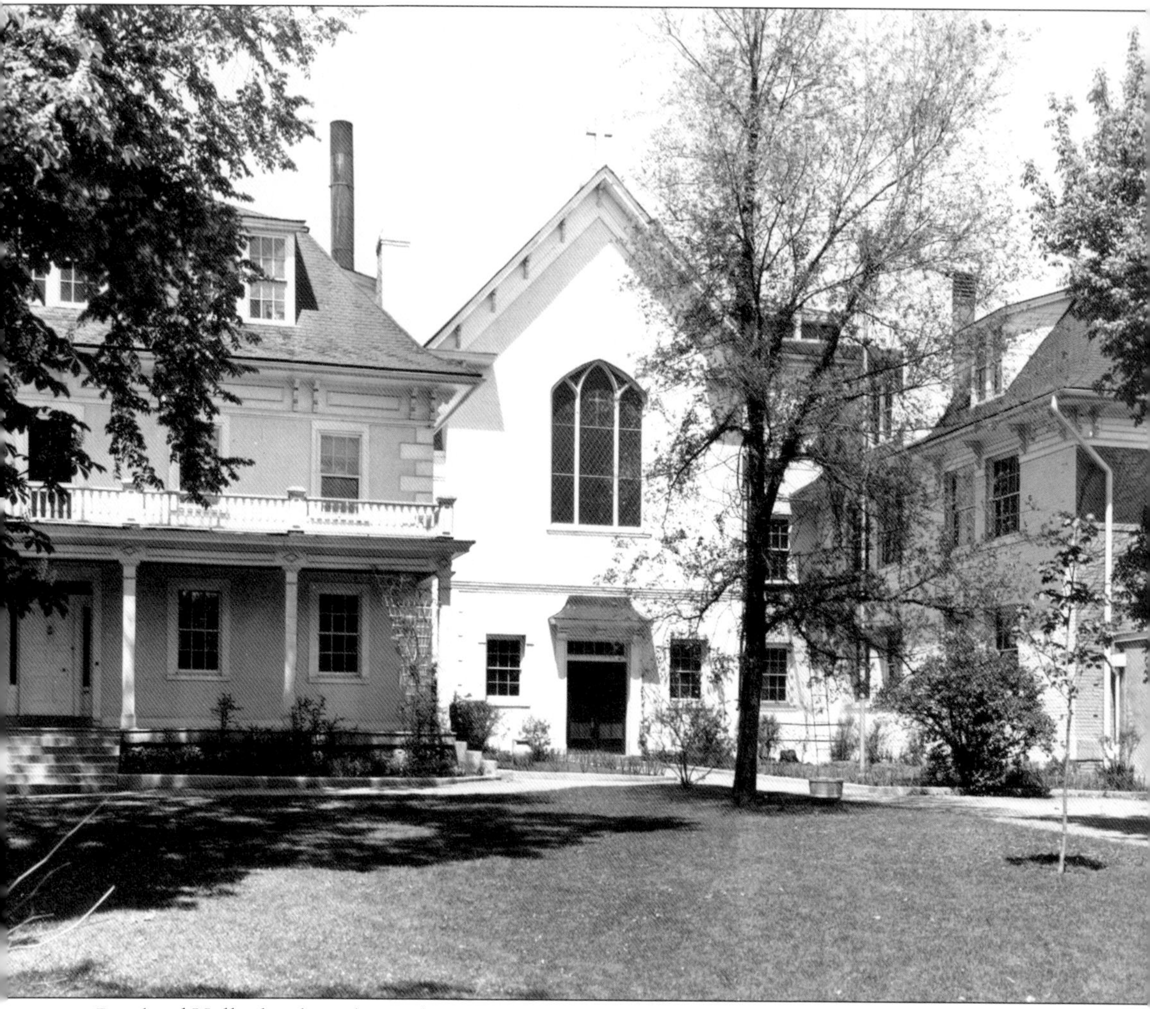

Rowland Hall school was located on First Avenue in the Avenues from 1906 until 2002. Originally, the school was operated by the local Episcopal church as a boarding school for girls. St. Marks School for boys was also operated by the church off and on during the last century. Eventually, the two schools merged. The original campus buildings are now owned by the Catholic Diocese of Salt Lake City. The Madeleine Choir school now operates at the location as a Catholic elementary school.

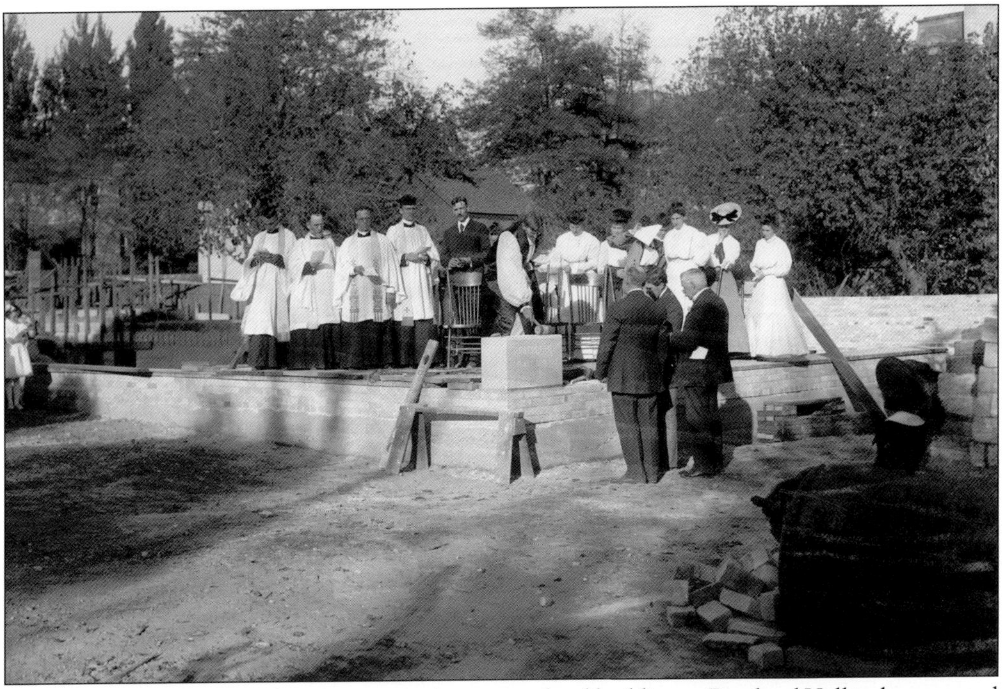

The ceremony dedicating the cornerstone for a new school building at Rowland Hall is documented in this 1906 photograph. Episcopal ministers, local government officials, and Rowland Hall administrators attend the event. The image below reveals the completed structure in 1907.

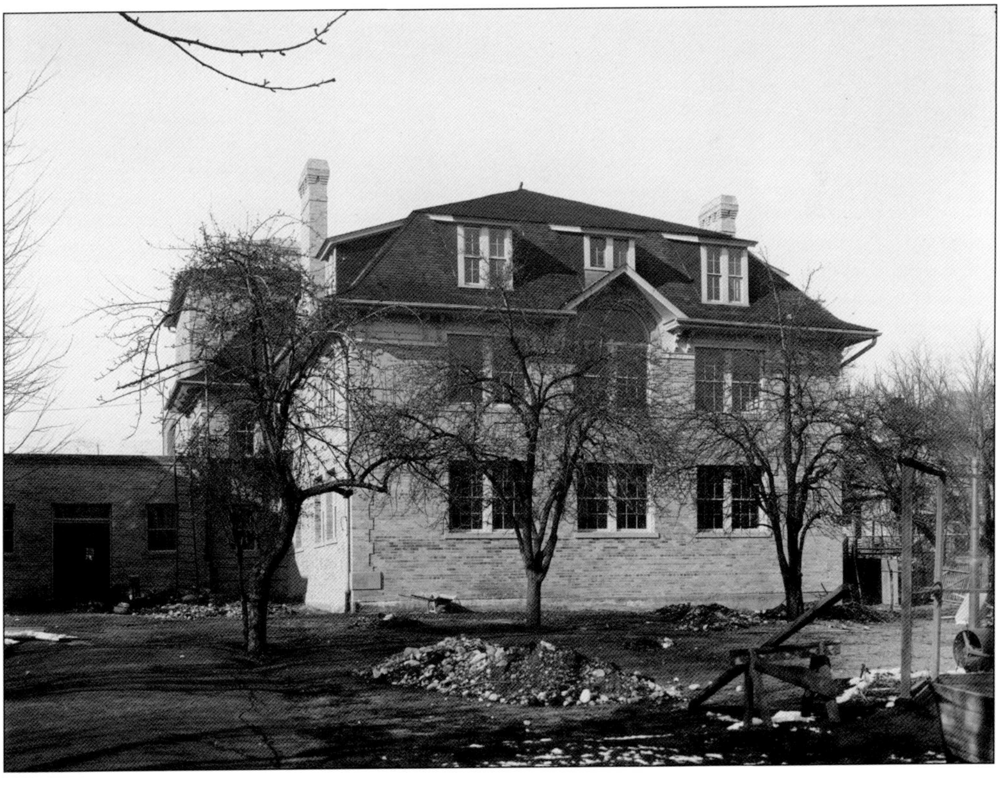

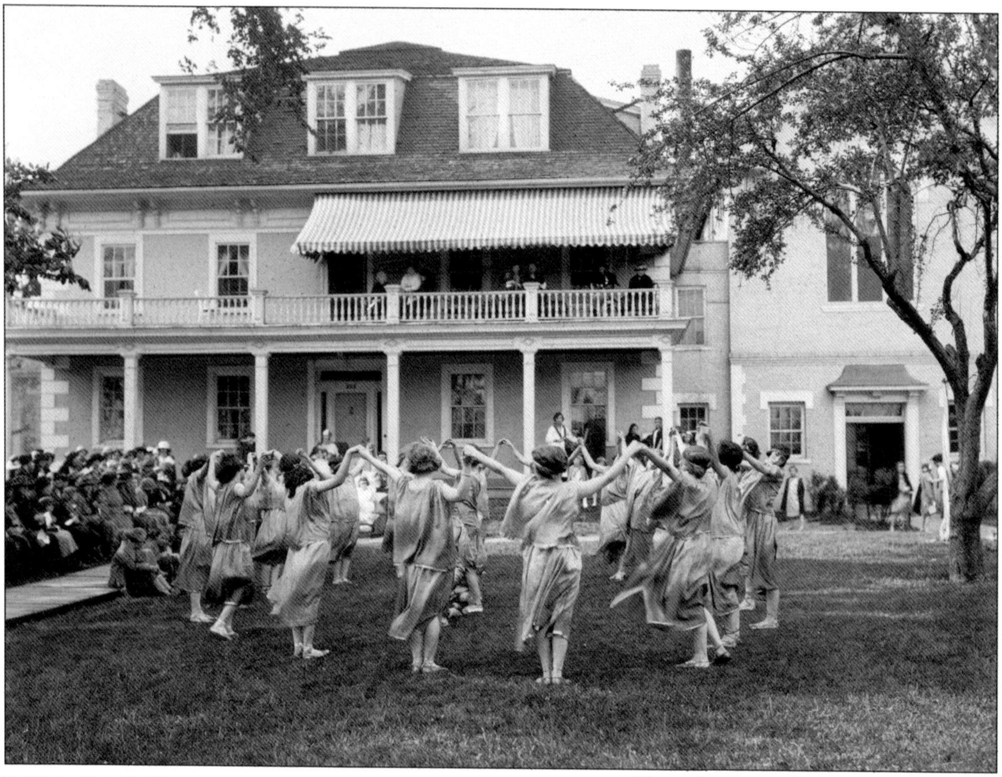

This photograph was taken in the yard between the school buildings at Rowland Hall in 1922. A group of girls participate in a dance routine.

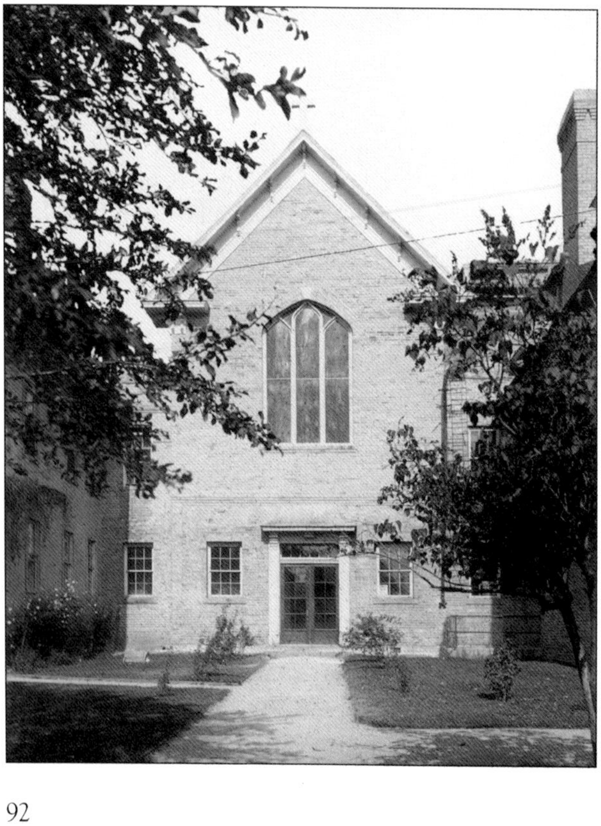

The Episcopal Chapel was an important part of Rowland Hall when this image was captured in 1910. This is the front of the building, as viewed from First Avenue.

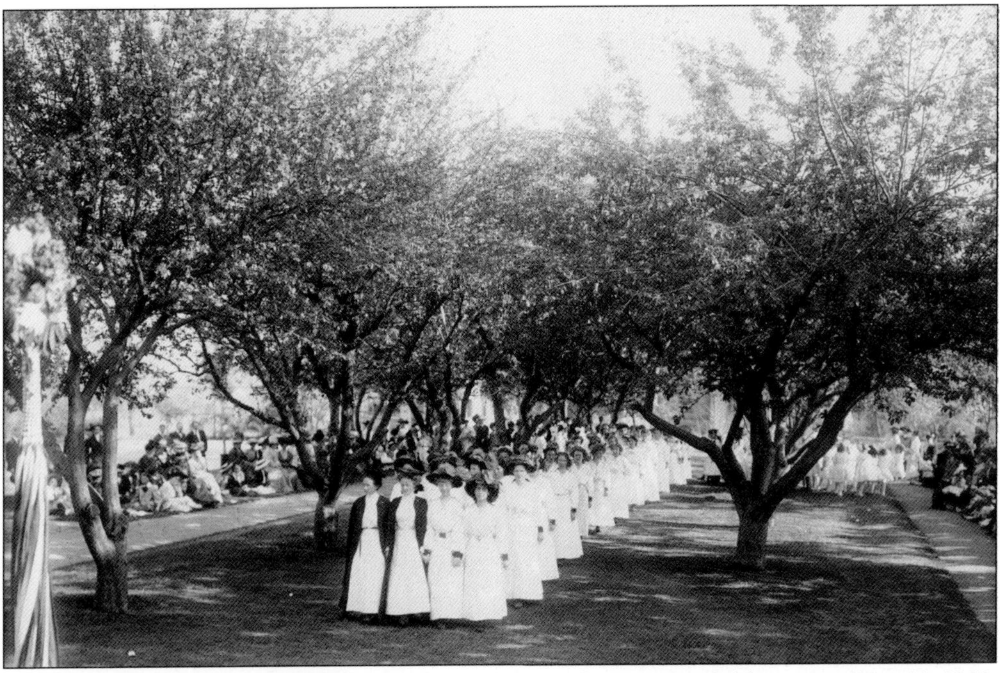

A group of Rowland Hall students march in what was known as a field meet on May 14, 1909. Parents and teachers sit on the sidelines as the girls go by. Pictured below, a group of uniformed girls walk around the maypole on the same day.

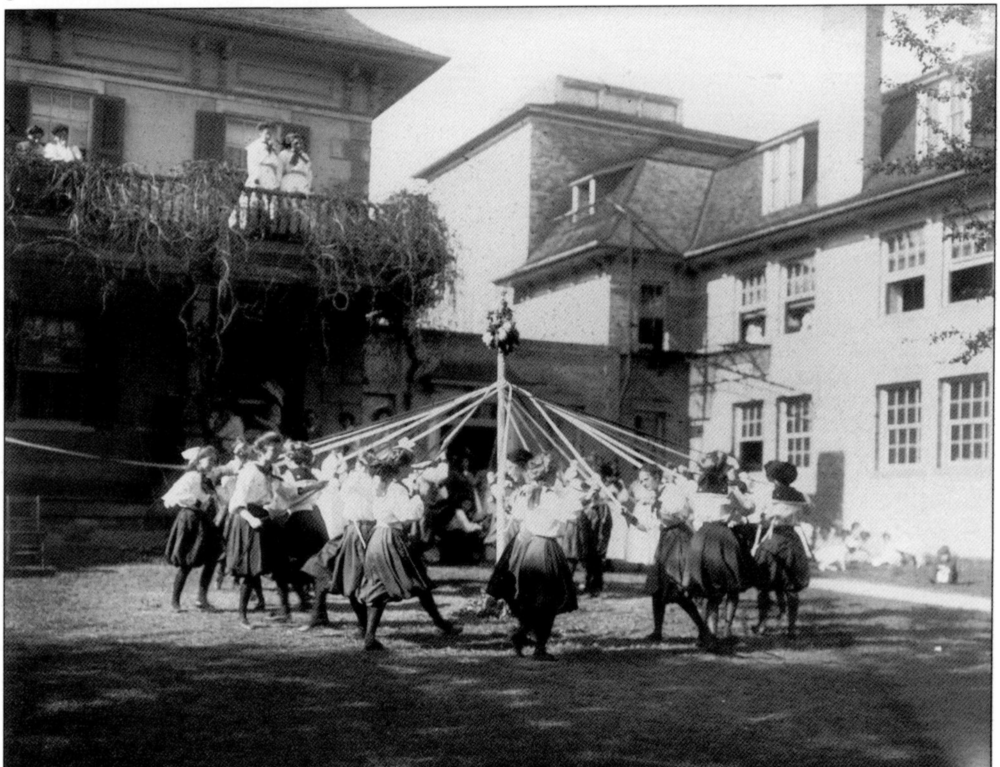

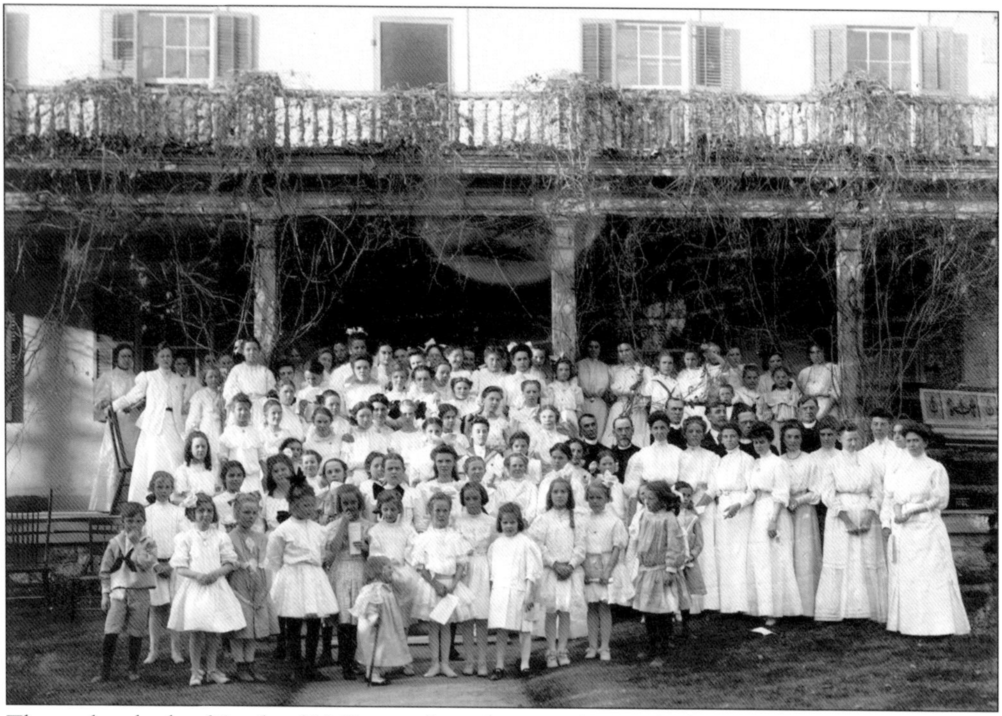

The student body of Rowland Hall poses for a photograph outside the original vine-covered main school building in 1906. Rowland Hall was an all-girls school at the time this image was captured. The school served grades kindergarten through high school. There is no known explanation for the one boy standing on the left side of the front row.

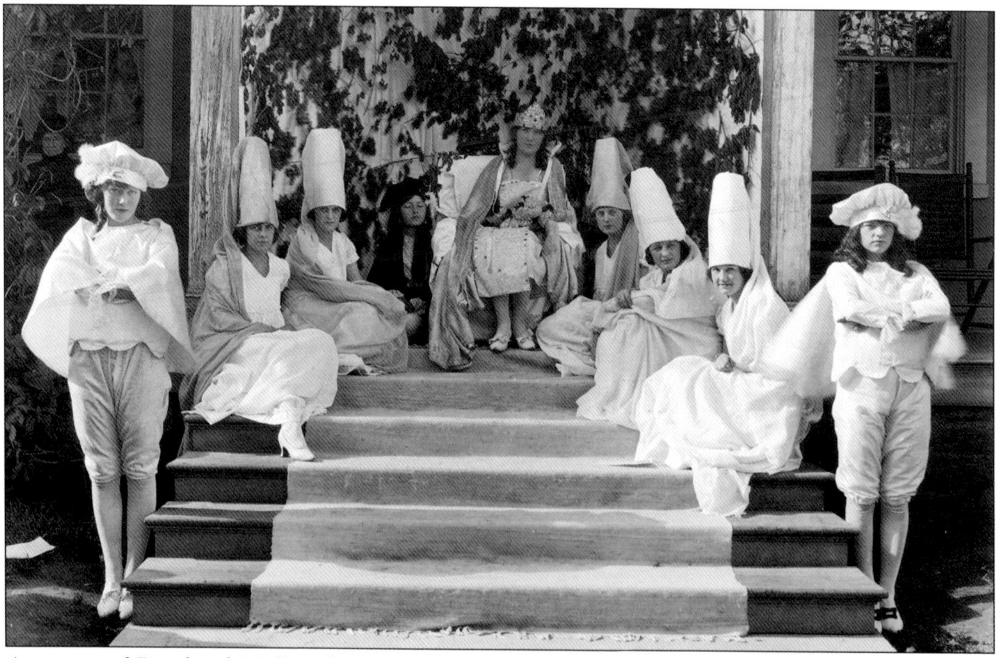

A group of Rowland Hall girls pose for a photograph before performing an outdoor play in 1922.

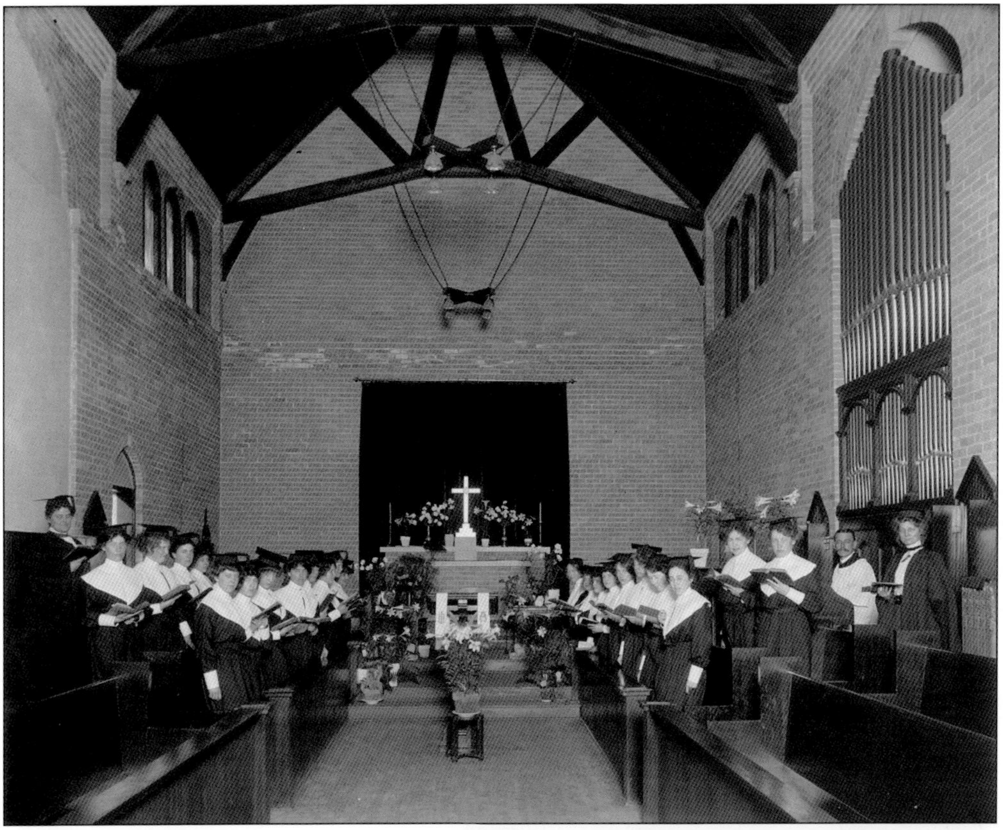

Choir students perform in the Rowland Hall chapel in 1912. The image at right shows the pipe organ on the side of the sanctuary.

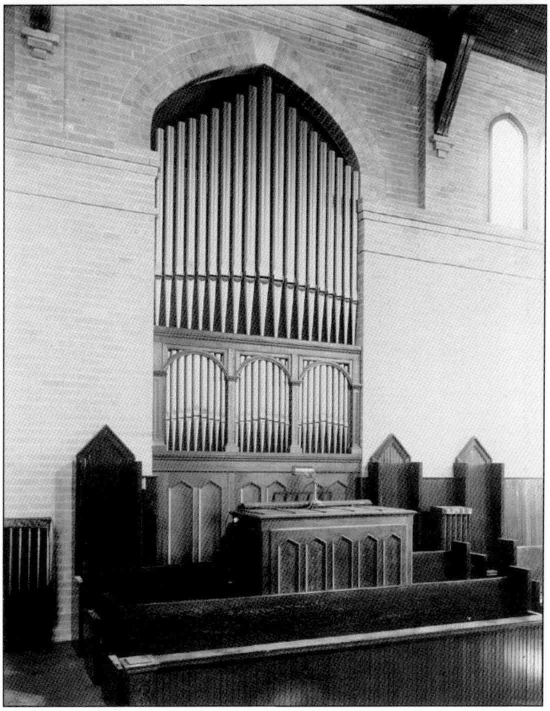

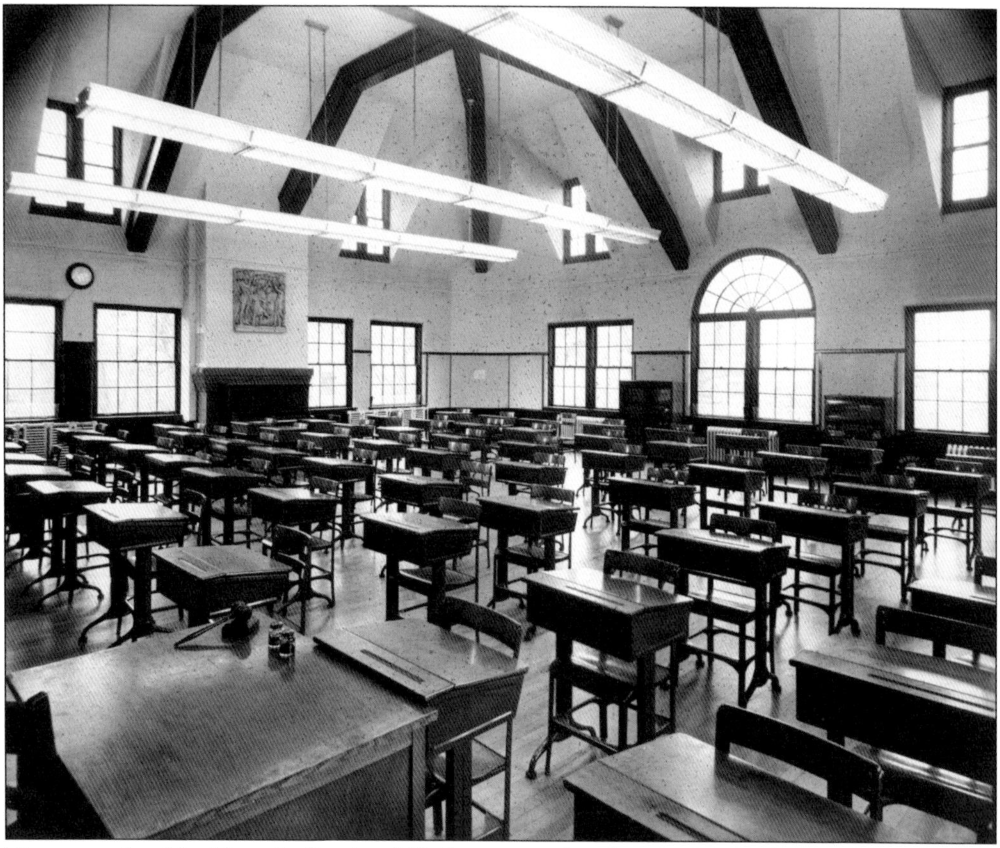

The new school building for Rowland Hall was completed in 1906. On the top floor were two very large classrooms that were also used for athletics and drama performances.

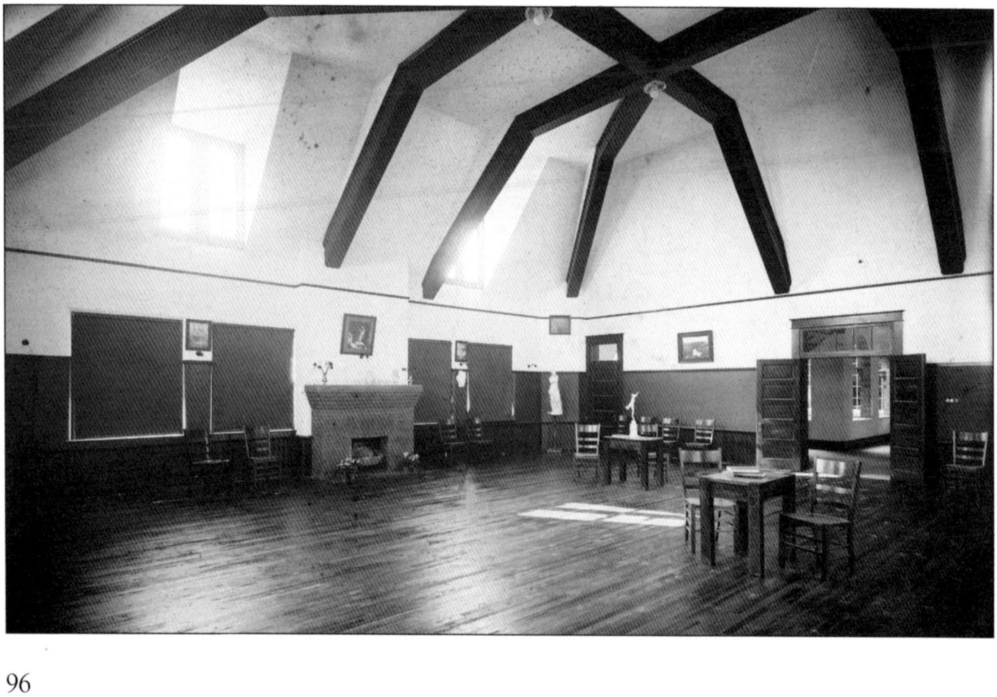

Five

PUBLIC PLACES AND PUBLIC SPACES

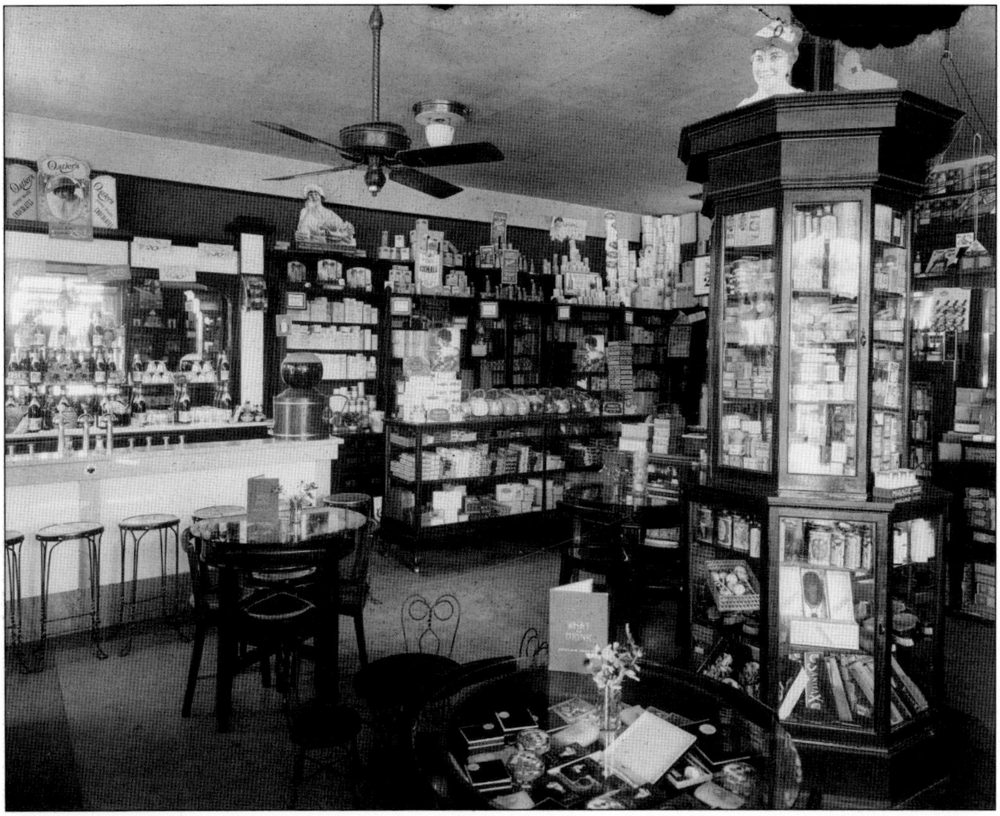

As the Avenues community grew, the need for public places and spaces grew as well. Convenient neighborhood general and grocery stores, such as Sixth Avenue Drug Store in this photograph, appeared near street corners. A small amusement park was established in the 1870s, providing neighbors with recreational opportunities. The city's main cemetery and hospital were built at the top of the neighborhood, above the polluted skies of the valley.

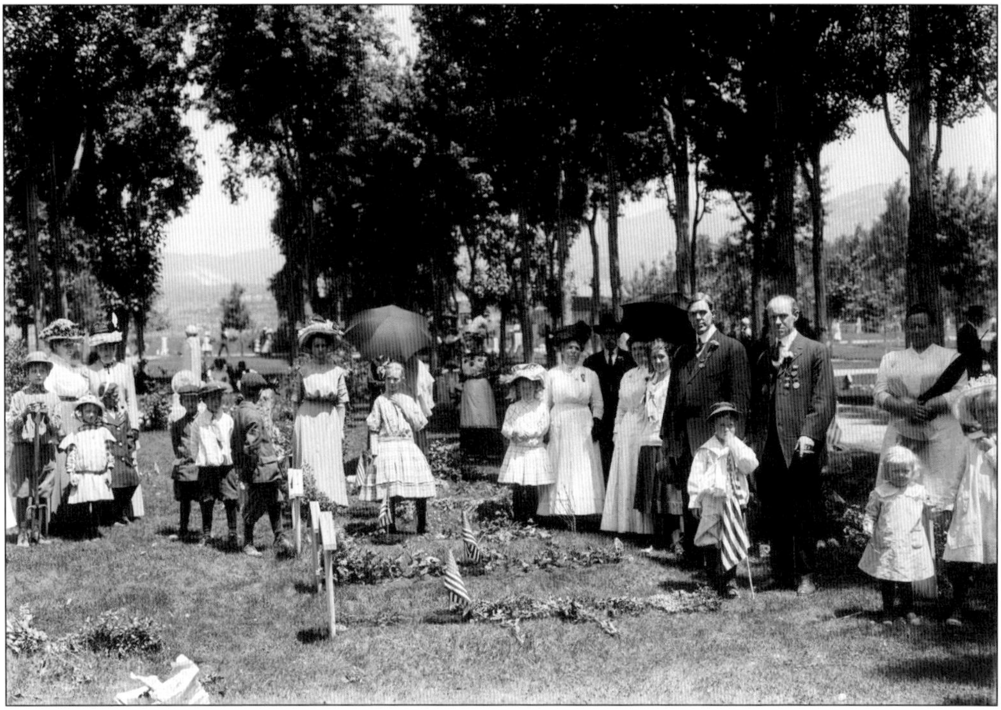

Men, women, and children gather in the Salt Lake City Cemetery for Decoration Day in 1911. The holiday was first celebrated in 1865 in memory of the soldiers killed in the Civil War. After World War II, the now recognized and preferred name for the holiday became Memorial Day.

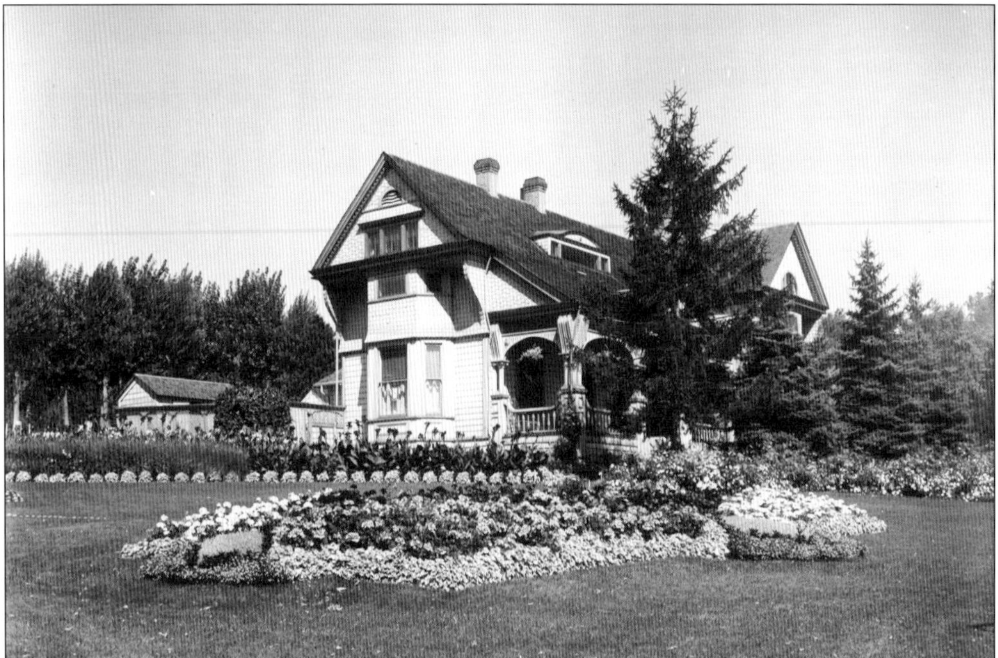

A lush flower garden surrounds the Salt Lake City Cemetery caretaker's home in 1918. The large Victorian house was replaced by a Tudor-style structure in the late 1920s.

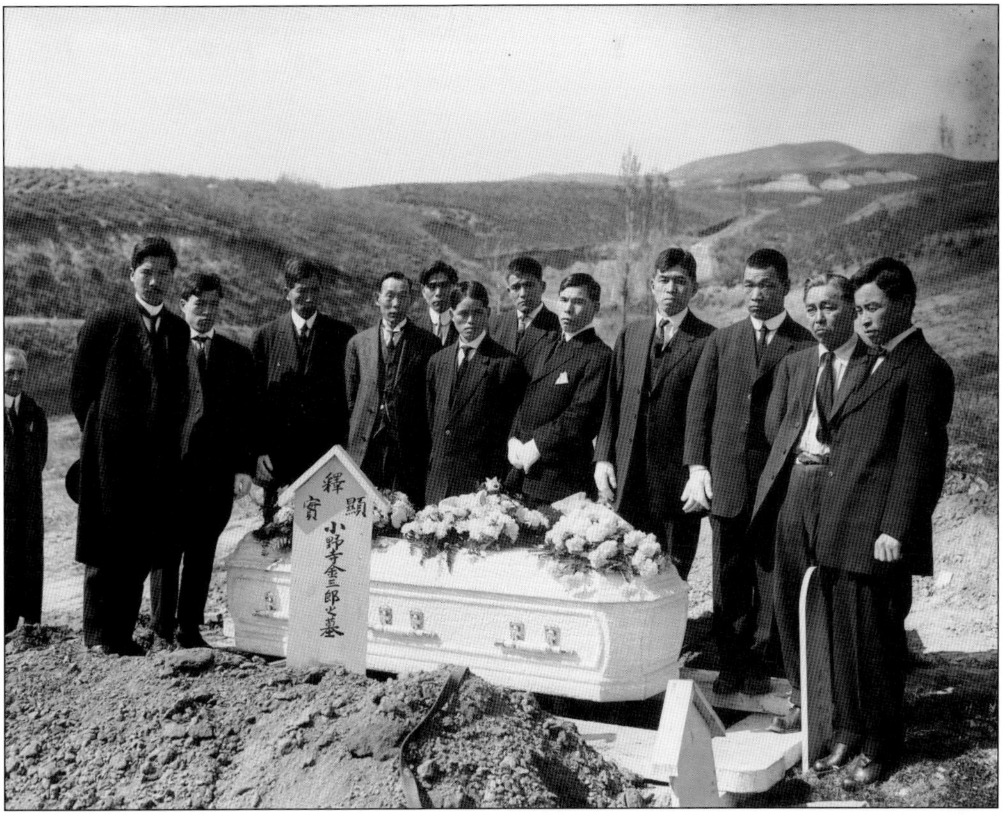

Portions of the Salt Lake City Cemetery were divided by ethnicity and religion. A group of Japanese men are pictured above during a 1914 funeral in the Japanese section of the cemetery and across from the main cemetery on 11th Avenue. The cemetery also has Catholic, Jewish, and military sections. The 1915 photograph below shows a group of people attending a funeral in the Catholic portion of the cemetery on a snowy day.

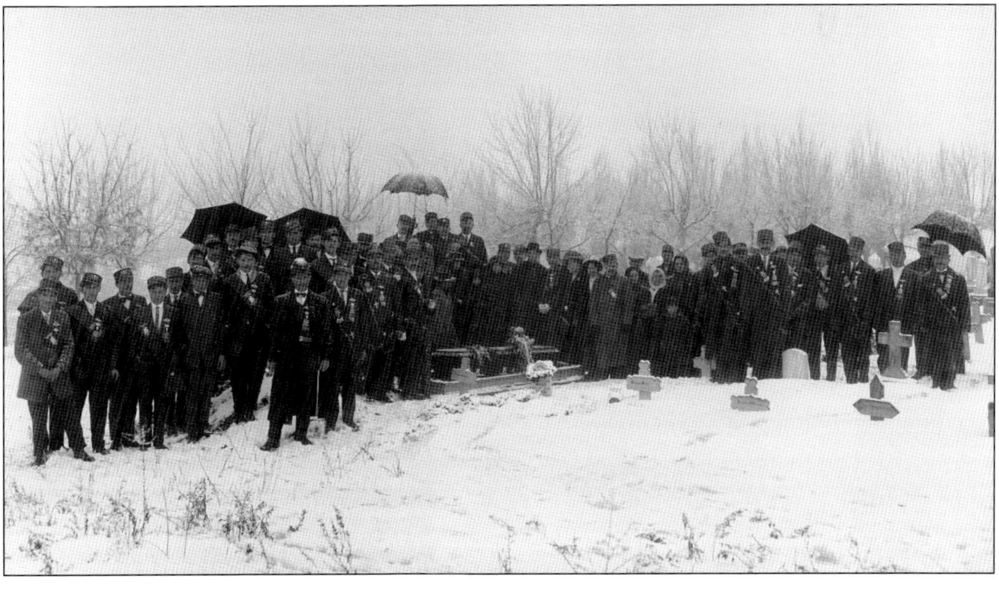

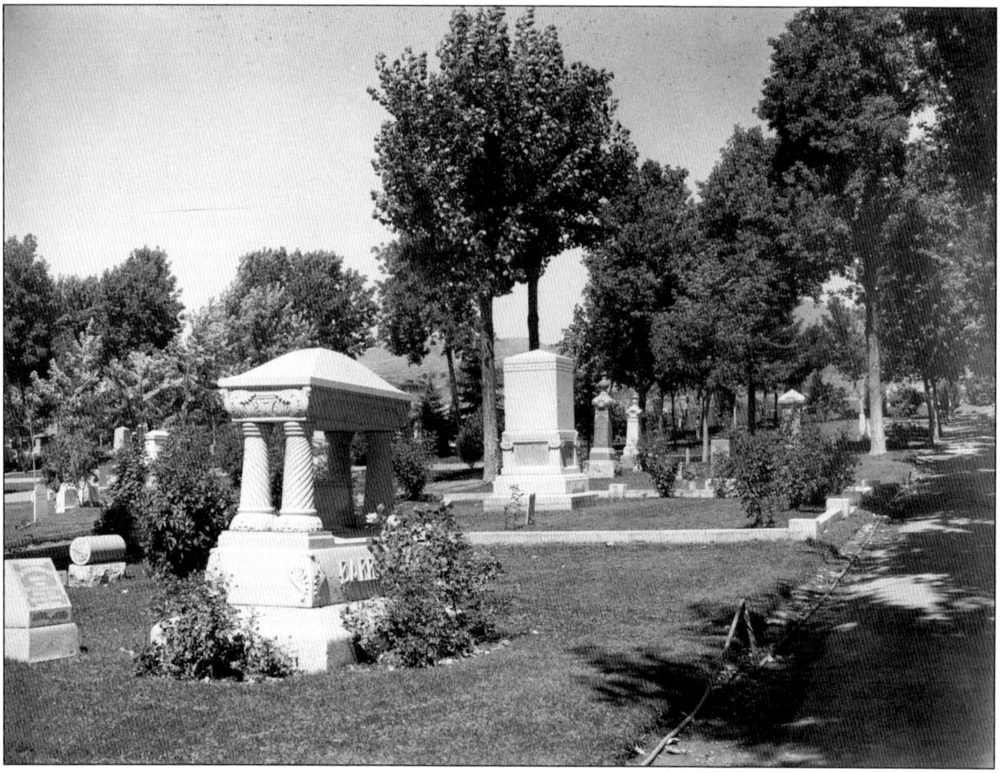

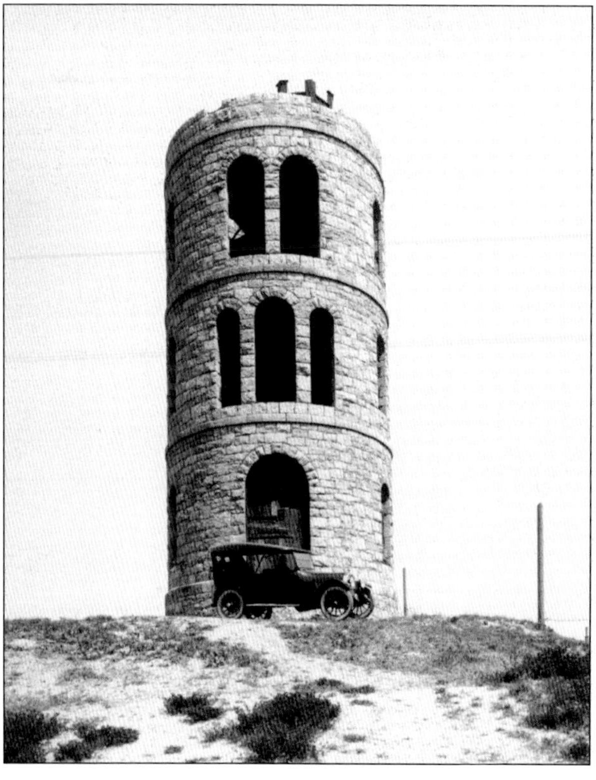

This September 1917 image shows the ornate granite monuments that line the narrow streets of the Salt Lake City Cemetery.

In 1919, a car sits in front of Anderson's Tower overlooking Salt Lake City. This stone tourist attraction stood at Sixth Avenue and A Street until 1932. The city demolished the structure because it was considered a hazard. Tourists never flocked to the top of the tower as Anderson had hoped. It became a subject of photographs more so than the beautiful view from the top.

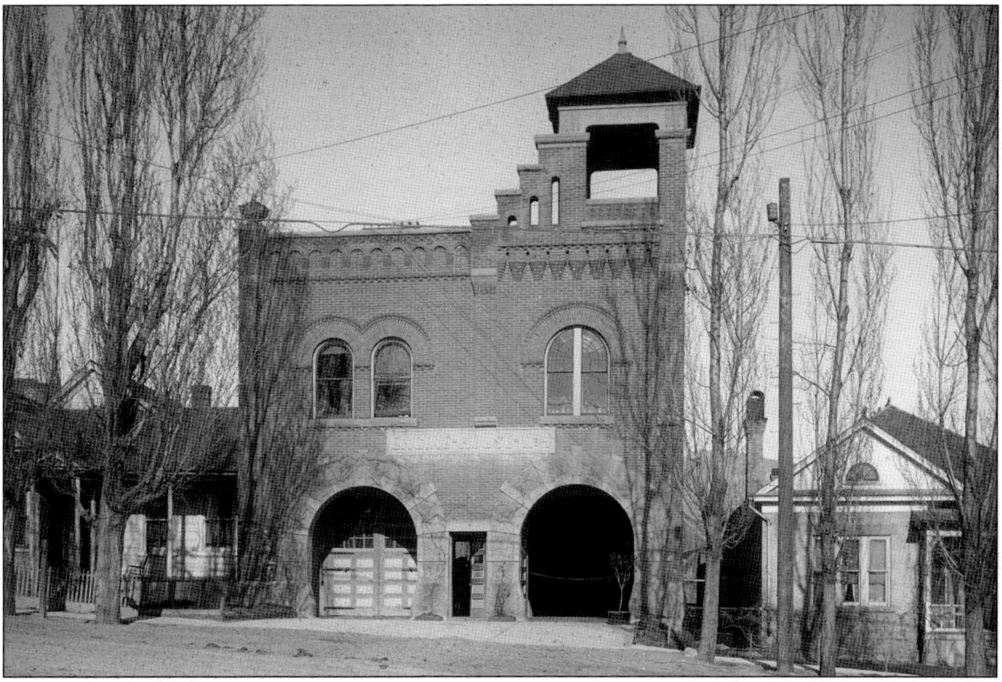

Built in 1900, Engine House No. 4 served the Salt Lake City Avenues neighborhood until the early 1980s. The original structure built of bricks and sandstone had a dramatic tower on the south end. This building was heavily remodeled in 1940. The new station had Art Moderne architectural characteristics. A new fire station was constructed for the Avenues on 11th Avenue in the 1980s. This building is currently used as a residence.

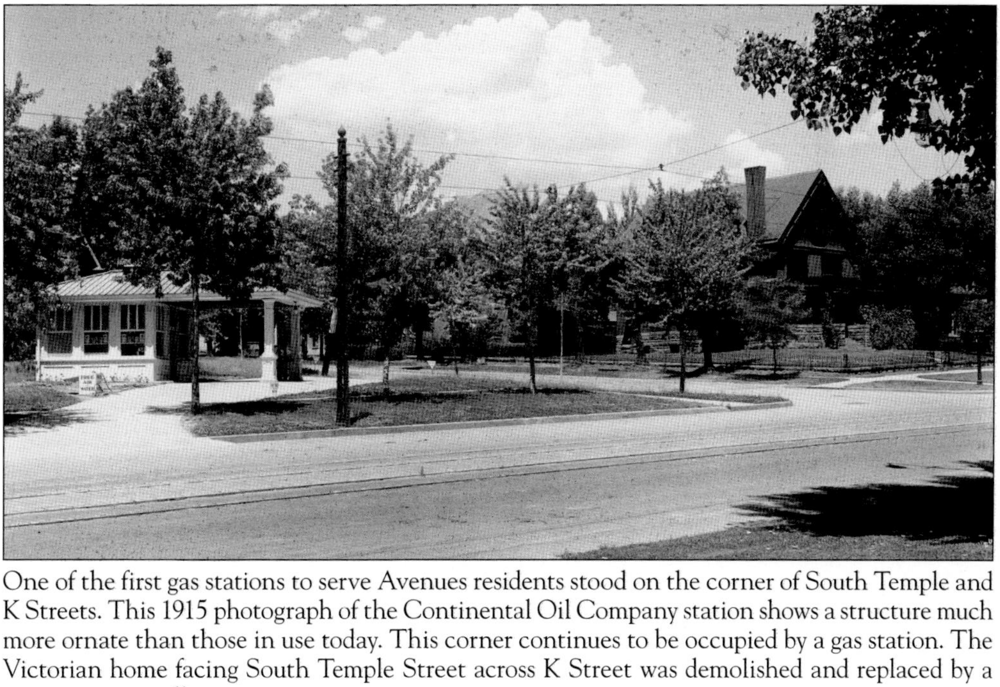

One of the first gas stations to serve Avenues residents stood on the corner of South Temple and K Streets. This 1915 photograph of the Continental Oil Company station shows a structure much more ornate than those in use today. This corner continues to be occupied by a gas station. The Victorian home facing South Temple Street across K Street was demolished and replaced by a gas station as well.

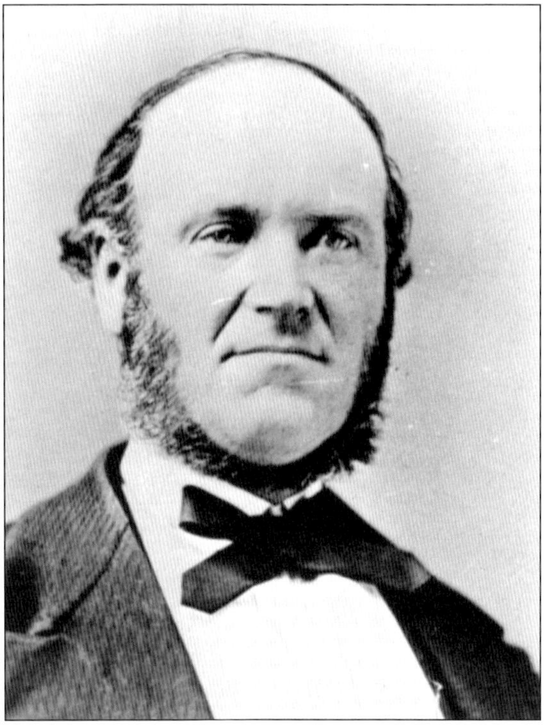

Avenues resident Mark Lindsey is pictured here. The Lindsey family established one of the first amusement parks in the Utah Territory on part of their original 160-acre homestead. Today, Lindsey Gardens is a popular park that starts near L Street and Sixth Avenue.

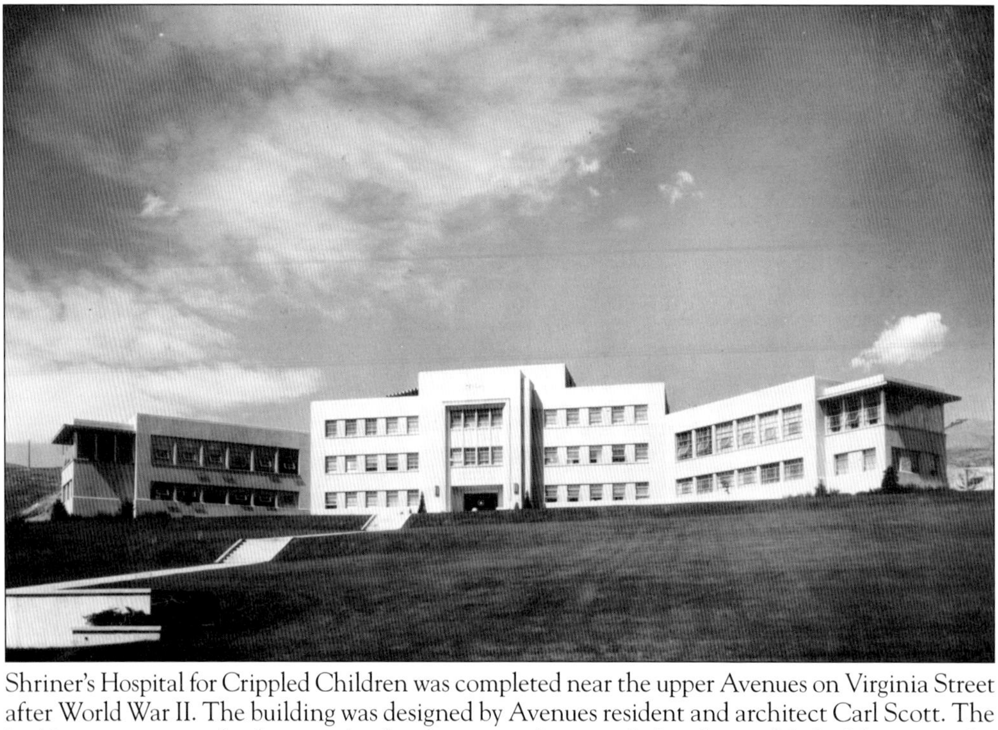

Shriner's Hospital for Crippled Children was completed near the upper Avenues on Virginia Street after World War II. The building was designed by Avenues resident and architect Carl Scott. The building remains in this location but has been greatly expanded and remodeled, obliterating the original architecture.

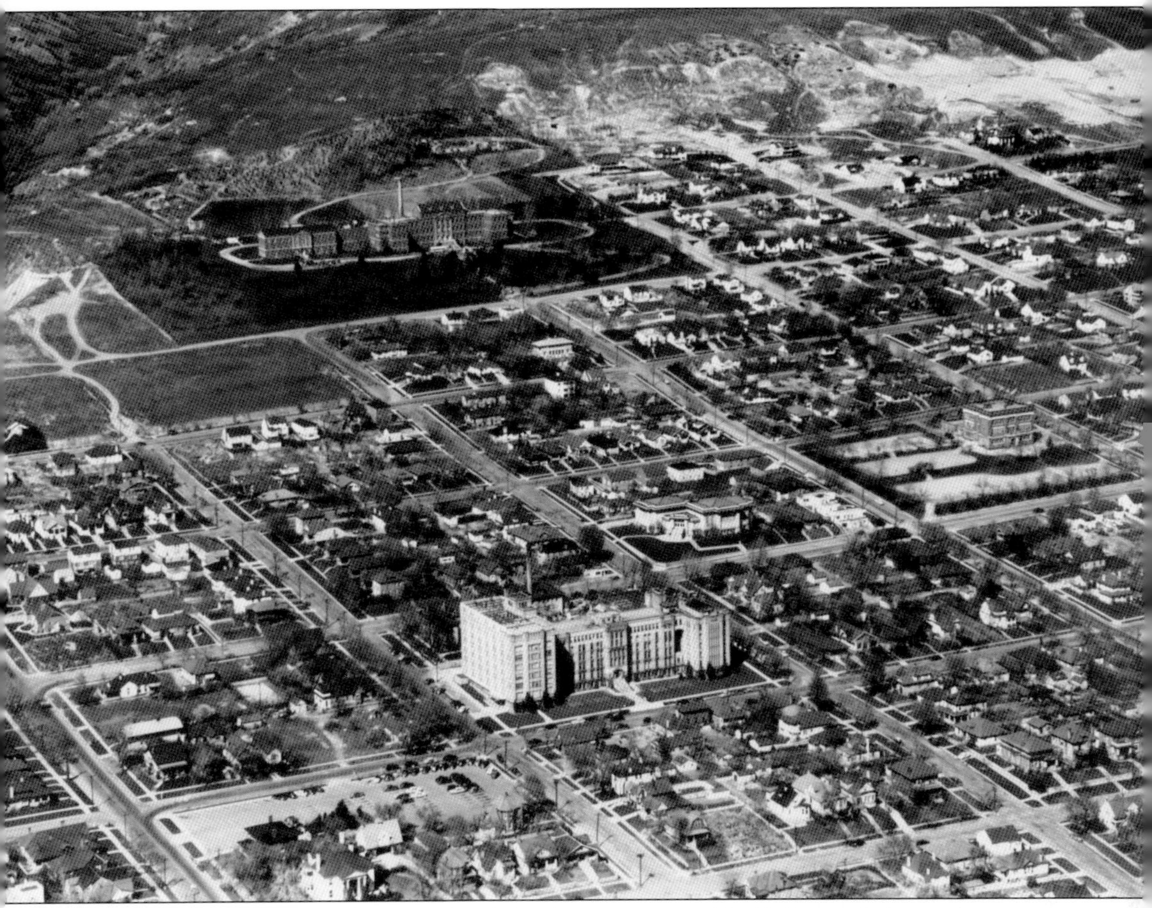

This revealing 1949 aerial photograph of the Avenues around LDS Hospital shows the extent of changes that have occurred in this portion of the neighborhood as the hospital expanded. Nearly all the homes on the blocks immediately surrounding the original structure have been demolished. Eighth Avenue no longer runs through C and D Streets. Ensign school and the Prairie-style Ensign ward building were demolished in the 1980s.

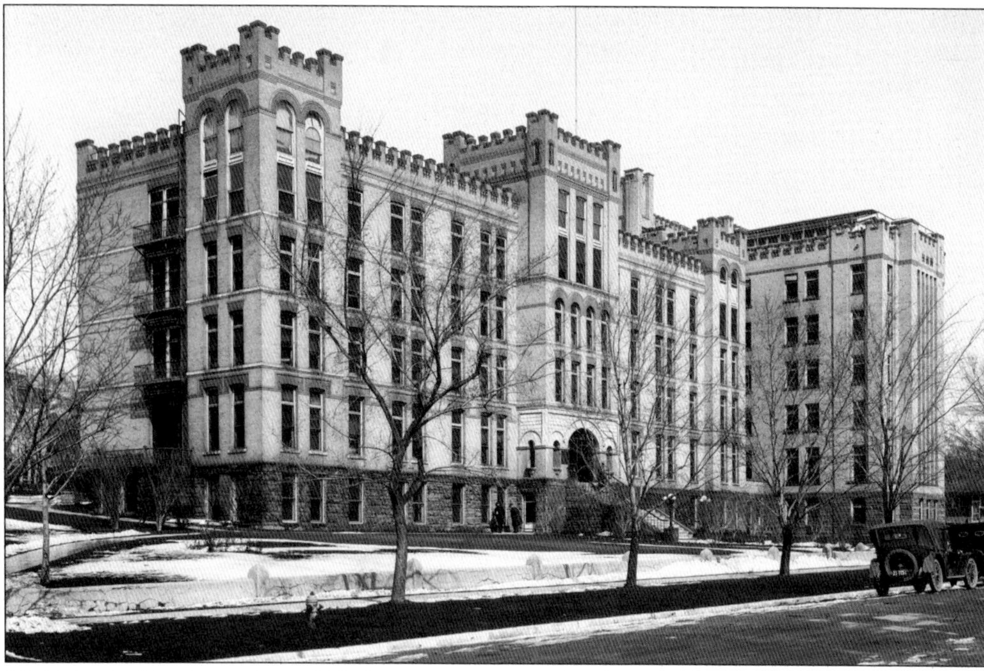

LDS Hospital is pictured in 1922. The eastern tower has been added to the original castle-like structure. A wing would soon be constructed on the west side. No part of the original hospital building is identifiable today. Eighth Avenue, where this photograph was taken, was closed as the hospital expanded to the south. The hospital was started in 1905 and named the W.H. Groves LDS Hospital. Groves was an LDS emigrant from England. He donated a large sum of money for the establishment of the hospital.

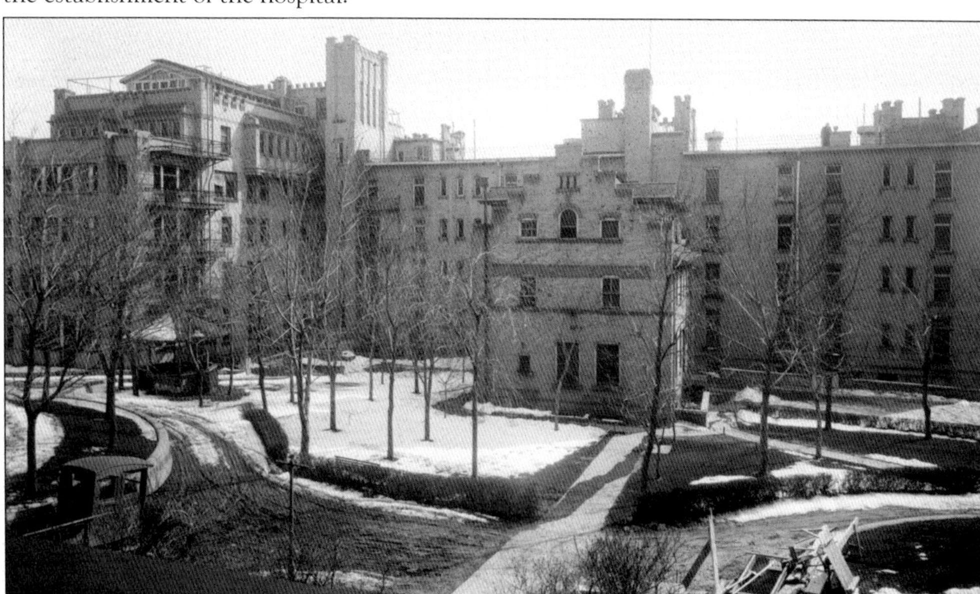

The rear of LDS Hospital is pictured as viewed from Ninth Avenue on March 14, 1922. The east tower of the hospital has been added to the structure. The old employees' dormitory is in the center of the photograph. A delivery truck makes a path around the muddy road.

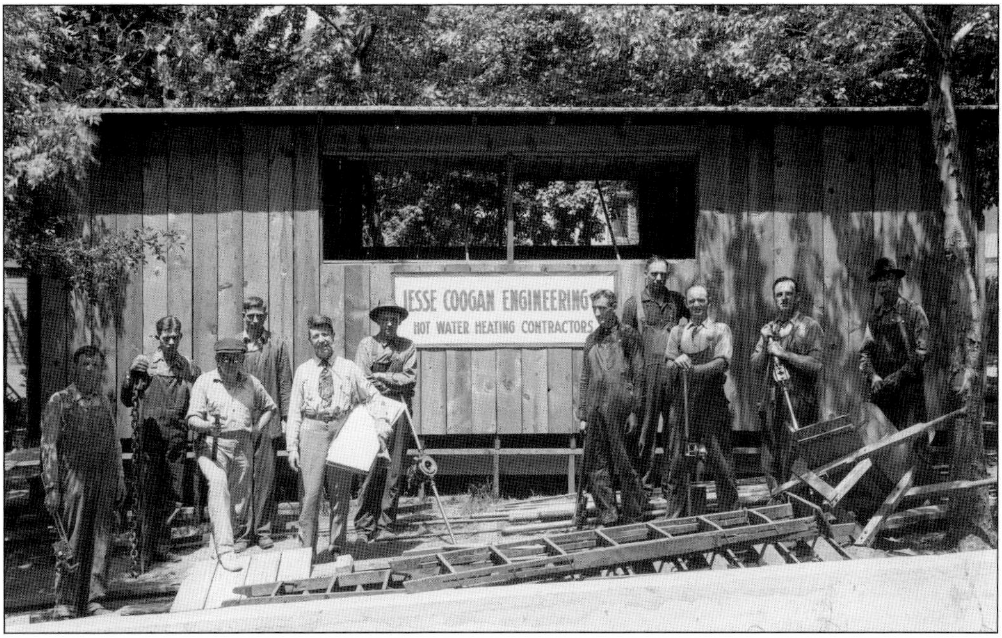

In the photograph above, workers with the Jesse Coogan Engineering Company pose with their equipment on a job site at LDS Hospital in 1921. In the photograph below, three of the men are testing the newly installed radiators in the hospital building.

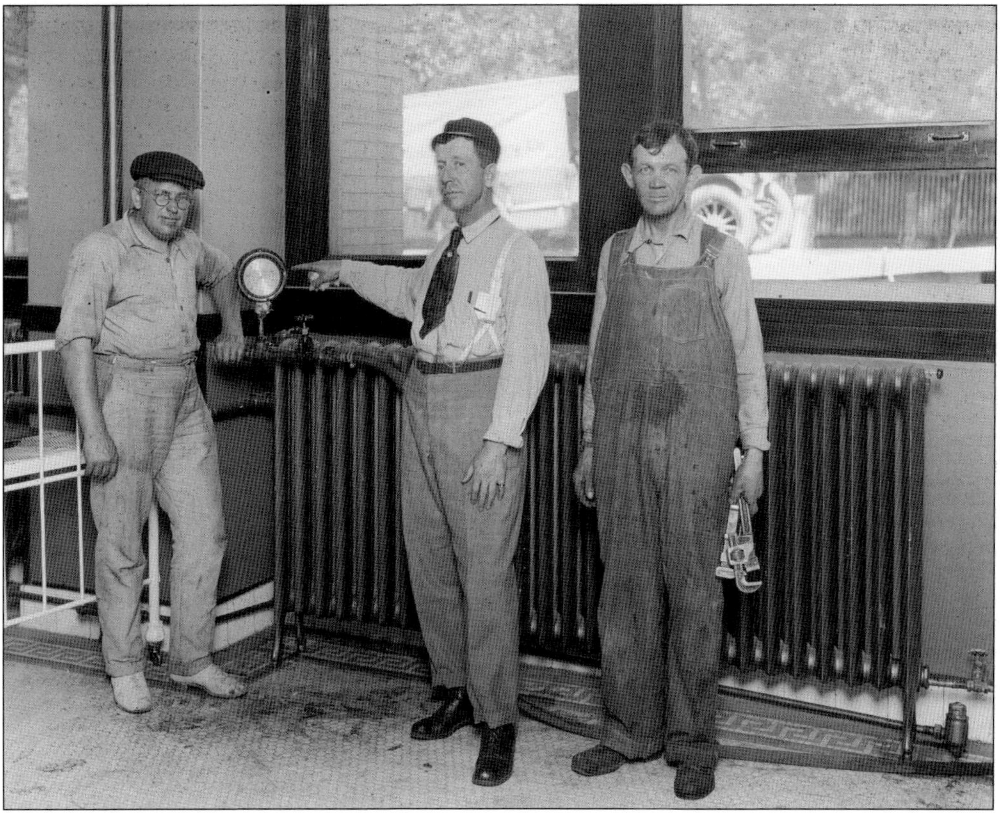

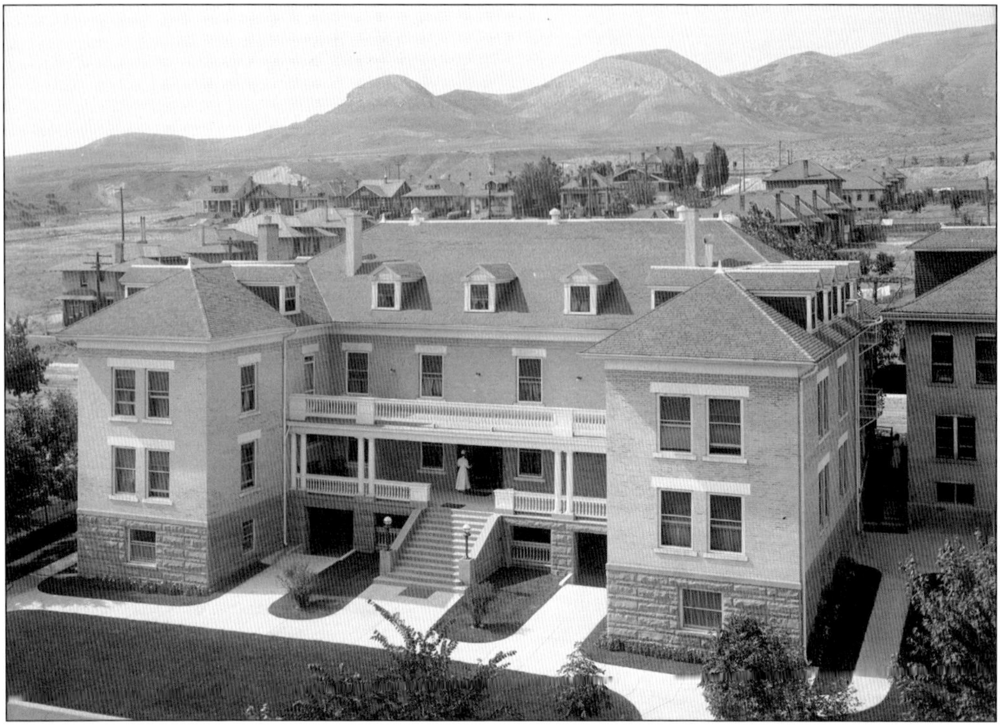

The image above, captured in July 1912, shows the LDS Hospital annex used as the home for the hospital's nurses. Ensign Peak rises above the barren foothills in the background. All the homes shown in this photograph are less than 10 years old. The picture below shows the LDS Hospital employees' dormitory behind the original hospital building.

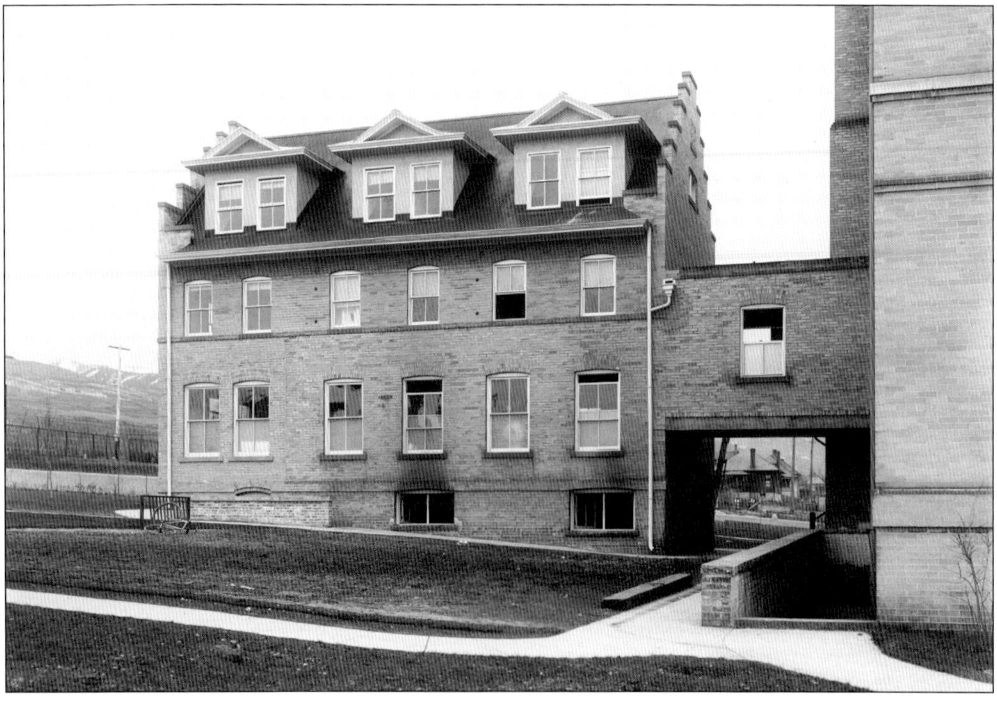

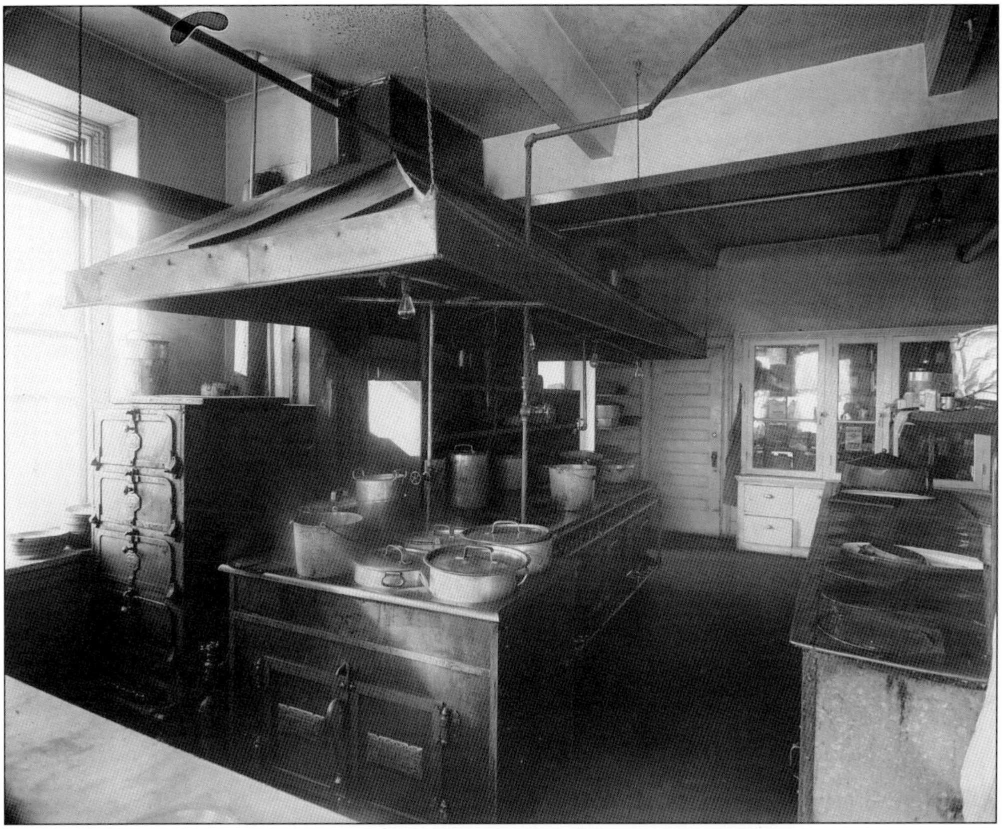

The Utah Gas and Coke Company built this kitchen for LDS Hospital. This 1910 photograph shows the most modern equipment available at the time for cooking a large number of meals. Pictured below is the hospital laundry with its steam and electric equipment.

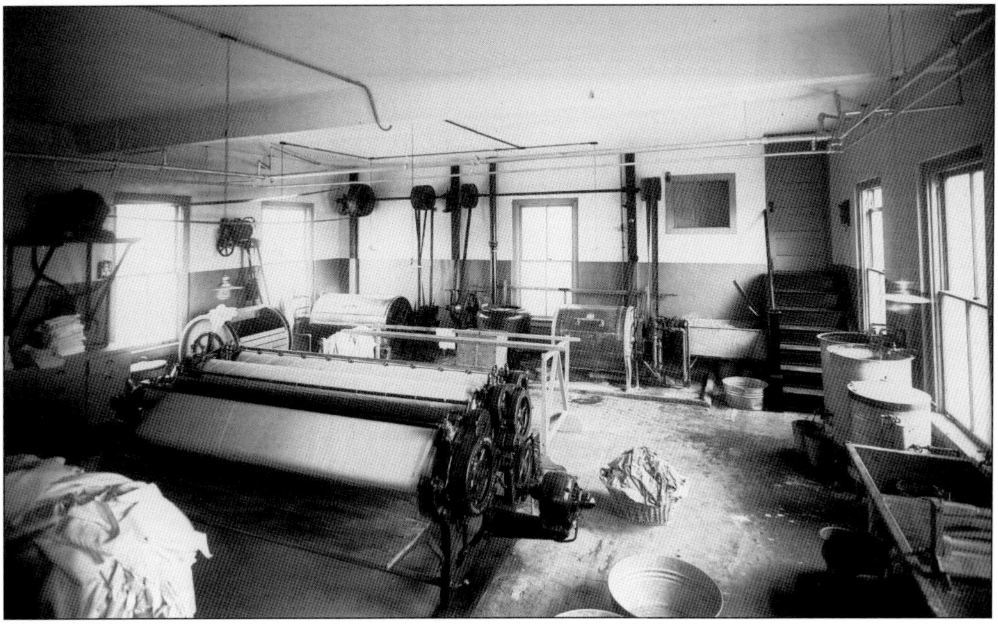

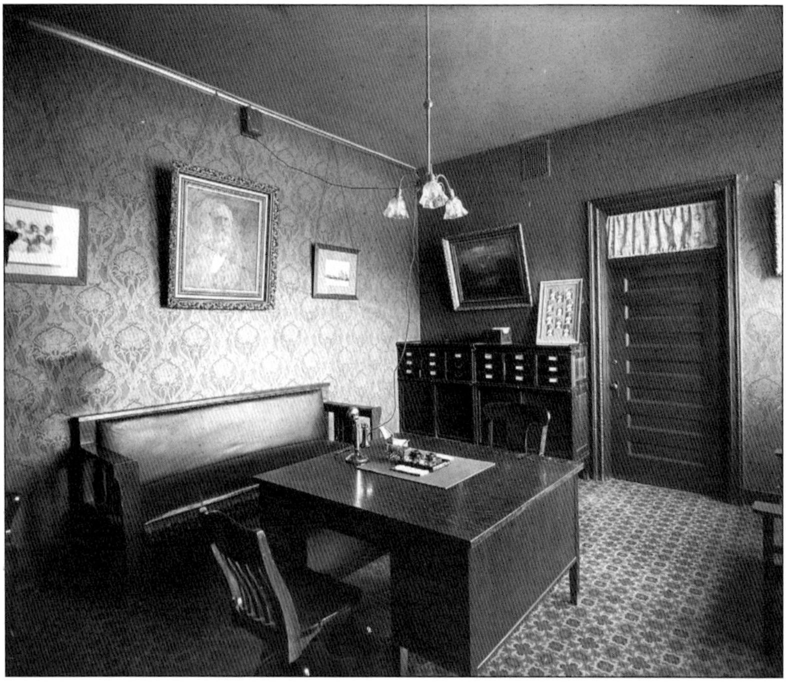

The office of the superintendent of nurses is pictured in 1912. An early telephone with its chord draped through the overhead light can be seen on the desk.

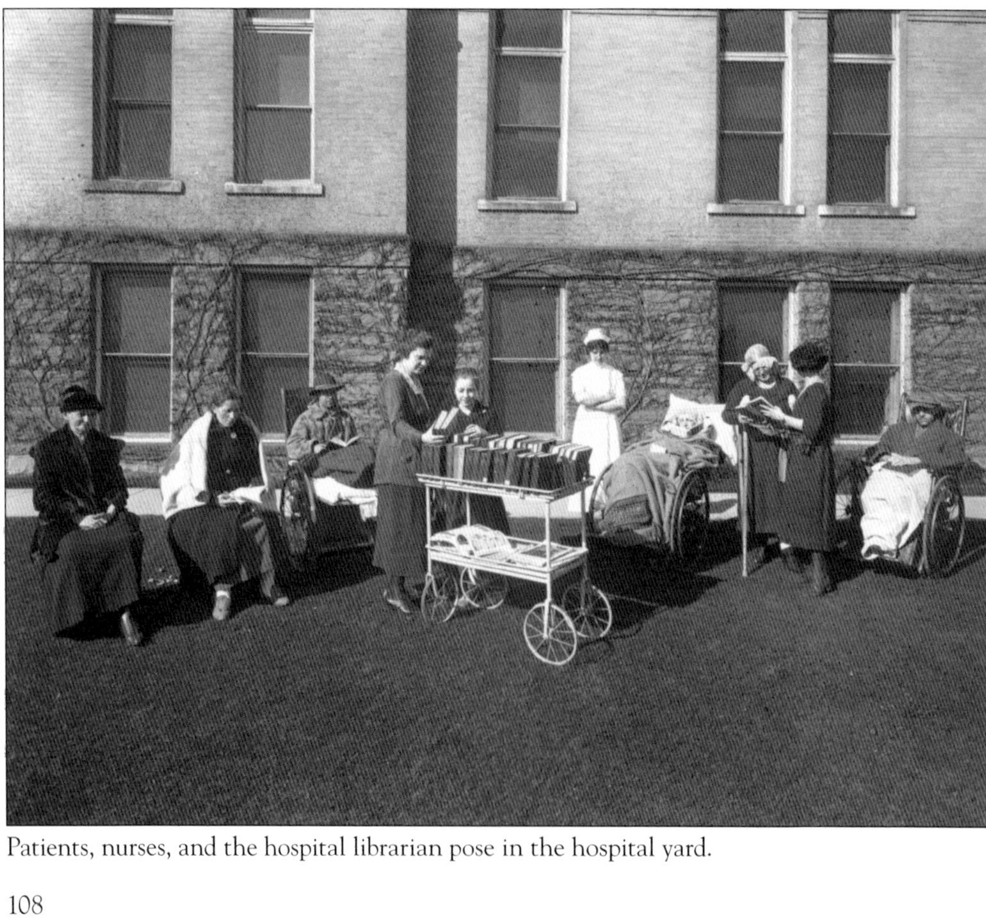

Patients, nurses, and the hospital librarian pose in the hospital yard.

With a brick fireplace and built-in bookcases with art glass doors, the room in this photograph could be the living room of any Avenues bungalow. However, it is the nurses' parlor at LDS Hospital in 1912. In contrast to the cozy environment in the image at right, the stark sterile room pictured below is an operating room at LDS Hospital in 1912.

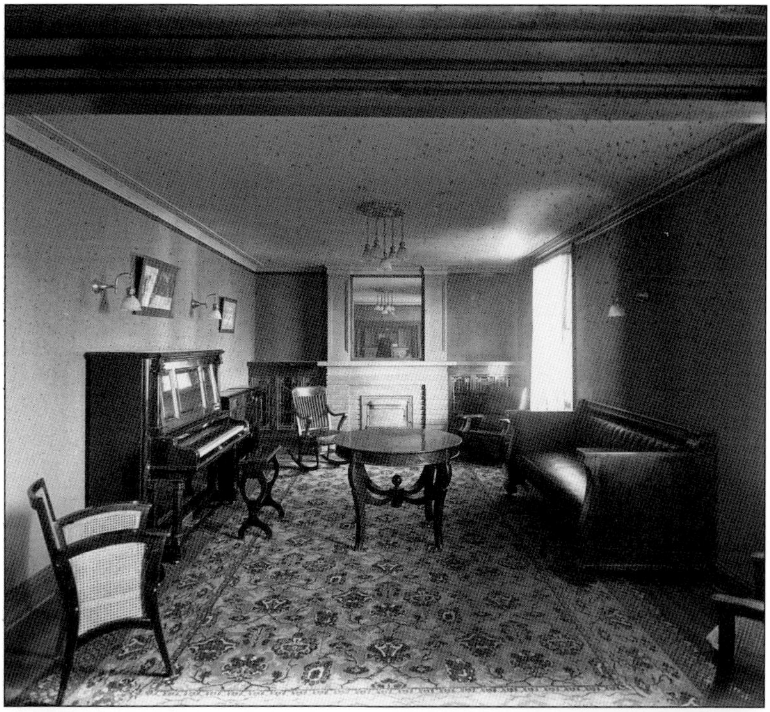

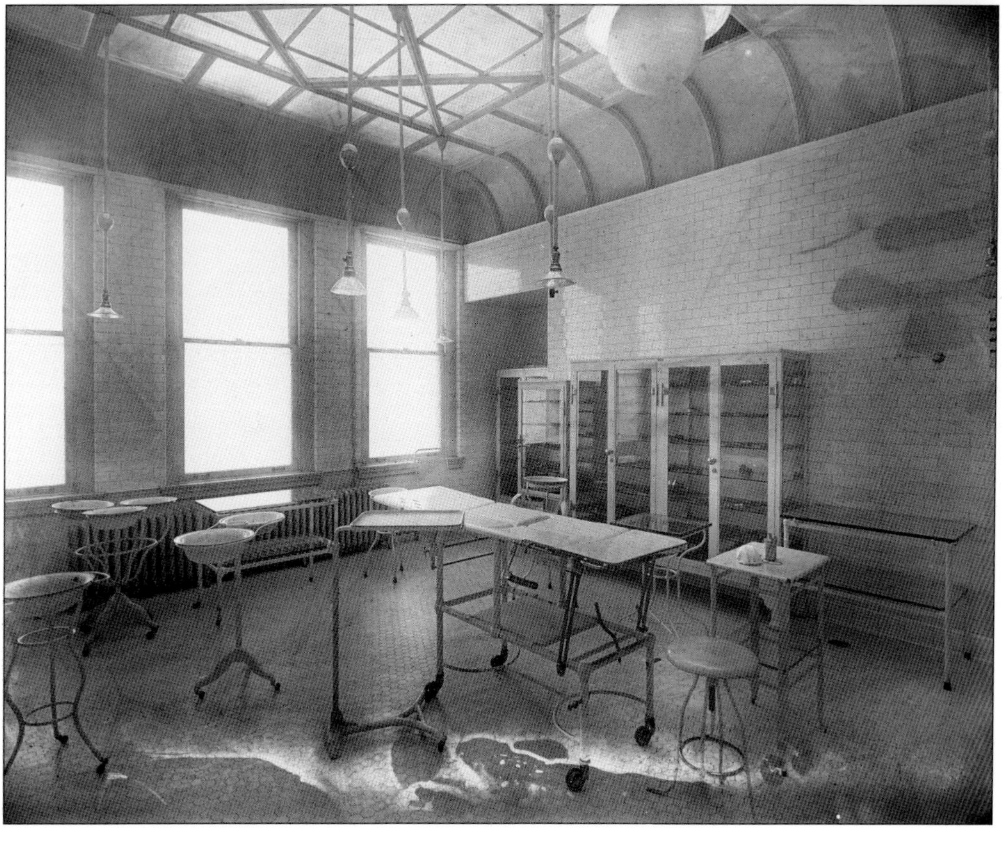

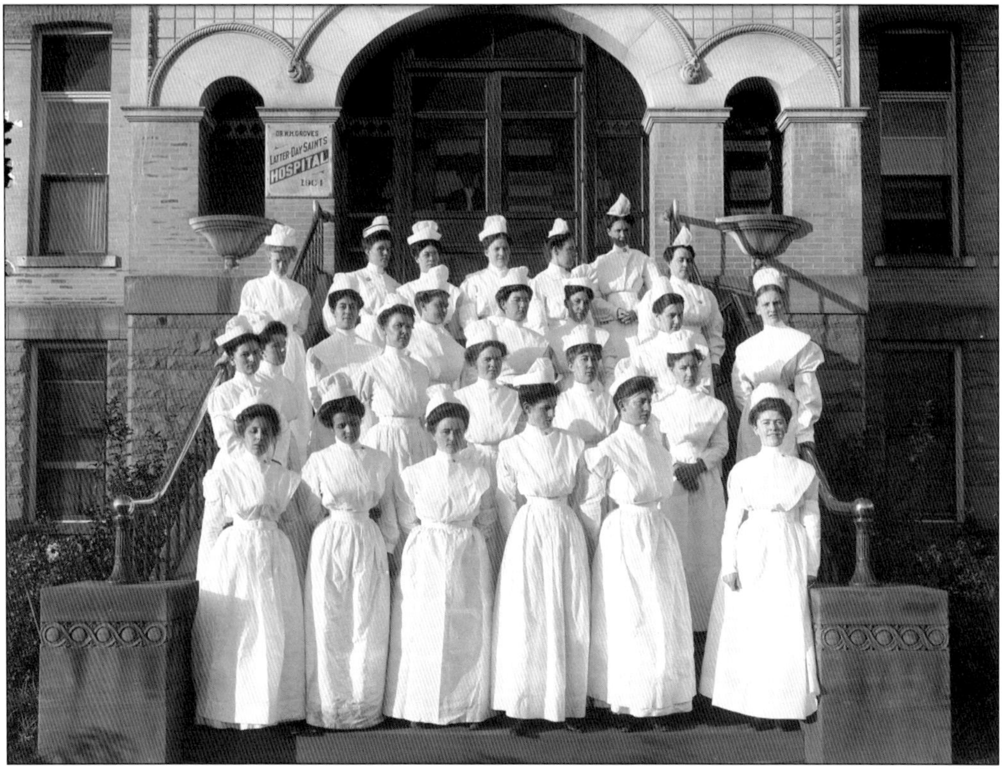

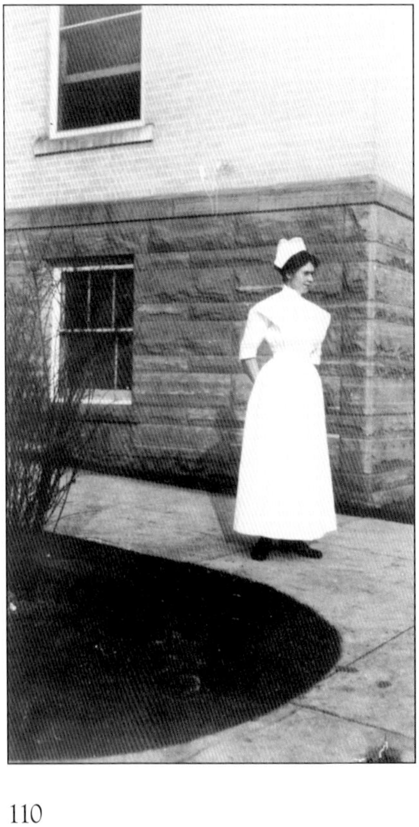

In the photograph above, the nurses of LDS Hospital pose for a group portrait on the front steps of the main building in 1907. The sign on the right reads, "Dr. W.H. Groves Latter-day Saints Hospital 1904." Nurse Anna Taylor poses in her white uniform in the image at left.

Six

Apartments in the Avenues

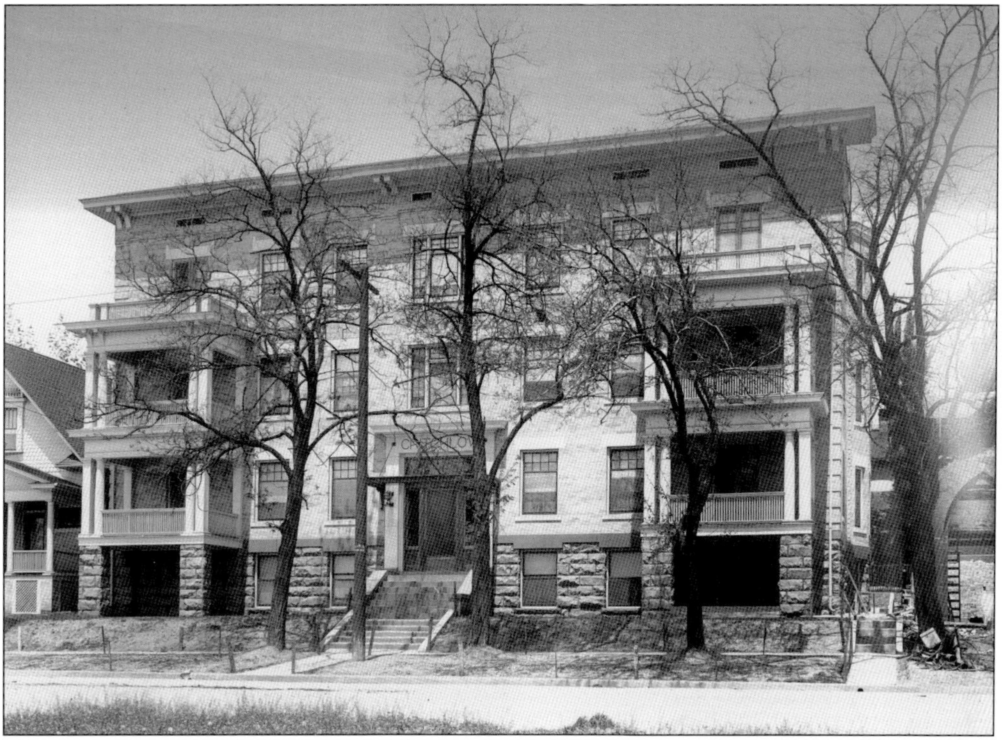

By 1908, increasing demand for housing close to the city and the normal urbanization of neighborhoods near downtown led to the development of apartment blocks in the Avenues. Frank McGurrin's Salt Lake Security and Trust Company was known for building numerous homes on speculation in Salt Lake City. As the demand for multifamily residences increased in the Avenues, the company constructed apartment buildings, such as the Critchlow.

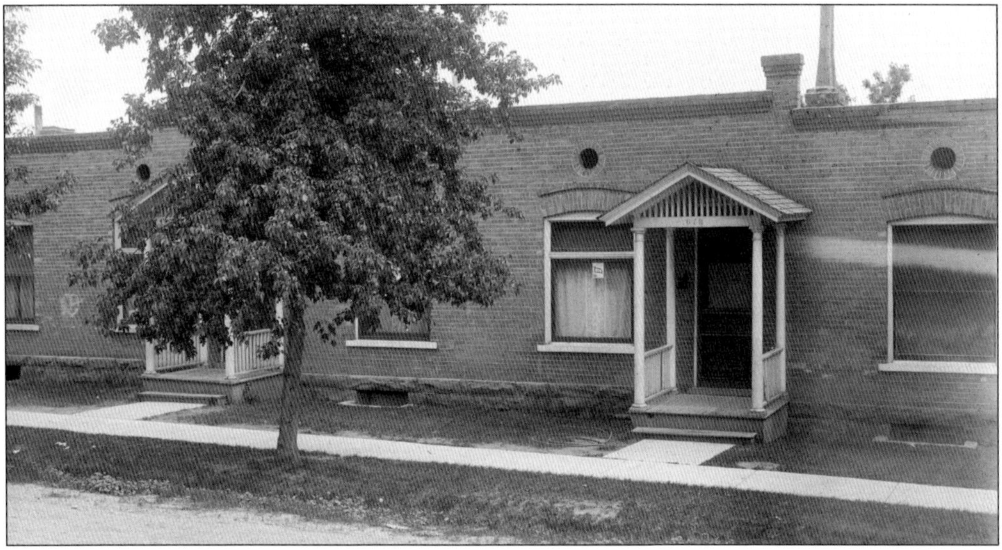

This is a unique one-story row house apartment block built in 1907. The building, located at Seventh Avenue and I Street, was erected for Lucy Watkins, owner of the Palace Cafe in downtown Salt Lake City. The entrance to each of the six apartments is covered by a gable-roofed front porch.

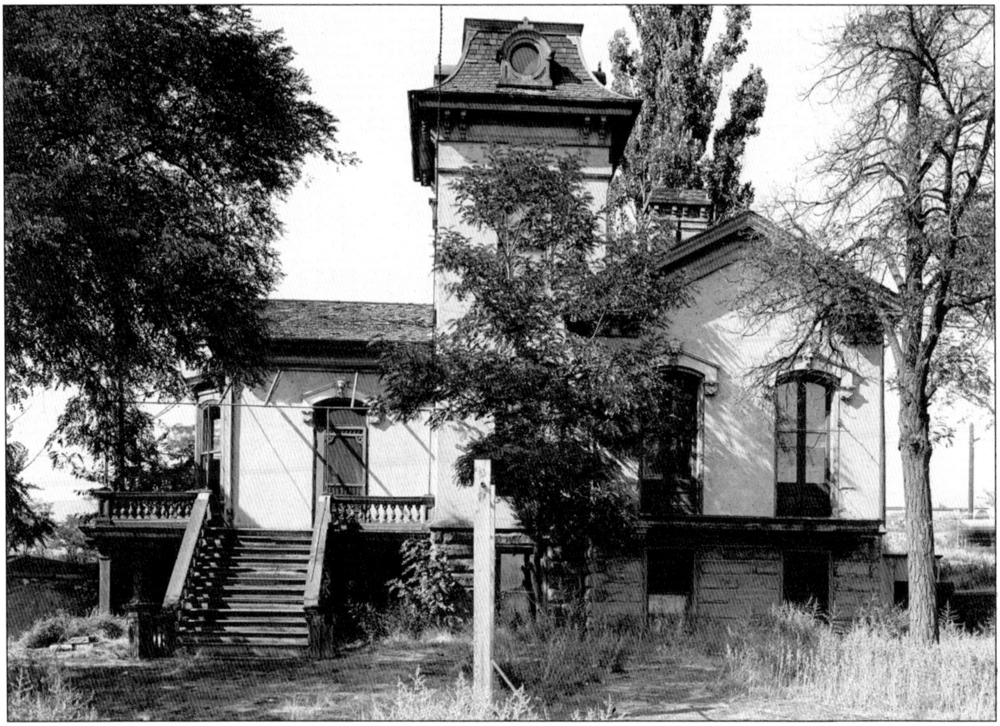

The Oliver Meredith home was constructed in the 1870s and stood at 160 First Avenue. This photograph was taken prior to its demolition in 1908. The proximity of the Meredith residence to downtown Salt Lake City led to its demise. Demand for apartments in the area started in the first decade of the 20th century and would continue into the 1980s. This home was the first of hundreds to fall to construction of apartments throughout the Avenues. The Meredith Apartments continue to stand on this sight.

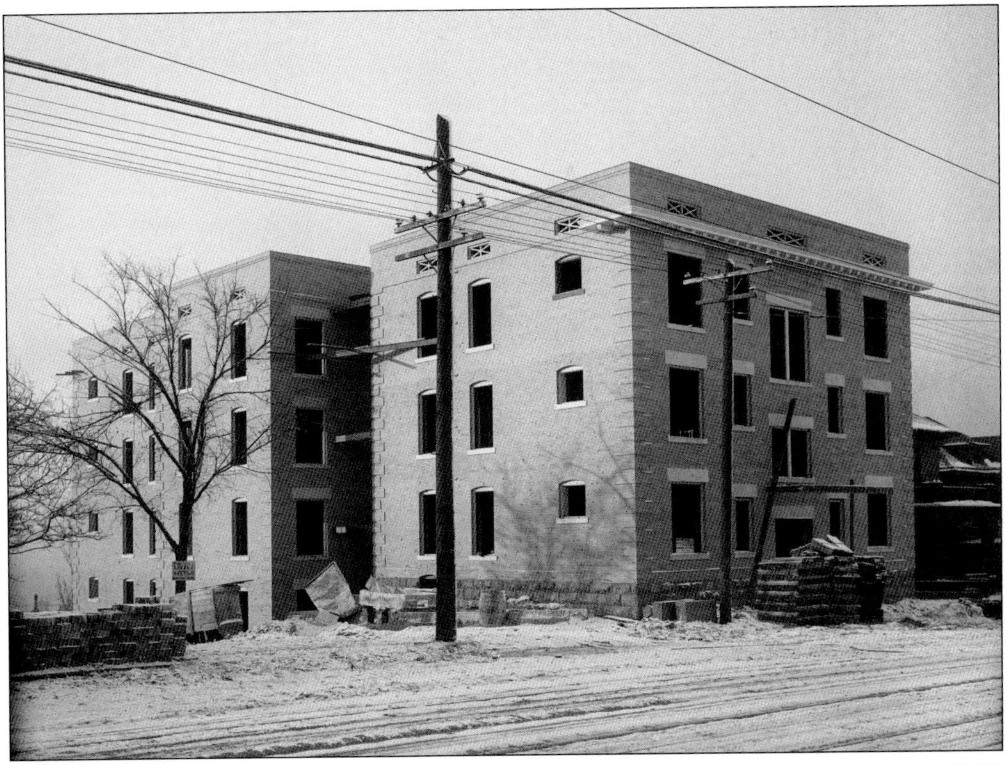

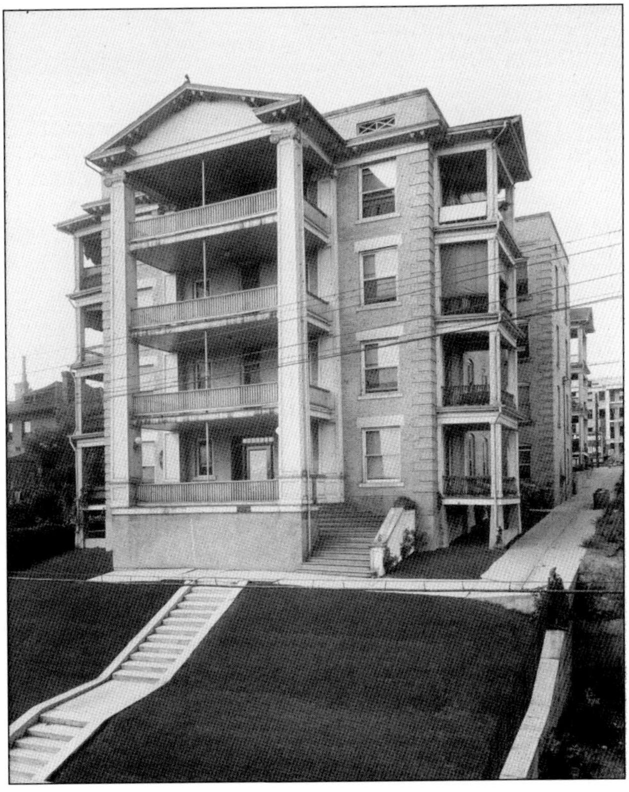

The Meredith Apartment complex is viewed from First Avenue during construction in 1908. This is the sight of the old Oliver Meredith family home. These apartments stretch through the block and also face out on South Temple Street. The photograph at right shows the South Temple facade with its four-story, Classical-style porch after construction is completed.

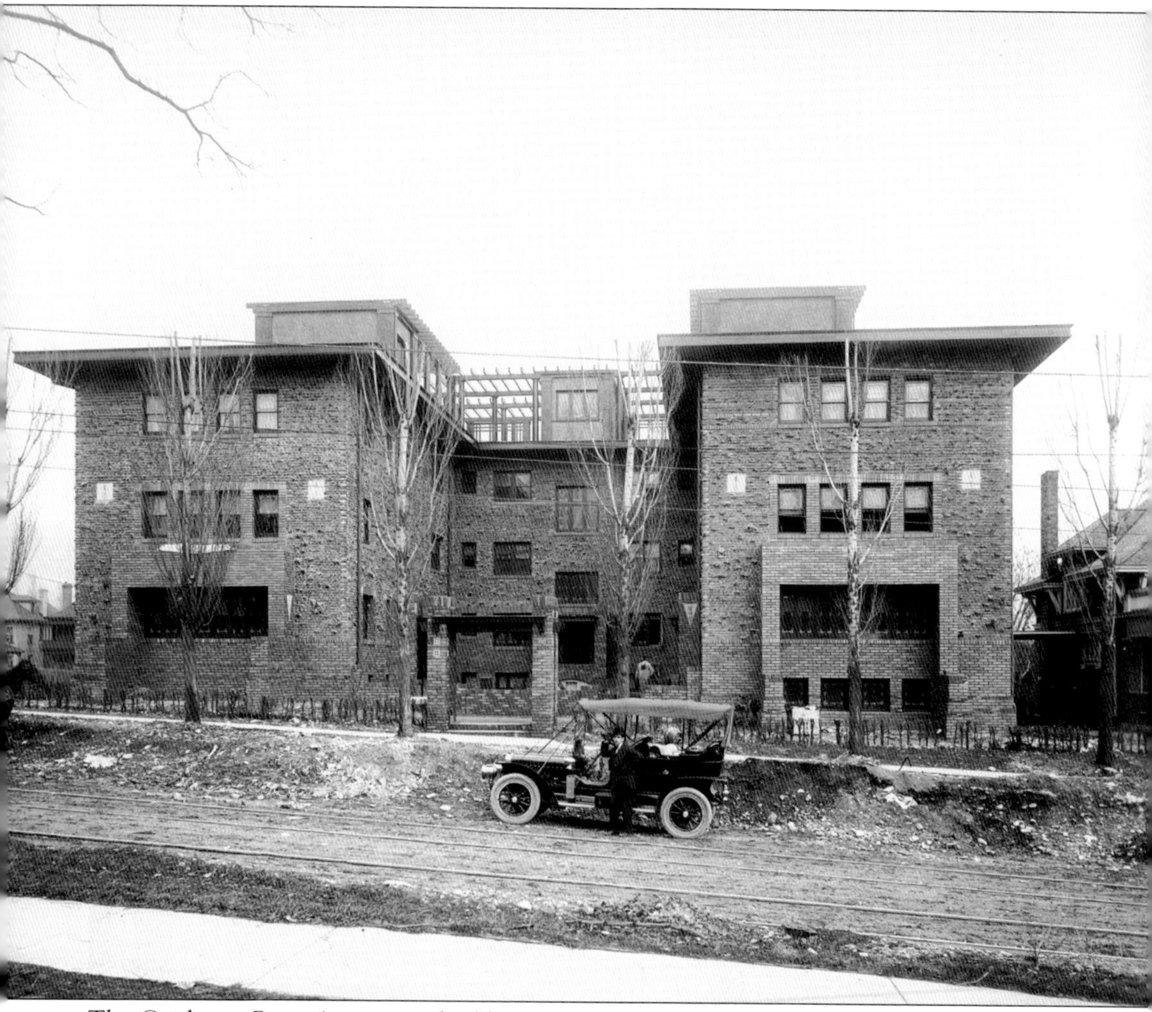

The Caithness-Riter Apartment building, a Prairie-style landmark, was nearly completed on the corner of B Street and Second Avenue when this 1908 photograph was taken. Upon its completion, architectural critics recognized the building as one of the finest in the Intermountain West. Walter Ware and Alberto Treganza designed the building for Lynville and Isabella Riter. The Riter family was made up of Scottish emigrants and successful engineers in Salt Lake City. The building's exterior is covered in clinker bricks. Rows of stained-glass windows open to the street. A roof garden existed until 1964, and the entrance pergola no longer exists.

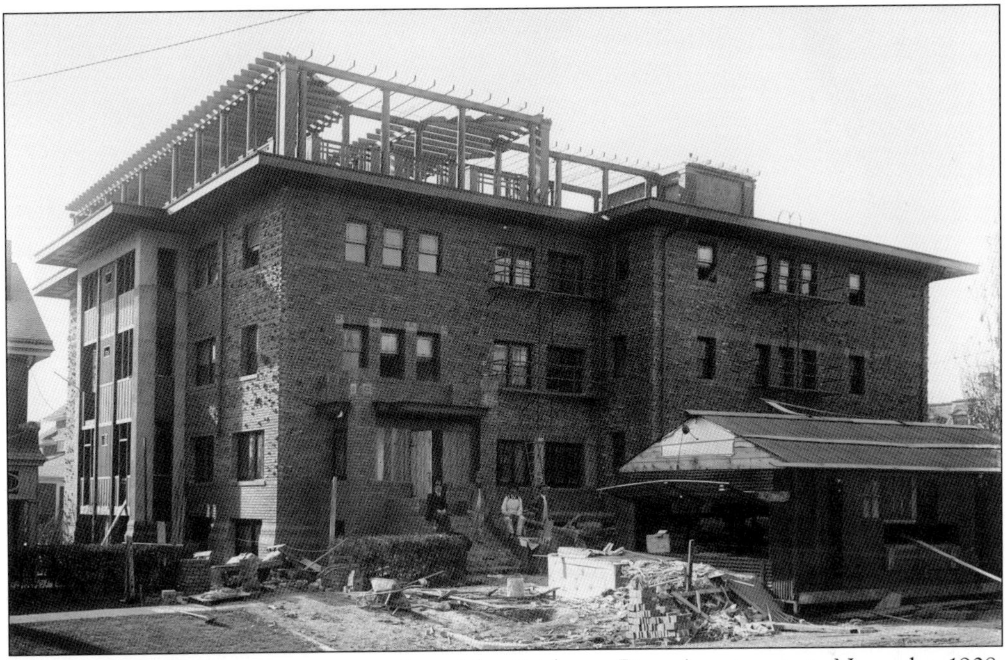

Workers take a break during construction of the Caithness-Riter Apartments in November 1908. Second Avenue remains unpaved in this image. The extent of the roof garden is clearly visible in this view of the north side of the building.

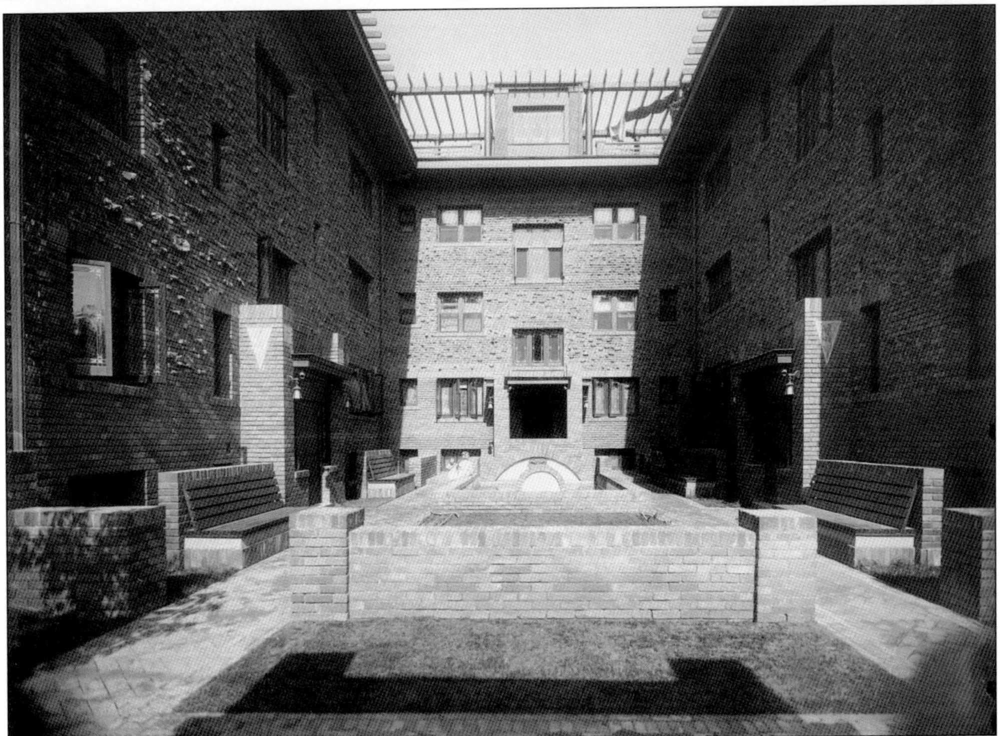

Sun drenches the new courtyard and fountain of the Caithness-Riter Apartments. Today, this courtyard appears very similar to its original condition.

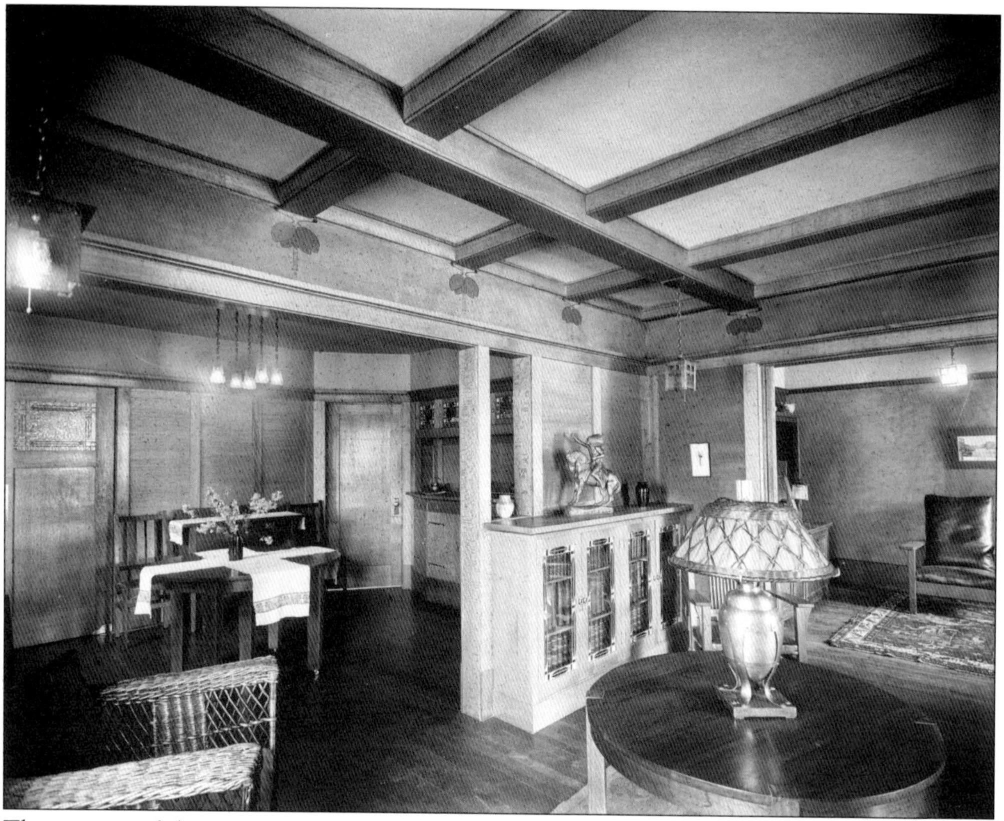

The interior of this unit in the Caithness-Riter Apartment building shows classic elements of Craftsman interior architecture. Built-in bookcases, box-beamed ceiling, built-in sideboard, high wainscoting, and Art Nouveau wallpaper were all popular when this image was captured in 1909. Sadly, nearly all of these elements have been lost over the last 100 years. In the past decade, the building was converted into condominium units.

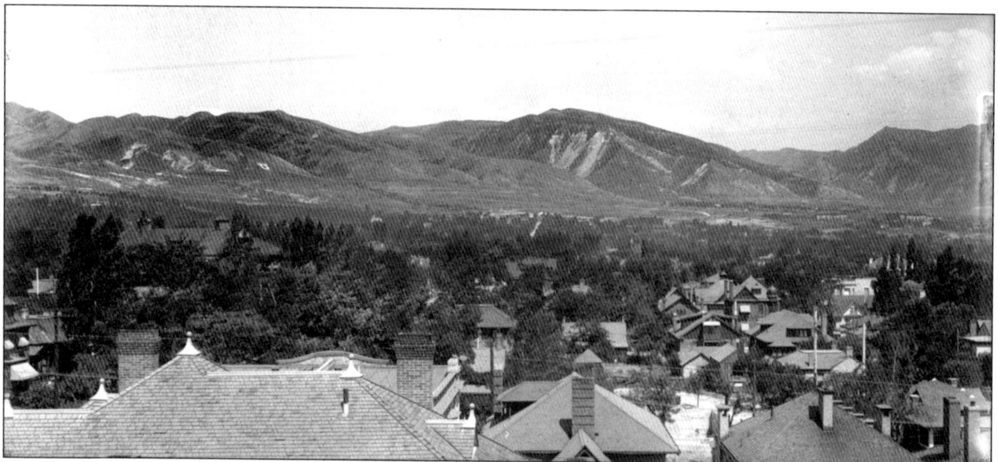

This is the view east from the roof garden of the Caithness-Riter Apartment building in 1909. The Wasatch Mountains are seen in the distance. The University of Utah campus is located on the foothills on the right side of the photograph. The landmark block "U" built into the mountain for the University of Utah overlooks Salt Lake Valley.

Space-saving built-in furniture was popular during the bungalow era of the early 20th century. These two photographs show the interior of a studio apartment in the Critchlow Apartment building located on First Avenue between D and E Streets. The building, completed in 1909, still stands with a slightly modernized exterior. The Craftsman-style drop-down desk doubles as a pullout bed.

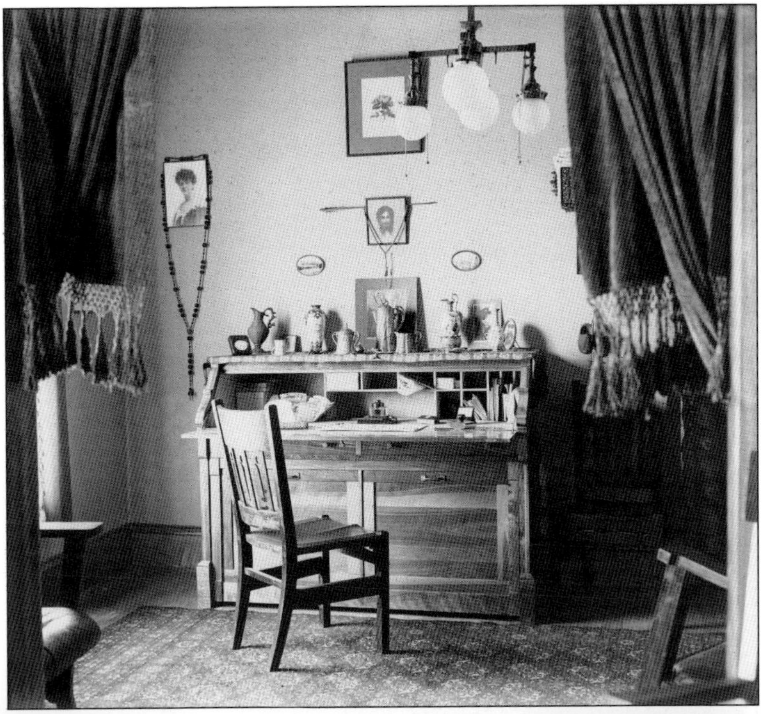

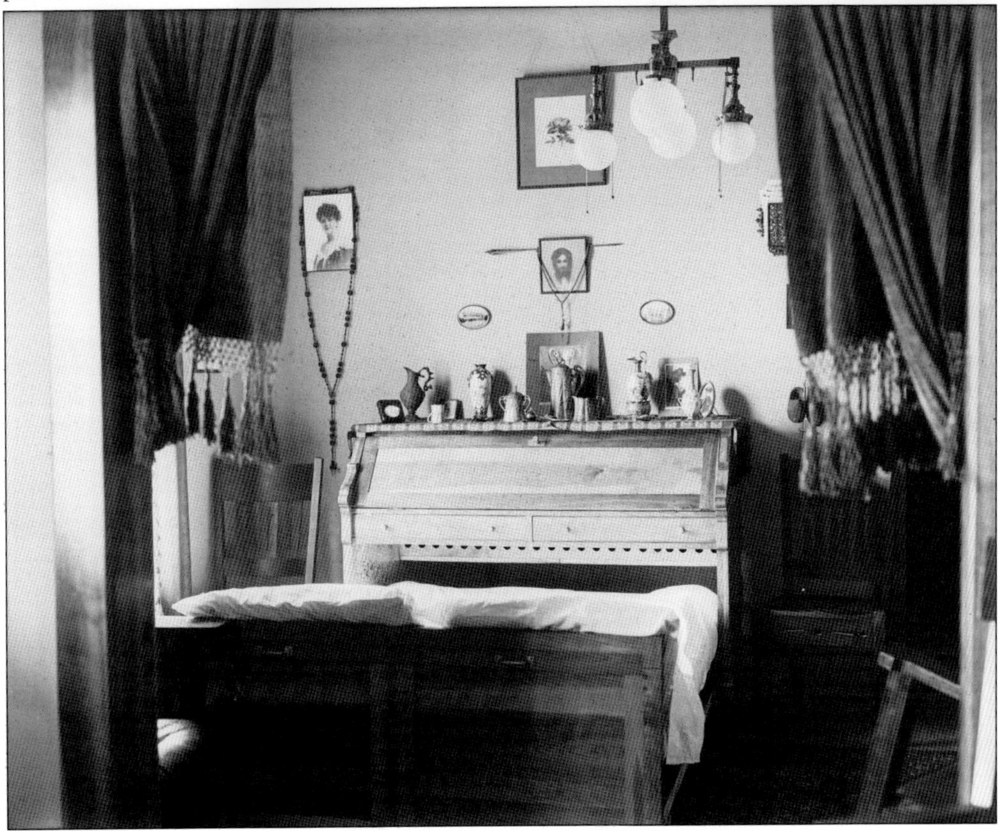

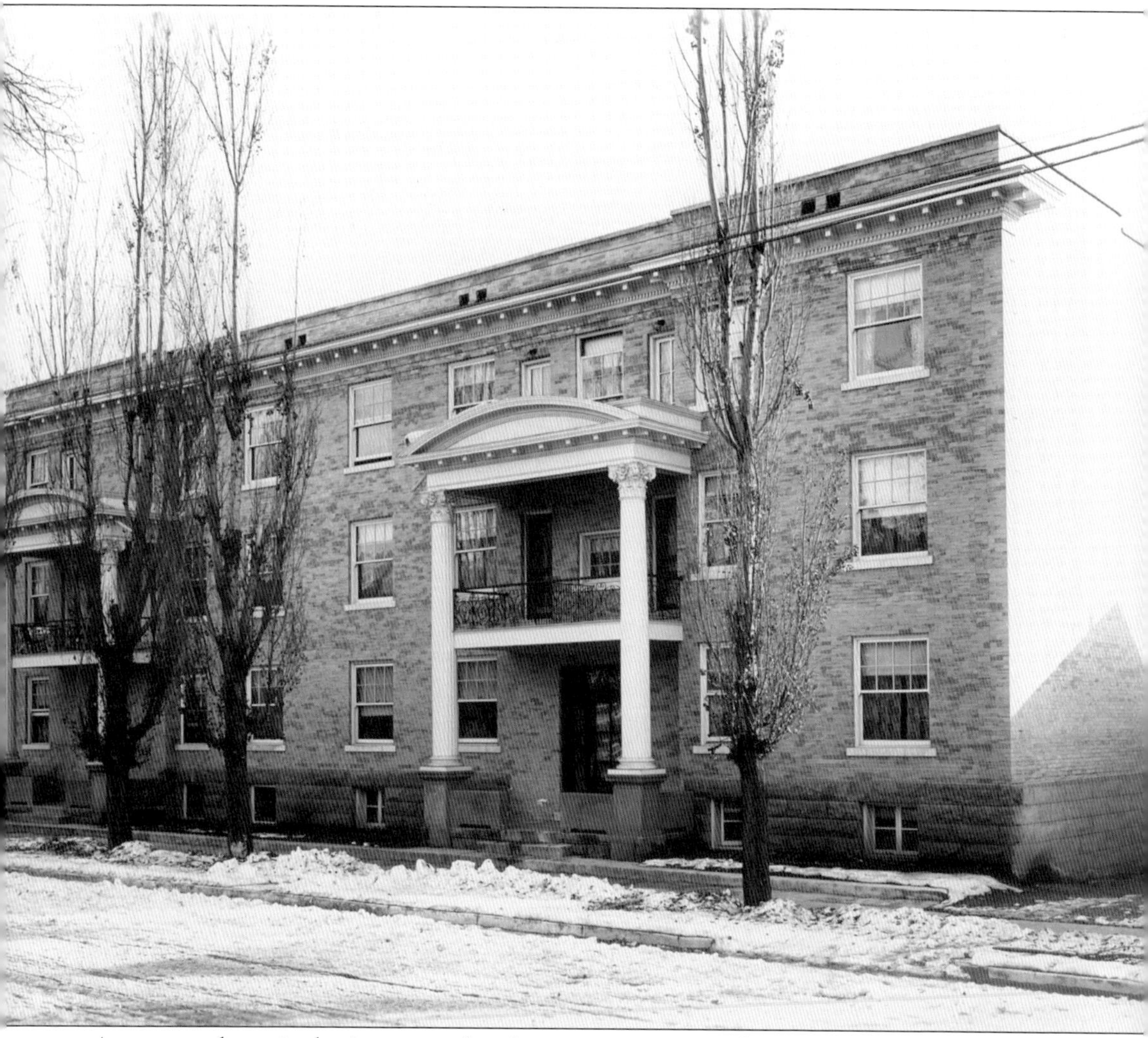

A common theme in the Avenues is that there is no common architectural theme. The Cummings Apartments, built around 1913 on the corner of D Street and First Avenue, exhibit an eclectic blend of style features. A brick parapet surrounds the flat roof. Below the parapet is a cornice with dentil molding and modillion brackets. Corinthian columns support the two-story porches. Multicolored bricks add to the building's character. This structure has since been demolished. The Chapel Hill Apartments, built the same year on Third Avenue, are nearly identical in design.

The Eagle Gate Apartments were once located at the base of the Avenues at the corner of State Street and First Avenue. The building was an eclectic blend of Classical and Prairie styles. The decorative detailing on the exterior of the structure was very similar to the designs of famed architects Louis Sullivan, William Purcell, and George Elmslie. The original owner of the building was Wallace M. Bransford, who had gained his wealth through Utah mining interests. In the late 1940s, the building was renamed the Gateway Apartments. Despite efforts to save the structure, it was demolished in the 1980s and replaced by a new building of the same name. Some of the architectural design elements from the original building were placed on the exterior of the new Gateway Apartments.

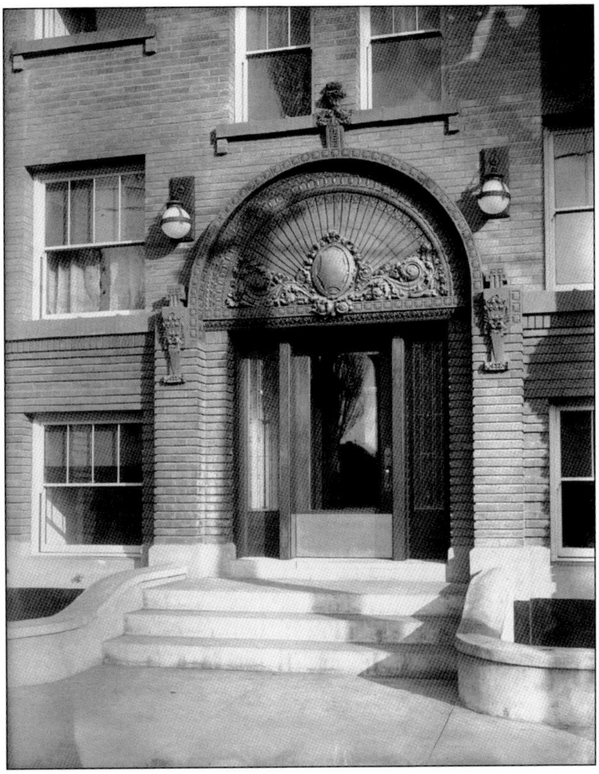

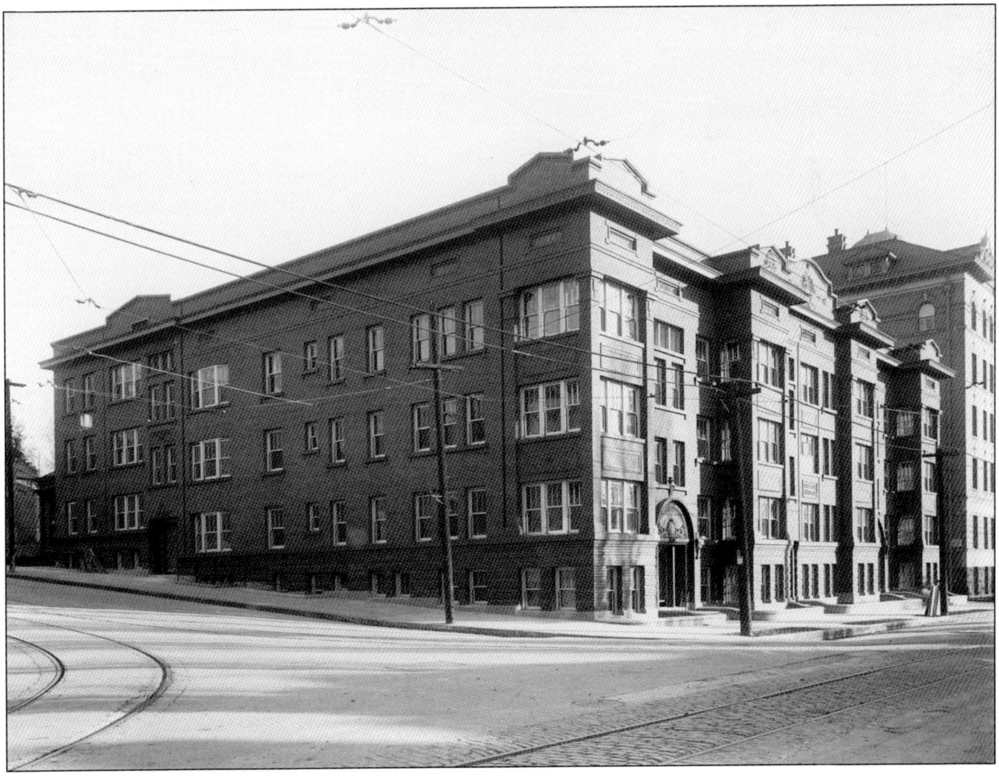

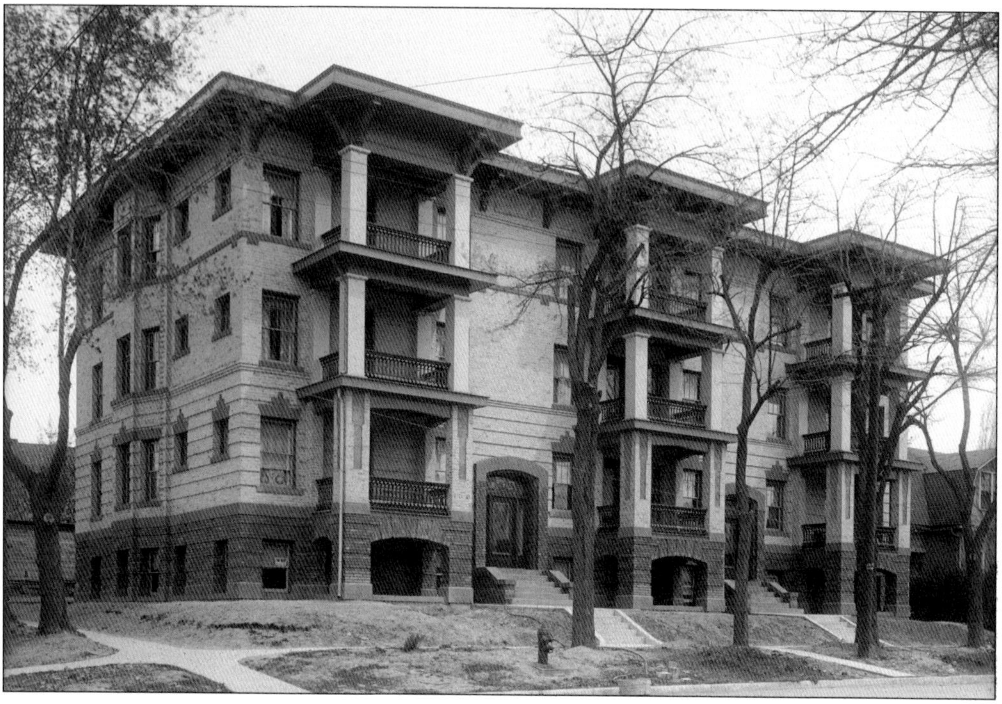

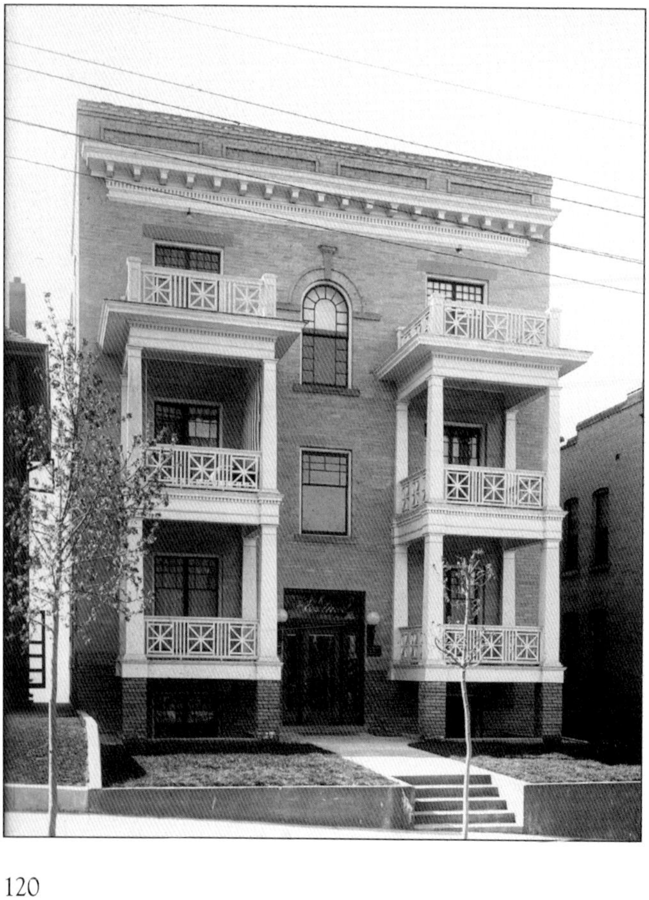

The Dorius Apartment block stands on the corner of H Street and First Avenue in 1909. Developer John Dorius built several homes in the Avenues. They are mostly located on the eastern end of First Avenue. With the growing demand for multifamily housing, Dorius had this building constructed. Architecturally, the building possesses elements of Classical, Prairie, and Craftsman styles. The well-preserved structure still stands today.

The small Esther Apartments were built on the west end of First Avenue, close to downtown Salt Lake City. By 1910, some of the earliest Avenues residences closer to the city were being replaced by apartment blocks, such as the Esther.

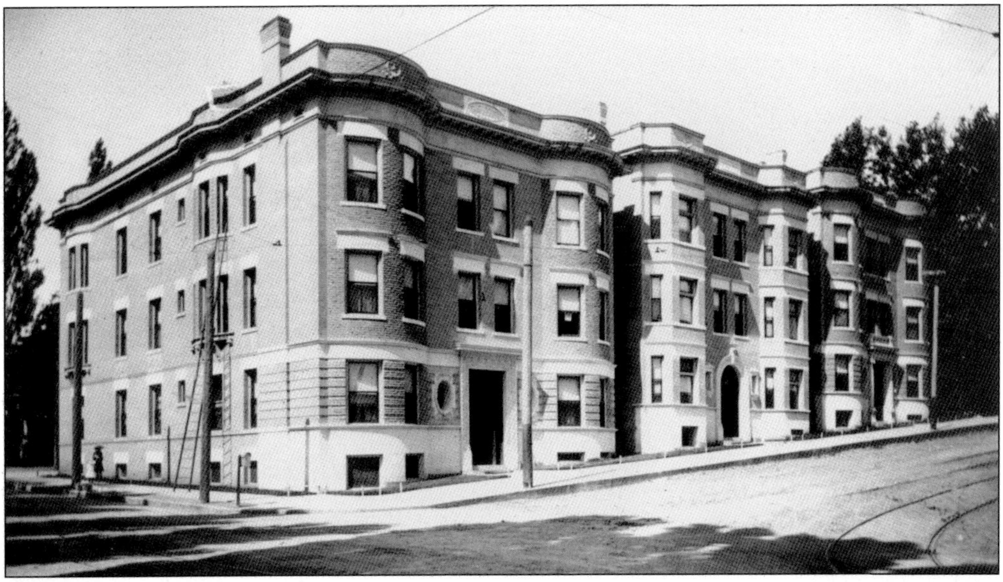

The Grace Louise Emery Apartments stood on the corner of First Avenue and State Street. The building was constructed for Susanna Bransford Emery Holmes, who was also known as the "Silver Queen of Utah." She named the building after her daughter. The structure was designed by John C. Craig, and he added several new innovations for the day, including mailboxes, speaking tubes, electric lights, and button-operated front doors. The building was demolished in the 1980s, and a park currently occupies the site.

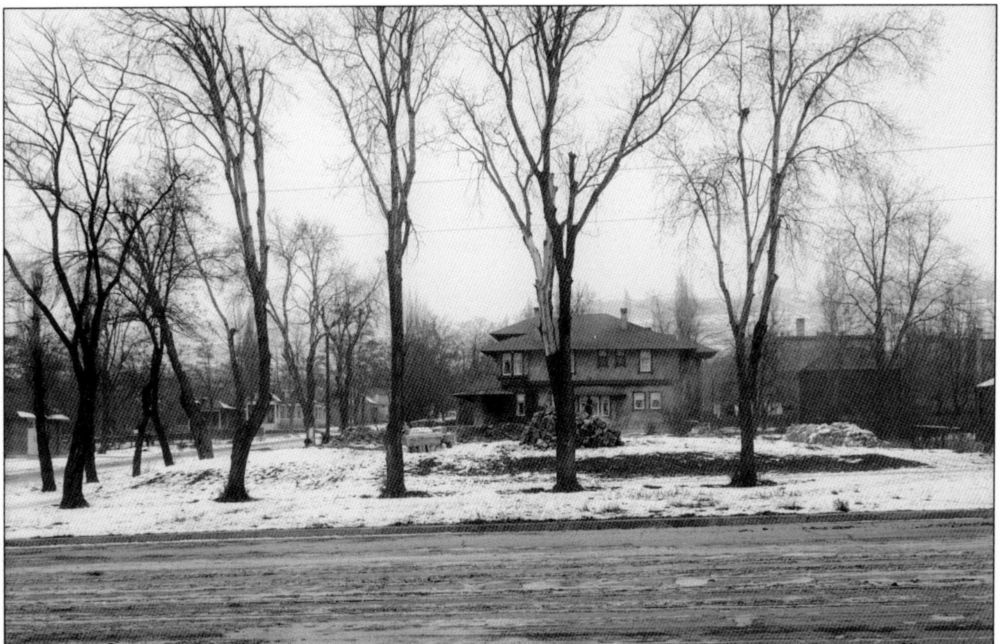

This site is cleared for construction of the Mecklenburg Apartments on the corner of L Street and South Temple Street in 1910. Because of its German name, the building would be renamed the Maryland Apartments during World War I. The Joseph E. Galligher residence is seen in the center of the photograph.

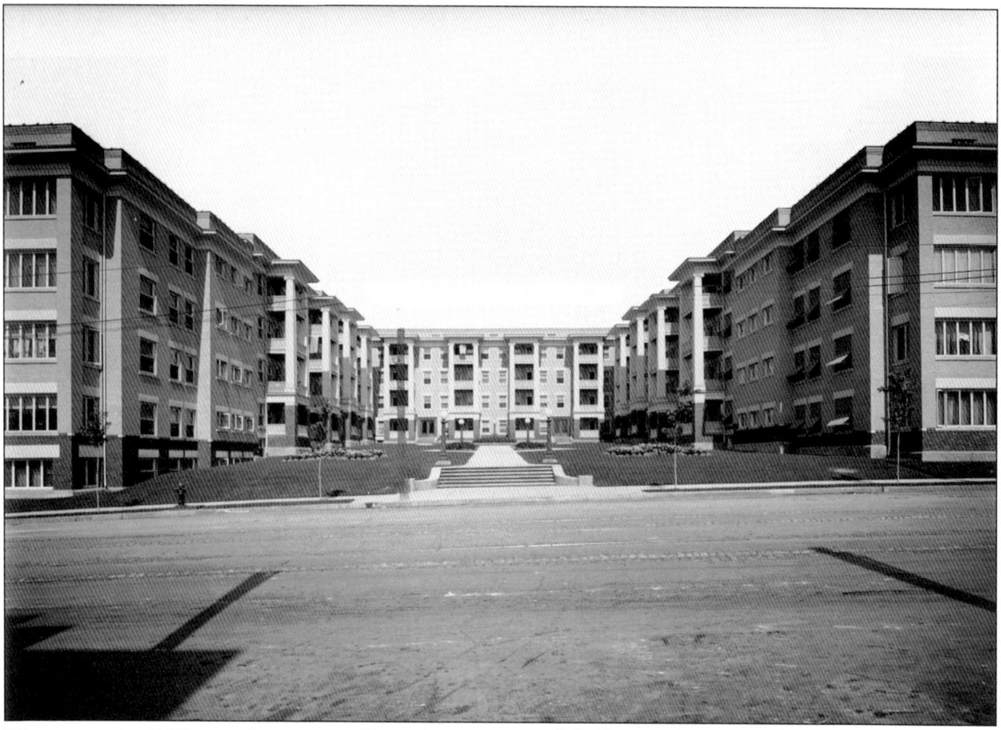

The expansive Hillcrest Apartment Complex was one of the largest apartment buildings constructed in Salt Lake City during the first half of the 20th century. The main structure was completed in 1916. A garage and an additional building were added on the Second Avenue side of the complex in 1925. Full-height porch piers supported by square columns and topped by Ionic capitals make the structure unique.

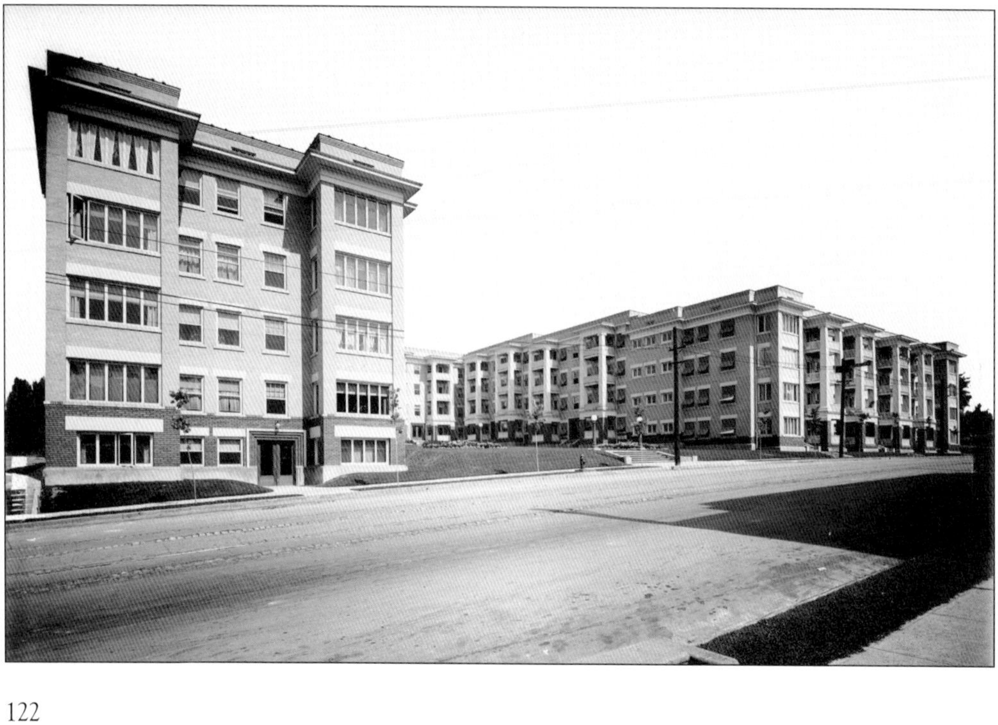

This 1918 photograph shows the interior of a unit at the Hillcrest Apartments. Thick gumwood moldings, a plate rail, and a simple colonnade add character to the apartment.

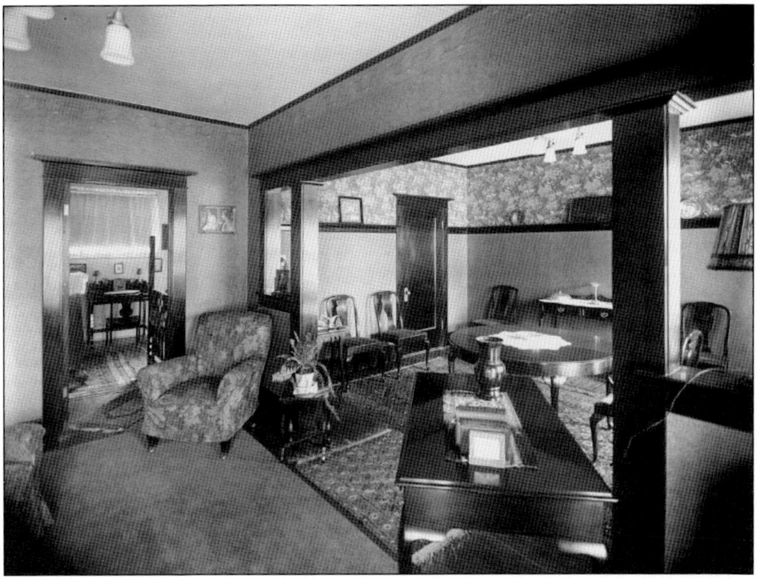

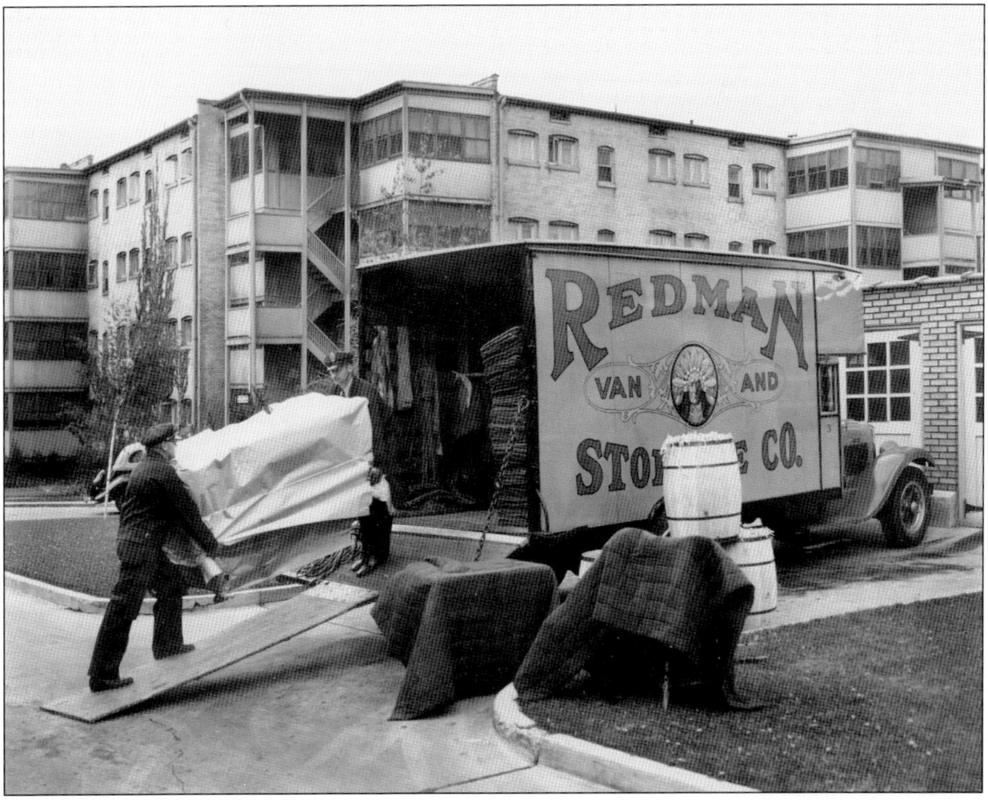

A moving truck from the Redman Van and Storage Company unloads furniture for a new resident of the Hillcrest Apartments in 1935. The Redman Van and Storage Company was headquartered in Sugar House. Their former building was recently converted into condominiums.

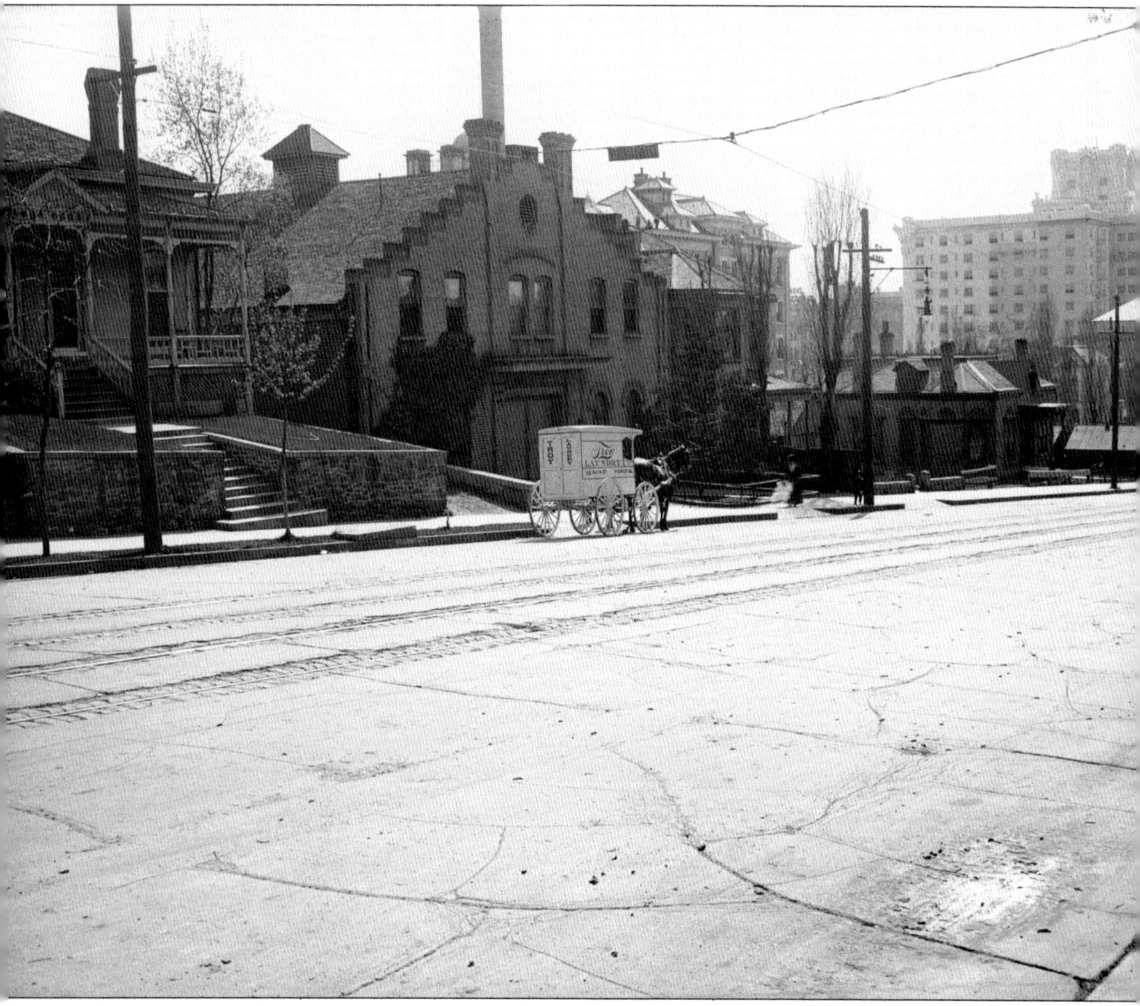

This photograph shows the proximity of the southwest Avenues to downtown Salt Lake City and Temple Square. A wagon from the Troy Laundry Company is parked on the south side of First Avenue in 1911. Executives of the company were Avenues residents. The Hotel Utah is nearing completion and is shown partially covered in its white stone finish. The Craig Apartments, located on the corner of South Temple and State Streets, is seen in the distance.

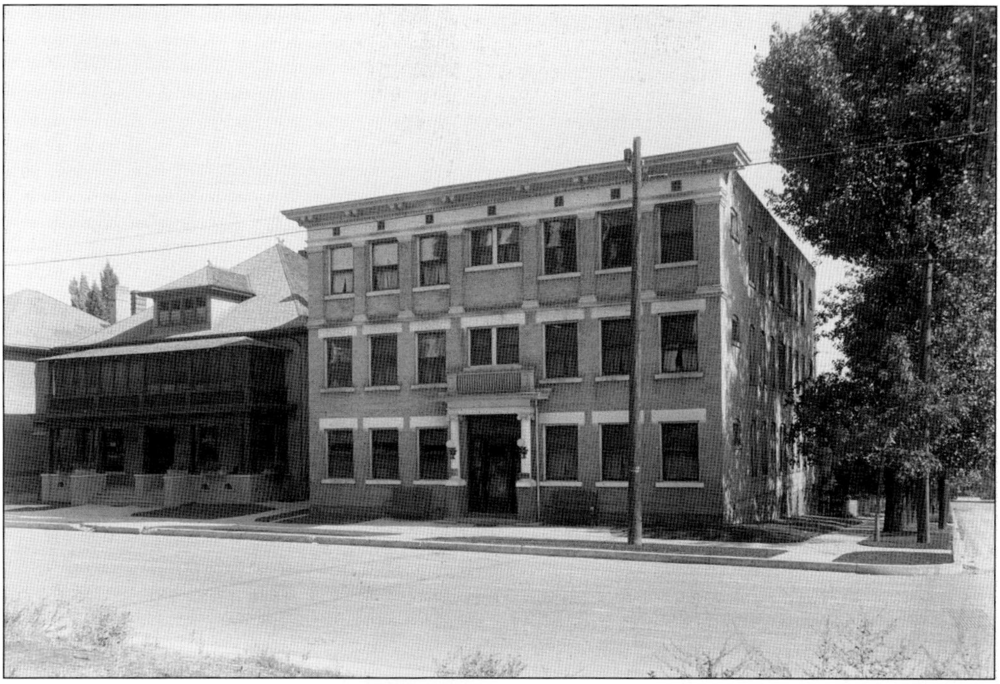

The Zimmerman Apartments stood on the southeast corner of First Avenue and E Street. A parking lot currently occupies the site.

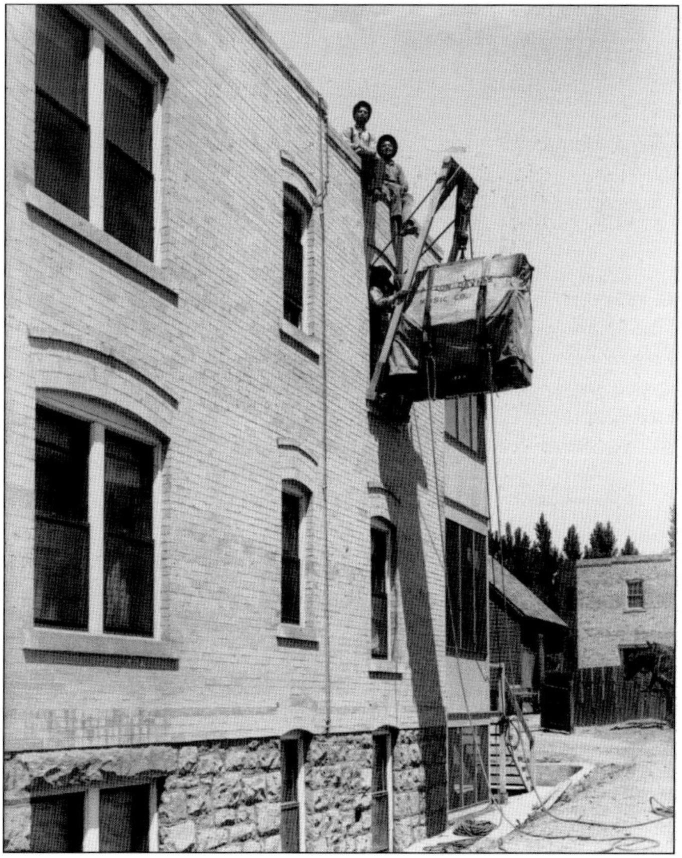

Delivering a piano to a second-story apartment was a challenge for this crew from the Daynes Music Company. Members of the Daynes family lived in the Avenues for many years.

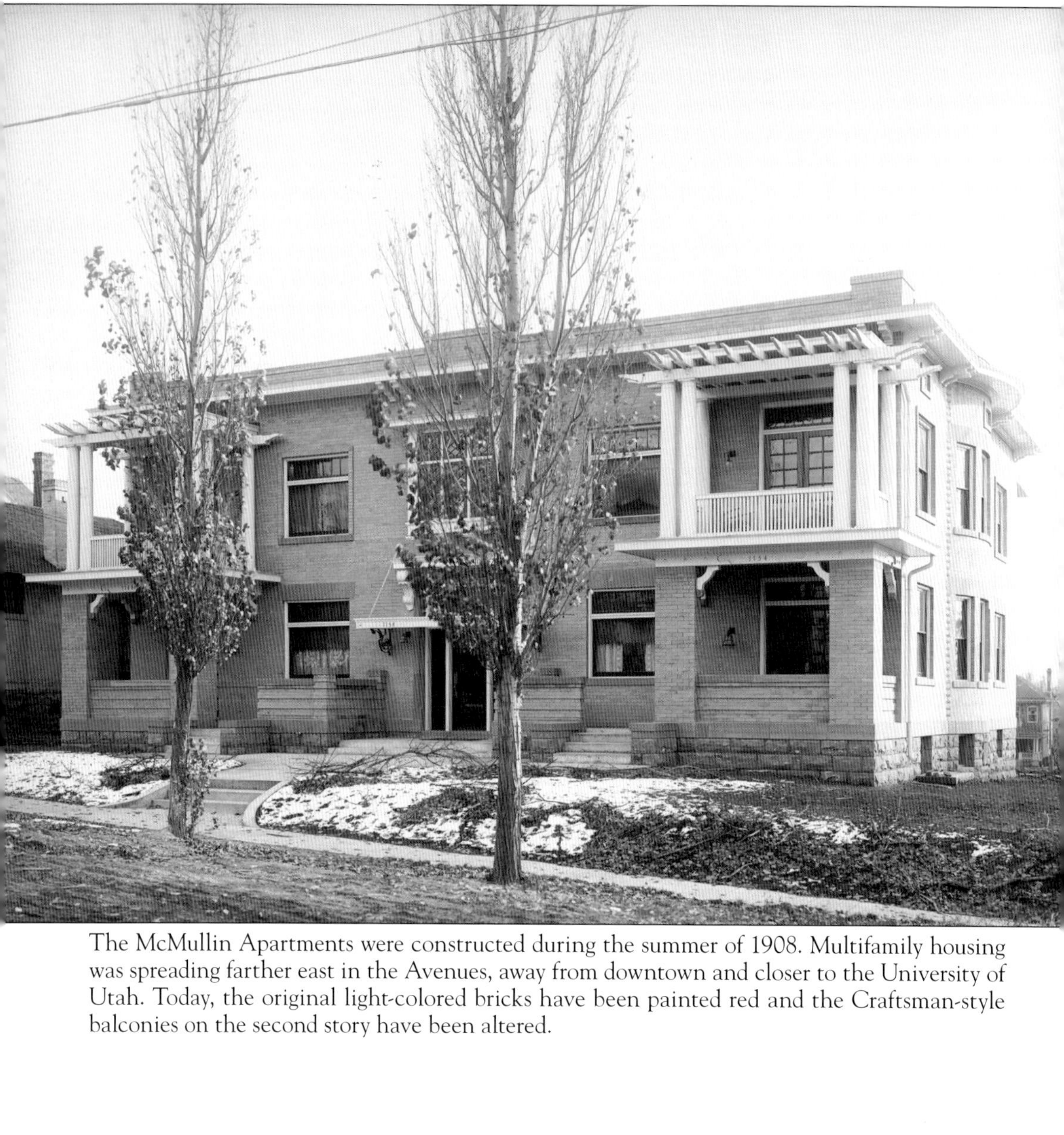

The McMullin Apartments were constructed during the summer of 1908. Multifamily housing was spreading farther east in the Avenues, away from downtown and closer to the University of Utah. Today, the original light-colored bricks have been painted red and the Craftsman-style balconies on the second story have been altered.

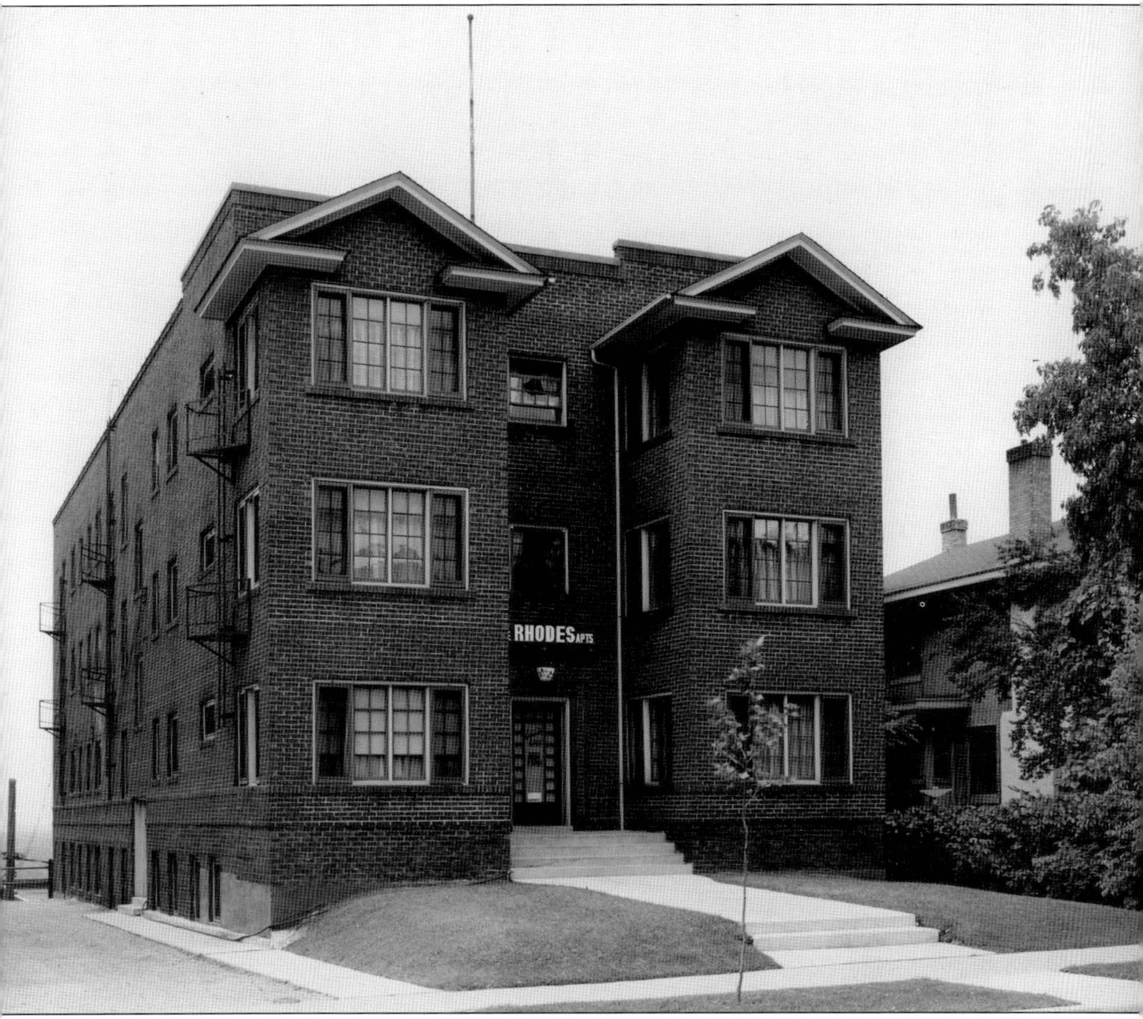

The Rhodes Apartments replaced an adobe home at 228 First Avenue in 1937. The Great Depression accelerated the decline of the Avenues neighborhood. Home owners needing additional income often split their houses into apartments or sold their property to developers.

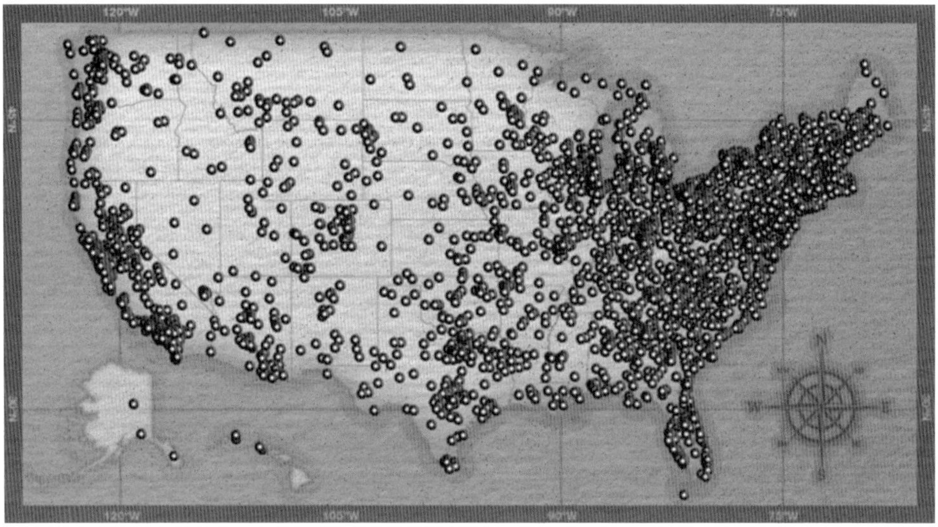

Consistent with our mission to preserve history on a local level, this book was printed in South Carolina on American-made paper and manufactured entirely in the United States. Products carrying the accredited Forest Stewardship Council (FSC) label are printed on 100 percent FSC-certified paper.

MADE IN THE USA